Adventures in the Supernormal

Adventures in the Supernormal

by

Eileen J. Garrett

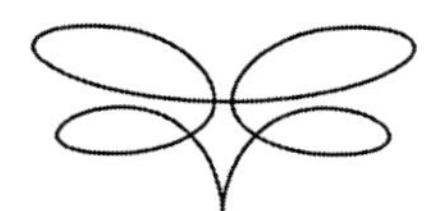

HELIX PRESS
NEW YORK

ISBN: 978-1-931747-01-1

Published by Helix Press
an imprint of the
Parapsychology Foundation, Inc.
P. O. Box 1562
New York, New York, 10021–0043, USA

TEL: 212-628-1550
FAX: 212-628-1559
office@parapsychology.org

www.parapsychology..org
www.pflyceum.org
www.psychicexplorers.org
www.psi-mart.com
www.ehe.org

Printed by Bookmasters
Ashland, Ohio, USA

Cover art designed by
Illuminations, Inc.
Greenport, New York, USA

Table of Contents

❖ PROLOGUE

Just who was Eileen J. Garrett? No simple answer emerges. Her personal memoir, reprinted here after many years, allows the lady herself to consider and contemplate her own experiences in her own words in her own *Adventures in the Supernormal.*

For those who experienced the force of her personality first-hand, Garrett was an essay in contradictions. Many know of her through her writings and good works within the fields of publishing and parapsychology. To us, her daughter and granddaughter, she was a beloved ever-present whirlwind of activity with a deeply centered core, almost the eye within the storm of a complex personality.

Author, publisher, entrepreneur, and foundation executive, Garrett never failed to elicit a response — more to the point, a strong reaction — from those she touched. In attempting to define more completely the essence of Eileen J. Garrett, in addition to reprinting her unique personal chronicle in which she dealt with the psychic elements in her life, we have collected a selection of remembrances from those who actually knew her. These vignettes appear at the end of the book. We have also reprinted a selected bibliography of works by and about her.

This new edition of her book is being published as part of the 50th Anniversary celebration of the Parapsychology Foundation, the non-profit organization Garrett founded in 1951 to act as a worldwide forum supporting scientific exploration of psychic phenomena, an organization which we are proud to currently administer.

It is our fond hope that new readers and old friends will enjoy the insights and commentary of this unique individual, as we welcome you to join us in continued *Adventures in the Supernormal.*

Eileen Coly
President

Lisette Coly
Executive Director
Parapsychology Foundation, Inc.

❖ TO MY NEW READERS

Some time has elapsed since the first edition of this book was published. The story it tells, however, will always be new to those, like myself, who have to travel in uncharted regions, defying the usual established conceptions of time and space.

Paranormal phenomena are alleged to belong to the world of dreams and fantasy, fading strangely away when exposed to the cold light of fact. In telling my own life story, I have sought to interpret paranormal aspects of personality, not in allegories or symbols, but in impersonal terms of thought and action. The process for such activity must become almost a dedicated one. For me, these chapters of my life are linked to the love of God and man.

The gift of vision belongs to all. It links man to the world he lives in, and by virtue of its magic not only permits him to uncover the secrets of nature herself, but may someday enable him to wrest the deep meaning of creation from the Universe. This can be an alarming thought. It might cause one to hope that the justice of the Universe will not reveal all, *for the history of man's discoveries of nature discloses that he has turned his knowledge against all living things, and eventually against his own kind. This has been the willful and destructive choice that man has made for himself in order to possess without love and understanding. He has made captive the elements, only to change them and dissipate them to his own undoing, bringing forth more and more destruction. He cannot plead ignorance of the laws of life, for every great human upheaval has brought with it teachers who have tried in vain to save him.*

The story of my life shows the ways by which I have endeavored to adapt it to a world of tradition, like the surroundings of my early years, and carry it through within a system of fixed laws. It shows how, as a child, I grasped the exciting interpretations that remained my own all through maturity. It tells how I have lived within a world of the immediate, and yet have been aware of the demands of time and action. It tells how it happened that I came to know the end before the beginning, and how the actions of others have often been a part of my own dream. Mine has been a life of adventures in the inner and outer world.

I am often asked what this vision does for me — how does it affect me? One feels that one is so busy sensing the pulse of life that one cannot write too clearly about it. Returning to the worldly and the usual from adventures in the paranormal, one does not bring back new language to clothe the shimmering thought. When one seems to be touching the stars, the cosmic dust which one desires to bring back as evidence of the adventure vanishes before man's sober gaze. The impact of one's vision may be lost when the experience has to be related in reasonable and cautious terms. I truly hope, however, that this new printing of my book will be read and understood as an invitation to a richer and more meaningful life.

Eileen J. Garrett
1969

❖ PREFACE

The writing of an autobiography is a perfectly defensible activity, but it is also an exercise in egotism of a kind in which I have no desire to indulge. To write of one's life may be excused either by reason of public eminence or of true greatness, and neither of these conditions fits me very neatly. I have, nevertheless, spoken of my own life in the pages of this book because, to achieve my special purpose, I could not avoid doing so. A word now about that purpose and the measure of personal revelation these pages contain.

I have a gift, a capacity — a delusion, if you will — which is called "psychic." I do not care what it may be called, for living with and utilizing this psychic capacity long ago inured me to a variety of epithets — ranging from expressions of almost reverence, through doubt and pity, to open vituperation. In short, I have been called many things: from a charlatan to a miracle woman. I am, at least, neither of these.

In this book I hope to tell the reader what I am. It is an answer to literally hundreds of requests for information concerning supernormal perception and how it functions. Because I am the agent of this perception, it has been necessary to search for the moment of its first incidence. This came in childhood, and thus it is that my book begins with childhood.

Here, then, is so much of my life as I believe necessary to an understanding of the origin and functioning of supernormal perception. Nothing that I felt to be pertinent to that understanding has been withheld; nothing not to the point willfully revealed. I have presented the truth as I have seen it.

E. J. G.
1949

❖ ONE

AN IRISH CHILDHOOD

My earliest recollections consist of deep feelings, beautiful smells and happy pictures of a child — at about the age of three — moving in a clear air and a green countryside which I later identified geographically as a spot in County Meath, in Ireland. I had no parents but lived with my aunt and uncle in a rambling old two-story farmhouse built of whitewashed stone with a thatched roof half-smothered in roses, woodbine, and sweet briar.

It is impossible to clarify and separate the details of those early days with any precision. House, garden, and farm were a world in which I moved with curiosity, and though my physical body might have been immured indoors, my mind was always out wandering in the lanes and woods, or watching the animals beyond in the paddock. There can now be no dividing of the imagined from the so-called "real," as there was no separation of them then, so far as I was concerned.

The garden was a mystic place, where sounds and smells were woven together like gossamer. I still possess clear memories of its myriad perfumes, heavy after a shower, and the colors of lilac, delphinium, roses, and hollyhocks, bright against dark , boxwood borders and deep hawthorn hedges. Herbs were placed along the soft, moss-covered walk glistening with dew, and they filled the morning air with sharp, fresh pungency. Early birds chattered everywhere, and the crows in the rookery added their hoarse caws to the sounds of the waking day. Gray smoke curled up from the cottages down beyond the paddock as the herdsmen rose to tend the animals, and a medley of sounds from the farm announced each day's beginning.

I remember the depth of color of the mornings before dawn, when the cacophony of sound from the farmyard greeted the day and the hedges were filled with bird song; the cherry and sloe trees that marked the vegetable garden beyond the orchard where the bees gave out a symphony of sound at high noon; the blue-black starry skies of autumn; at night, the scent of stock and briar mingling with the woodbine and wild roses that climbed everywhere, offering incense to the twilight hours. White mists hovered after summer showers. On the hills beyond, the multi-colored greens of trees and shrubs and the yellow gorse stood still like a painting, and over all, at the end of each day, spread the silent, scented night. Heaven, of which I heard much in those early days, could not compare with the sweet realities of those country scenes, as fresh in my memory today as they were then.

My life consisted of day-to-day adventures, both grave and gay. Outside that little arena of distresses and happiness, the Universe was mysterious. I saw the sun, the moon and the stars, and I was possessed to reach out and touch them. I suppose every child lives in a similar world of mixed realities.

Beyond the house and garden was the barnyard, with its sheds housing the cattle and horses and its barns filled with fodder. A lane led to the fields beyond the farm — a lane which was always lovely with the bloom of hawthorn and crab apple or with blossoms of snow or ice that the trees bore in winter. It marked the boundary of my physical world. A gate opened into the paddock, where there were horses, cows and pigs and fowl of all varieties and sizes. There were many men at work around the farm, but they were dim figures compared with the animals.

I must have learned to ride early. I know that by the time I went to school, I was at ease on horseback. This is not strange, as children learn to ride at a very early age in Ireland, and Meath, where I was born, was then the second most important hunting county in Ireland.

My uncle bred dogs — terriers and collies. Their kennels were at the bottom of the garden. To terriers I never became attached; they were just well-bred dogs for show purposes. The collies were different. There was one named Ida, shaggy and golden-haired. Her chest was white and silken, and her eyes twinkled with kindness and understanding. She and her family were my friends, and I loved them more than the other animals.

I loved my uncle with a deep devotion. I was happy when I could walk behind him for hours (as did the collies) when, gun on shoulder, he strolled across the fields. He was never cross with me, though I must have tried his patience with my endless questioning. He did not always answer but replied with a nod —

an assurance that I was probably right. He had kind, gray eyes and was always cheerful in spite of the coughing spells that overcame him, which never detracted from his dignified bearing. Photographs of him in my room, with white hair and a full, well-groomed beard, definitely connected him with my remote conception of God.

I first understood the outside world through his words and, because he taught me that nothing in life existed to hurt me, I knew no fear of the woods, the animals, or the dark. I looked forward to those nights when he allowed me to accompany him to the woods in search of poachers and thrilled with excitement when he taught me to hold his rifle. I would have died rather than let him know that its weight was too much for me. His word was law, and it never entered my head to disobey him.

My aunt appeared to me as a lovely and statuesque creature, even when she was cross. She had tawny hair dressed high in a twisted knot. When she scolded me — almost every day — I did not mind so much if I could take refuge in gazing at her coils of red hair, which I always longed to touch. I think of her still as tall and unbending, gowned in her crisp black taffeta dress whose rustling always warned me of her approach. The glasses, which she wore on a black silk cord, were a part of her presence and froze me when her cold hands did not.

I remember running up to her, when she was gay with my uncle and others, and trying to get her to share her laughter with me; without any interruption or diversion of her attention to the others, her firm hands would take hold of my shoulders and turn me quietly aside. She never pushed me from her roughly, but the lack of response hurt.

Within the rambling old house, my own room was situated at the top of a winding staircase, a place of withdrawn quiet that knew all the wonders and secrets of my life. Roses and woodbine came in at the windows and, just above, the swallows had their nests in the thatched eaves. Looking below, I saw the gleaming blue and yellow borders of the kitchen garden, beyond which the orchard bloomed. My room, with its outlook, was my real home. The rest of the spreading structure was just "the house."

There, in an old chest of drawers, adventure was to be found. Peeping into the polished darkness, or following the grain of the wood with my finger, I was led away into the hills and forests of strange lands to forget my aunt's coldness. A little, old lady would visit this chest. She was tired and frail and never spoke. Nor could I converse with her, for I had been taught that I must never address my elders until they spoke to me. When I asked my aunt about her, she looked at me reprovingly and reminded me that I had too lively an imagination.

There was a large oval mirror in my room. I never looked into it without first breathing on the glass. Then, all the familiar colors and shapes of things caught in its misty focus would no longer be quite themselves, and I would imagine myself living in another room in another house, which I could people according to my heart's desire.

Besides the chest of drawers, the mirror, and the bed, the only other objects that I distinctly remember within the room were two small photographs that stood side by side on top of the chest. Once I heard my aunt refer to them as "poor Anthony and Anna" in a tone that held both pity and disapproval, and a sympathy for them stirred within me. Like the little old lady who hovered about the chest of drawers, they too shared my room, and though they were no more communicative than she was, my aunt's remark had acknowledged their real existence and stirred my curiosity. Their names held a dim, indefinable significance for me, and for a long time I gave their names to all the pairs of things that I found around me. Two trees standing side by side in the wood, two plants in the garden, pairs of puppies and rabbits — to these I gave the names of Anthony and Anna.

I don't remember ever having been curious about my parents or why I had none, but it was explained to me later that Anna and Anthony were my dead parents. I was glad then that I had given their names to so many living things that I had cherished.

There are many other memories, scattered and discontinuous, of the hunt meets: the wild excitement of the hounds, the breath of the horses making a fog in the cold morning air as they neighed to one another and pawed the earth, restless to be off. I remember the old statesman, his legs as crooked as a shillelagh, who lifted me to his shoulders to see the flash of morning light on the tankards, and I recall gazing from that lofty height out over the crowd of mounted men in scarlet and women in black.

In those days, the English Court and many members of continental nobility crossed to Ireland for the hunting and fishing seasons. The meet of the fox hunt was often held near the house, and the huntsmen rode over the farm almost daily. I found their fine horses and the bright coats of the riders exciting. I would hurry to hold the paddock open for them to pass through. More than once I was lifted up onto the saddle of one of these gaily attired gentlemen, but their crude caresses frightened me, and I resisted in the only way I knew — fighting with tooth and nail against rough petting — until at last they would let me go, laughing and chiding me for my wildcat reactions.

After such experiences, I would run away. Alone in my room, up under the thatch, I would relax and breathe again — breathe in my own way, beyond my fingertips and body, above my head — and hug myself with a sense of satisfaction.

These were not the beginnings of my ability to withdraw from the world and live within myself. I think that I may have had that ability always, but as the practical outer world became more insistent in its demands, I developed the faculty for shutting it out, and this all unconsciously at first, in an active struggle for self-preservation. My aunt often scolded me. Every day, it now seems. In time I became aware that I could watch the movement of her lips without hearing the words she said. I could voluntarily shut away the sound and the sense of her harshness, and by closing my eyes I could cancel out her very existence and live in a place within myself where nothing could intrude. Was this, perhaps, the beginning of that cleavage which later developed into my having more than one personality to deal with?

As long as I can remember, I have been able, by lying quite still with my head pillowed in the crook of my arm, to reach out and touch the flowers, the trees, the horizon and even the sky. I could sense the breath of a distant bush, the vitality in far-off flowers, the sap moving in a remote tree. On a rainy day, I could feel the response of the grass to the rain, the tingling pelt of each drop as it fell, the cool dampness that stirred the roots and the waving welcome of the trees to every shower. Lying this way, I could banish hurt by joining myself to the pulse of the living world.

It was affirmed by neighbors that I was a strange and lonely child, but if I was I never knew it. Human nature will not suffer the prolonged denial of its needs, and mature people sometimes become "queer" or deranged under the continuing pressure of inner necessities which they are not able either to satisfy or sublimate. For the most part, children are not too conscious, especially not too self-conscious. They live at an instinctive level. They sense and feel as the animals do, and most of their mental activity occurs in the areas of wonder, fantasy, and imagination which are creative and serve their own purpose in the life of the child who experiences them.

When I was a child, far from being alone, I had my secret companions: two girls and a boy. The boy and one girl were younger than I, and the other girl was somewhat older. I called them "The Children." They sought me. I did not have to go to them in any particular place or make any adjustments within myself in order to see them, be with them, or communicate with them freely. I saw them first when I was about four years old. I was in the doorway of the house, and they were in the garden. I stood staring at them. I do not know how long we may have appraised each other, as children do, but nothing definite passed between us at that encounter. I wanted to go out and join them, but I was unaccustomed to mixing with other children, and I suppose I must have turned shyly away. But the next day I saw them out-of-doors, and again we stood and examined one another intently. Nothing occurred between us other than that strange feeling by which children sense each other's qualities and find their basis of companionship.

"The Children" continued to appear, and I accepted them. We communicated freely but without words. Sometimes they stayed for hours, sometimes only for a short time. Suddenly, I would realize their presence, and as suddenly they'd be gone. Everything that I cared for was subject to change — the animals grew up and grew old, the flowers in the garden withered — but "The Children" did not. When the time came for me to go to boarding school, I was fearful I might lose them, but they promised me that they would visit there.

When I told my aunt about "The Children" in the early days of their coming, she ridiculed the idea of my playmates whom she had neither heard of nor seen. "What are their names? Where do they come from? Where do they live?" she asked. When I admitted I did not know, she replied sharply, "I thought so!"

"But come and see them for yourself," I begged.

"That will do now," she told me coldly. "I've no time to waste on your fancies. Just try to touch one of these children. You'll find there's nothing there to touch. And I'll not have you telling lies, Eileen," she would warn me finally.

"The Children" laughed when I told them that my aunt did not believe that they existed. "We are wiser than she is," they confided. It was easy for me to believe this, for I knew that they did exist and that my aunt was mistaken. However, I followed her suggestion and touched "The Children." Their bodies were soft and warm. Yet they were different. I saw all bodies surrounded by a nimbus of light, but "The Children" were gauze-like. Light permeated their substance. When I once tried to explain this to my uncle, he said, "Yes? Well, maybe so," and I realized that even he did not understand.

"The Children" taught me not to regard too seriously everything that grownups said, and, finding my elders so often lacking in sympathy for the things that I knew to be true, I gathered courage to face the consequences of insisting that I was right.

"The Children" also taught me to watch changing expressions of anger, fear, and uncertainty in people's faces — to listen to their voices and catch the meanings of varying tones and cadences. Together we watched my aunt and listened, and though she was still the power that controlled my immediate destiny, I gradually lost my awe of her. By the time I went to school I had come to know that human beings never quite speak the truth, saying always too little or too much, overemphasizing one point or omitting another.

There came a time when I did not want to talk about "The Children" to anyone but became cautious and secretive, at times more obedient to my aunt's wishes, for with companionship I could afford to make concessions. They often came in the night, and this was one cause of my unusual obedience, for I now made no protest at being sent to bed while it was still light. Such good behavior made my aunt suspicious, however, and in an attempt to discover what made me so amenable she watched me closely. When she looked into my room I pretended to be asleep, whereupon she would go away satisfied. When they came, I would climb through the window, slide down the low wall into the garden, and join them in the moonlight or the deep darkness.

More than once I was discovered outside the house when my aunt and uncle had supposed I was asleep in my bed and was promptly punished for such escapades. My aunt reasoned with me. "What makes you do this?" she would ask. "Surely, it would be better to ask permission to stay up longer than to go to bed, get up again, and go out without being properly clad. Do you want to catch cold and die? What makes you so disobedient?"

At first I tried to explain to her that "The Children" had come for me and I had to join them, but this only made her more angry. She called me stubborn, too imaginative, and she punished me further. So I learned to be silent, but the barrier between my aunt and me became stronger.

I was eager to go where "The Children" went when they left me, but, regarding me with a kind of pitying intentness, they were emphatic that I could not accompany them. I never clearly understood where their native place might be but just accepted the situation.

Undoubtedly, there was a difference between us, for they too had their peculiarities. They did not like water and would not cross the brook or paddle in it as I loved to do. Although they loved the trees and liked being near them, they did not approve of climbing. Trees were not to be assaulted or scaled. They possessed a hidden dignity that commanded respect. "The Children" loved everything that grew and flowered, and they helped develop my already acute sense of *knowing* things. Every lane and field, hill and valley, by-path and cave in the neighborhood held its adventure. They showed me where the first violets and crocuses bloomed in the spring, where the primroses grew thickest, where the cowslips flowered most profusely. Together we went mushrooming before dawn, and in the rain. They were the first to know when puppies arrived at the kennels. They hurried me away to see the newborn lambs or the first run of trout in the river. They showed me the bats, hidden away from the light of day in the high roof peak of the barn and in the belfry tower. When autumn came, they also knew where to find the finest blackberries.

I wandered through the countryside in the early morning and in the long twilight to discover the law and the lore of the animal world. I knew the birds by their plumage and their songs, for the very seasons became identified with their arrival and departure and marked each year's passing. I watched the wrens and robins build their nests. I knew when the first curlew arrived, when his lonely call foretold the rain. Spring came when the first cuckoo appeared, and I waited in trepidation for the sweet pea to bloom that would herald his departure.

In the woods I imitated the songs of the thrush and could distinguish the missel from the redwing or the rusty blackbird who sang in the evening. I protected their nests and broods from marauding cats, hawks, and weasels. I listened for the corncrake's night song that foretold the harvest ripening. I saved the young of corncrake and corn bunting from the reaper in the harvest, and they grew up to feather fully and fly away from a secret cache in the barnyard loft.

Jackeen, the jackdaw, taught me as much as I taught him. Smaller than a crow, though far more noisy and aggressive, he and his tribe pilfered everything that glittered in the farmhouses for miles around. Fortunately, his family made their nests in the trees and barns near the paddock, and so their loot was periodically recovered and returned to the owners.

Jackeen, so called by the farm hands who mocked his size, had been smaller even than his kind. He had tumbled out of the nest at a too-early age, and I fed him until he could fly and forage for himself. His soprano-like caw was distinguishable above the noise of the rookery which he joined in the spring. He came back at intervals to the farmyard, but his aggressively quarrelsome and noisy manner caused him to be chased by the domestic fowls, who were seldom so self-assertive. He grew wise in the ways of the farm hands and always knew when the grain was freshly sown or new crops were planted. From his treetop lookout, he warned the crows and starlings who stole the seeds from the furrows of the approach of danger. For his size, he acquired an amazing reputation.

One day I overheard my uncle say that Jackeen was a bad bird and would someday meet the fate that sooner or later overtook all telltales and bullies. This worried me, and I made up my mind that if he survived until winter I would do something to protect him. When the harvest was disposed of and the cold weather came, he was more humble and came into the house in search of food and playthings. Sometimes I would crochet coverings for his legs for the fun of seeing him lose his temper and unrip the yarn stitch by stitch. Before spring came again, I crocheted around his little body (leaving his wings free) a loose, red, yarn vest which later proved to be his undoing. He flew away from me into the trees, cawing aggressively and ordering the crows to obey him. However, nothing happened as it had in the past. His friends regarded him warily and sat apart from him. My uncle advised me that they had made him an outcast because of his changed appearance.

He sat alone until his red vest became frayed and his glossy black plumage no longer caught the sunlight. One day he flew down to join the fowls and, from then on, spent most of his time around the house. He imitated the human voices and called his own name. Occasionally he stole a thimble or a spoon, but as he grew older he occupied a good part of his day scolding his reflection in the mirror. After his death he was still remembered. Anybody with a blustering personality was told the story of Jackeen and how his pride was humbled.

❖ TWO

INTIMATIONS OF A DIFFERENCE

I have often been asked, "Did these playmates of your early childhood resemble other children?" When "The Children" first came, I knew no others intimately. I saw the village youngsters, but I was not allowed to play with them. Other people have suggested, "Were these children of yours fairies, perhaps?" But again, no. When "The Children" first appeared I was about four and knew nothing of fairies, nor did I hear any fairy stories before I could read them. Moreover, judging from what I later learned about "the little people," I am sure that "The Children" did not belong to any fairy clan.

"How did you communicate with the children?" I have been asked. "Did you talk together?" I can only say that I conversed with "The Children" as I did with everything. I knew what the trees and flowers and animals were conveying, and "The Children" and I communicated by means of understanding each other. It is my firm belief that there is a subtle means of communication available to all who are single-minded enough to overcome the distractions of their lives.

Words have only a secondary value for me. I am receptive to the thoughts and wishes of other people, even of those who may be quite distant from me. The inadequacy of words to express emotions, thoughts, and feelings has from time to time created a barrier between me and others and even made it seem impossible for me to explain myself and my method of functioning.

When as a child I expressed distrust of a person because of his touch or his "smell," I was reprimanded and punished for my insolence. I naturally judged people in just such ways, and they often confused me when all they did was stroke my hair or touch my face. While there were times when I was "out of key" with my environment, peace and happiness came when I was alone with growing things, the animals and "The Children."

My aunt continually told me that I was an unruly child, given to falsehood and disobedience, whose wild imagination was disturbing. It was not until many years later that I discovered that my perceptions were real and that my knowledge of subtle things was due to a type of sensing that was unusual but not abnormal.

I knew that school was something each youngster was exposed to, and I imagined it to be a dreary place of confinement where I was not going to be happy. I was surprised and relieved to find its rooms sunny, with books everywhere and bright maps and pictures on the walls. The teacher, a tall, gaunt, redheaded woman, was kindly enough, but up to that time my knowledge of people was limited to the household and those who worked on the farm, so the sea of young faces all turned in my direction overwhelmed me.

There was a three-mile journey between home and school. At first I was driven with a neighbor's child. Although I enjoyed the journey, I disliked the girl. She talked incessantly about her clothes, her hair ribbons, and her lace pinafores until one day, in angry desperation, I removed the ribbon and a good part of the lace from the pinafore and reduced her to a disheveled welter of tears.

My first public act of rebellion landed me in deep disgrace. I was punished at school and again by my aunt, and the atrocious child I had assailed was held up to me as a model of all the virtues that I lacked. I could not bear to ride with her anymore, and in response to my pleading my aunt permitted me to walk to school. In order to avoid even the sight of the detestable girl mornings and afternoons — I had to see her at school — I went alone by a roundabout route that was even longer than the way she drove. During the years that I remained at that school I never again took the shorter road, so deep was my dislike of this child and her mannerisms.

The schoolhouse was a long, roomy building of local quarried granite whose walls were covered with maps. It had many windows opening onto the playground and the road. The village was grouped around the chapel, in whose spacious grounds the schoolhouse itself stood, and there were trees. Beyond the confines of the chapel ground there was a stream where willows, pliable and restless, offered contrast to the oaks and elm and beech that were singularly like sentinels. The willow is a weed in comparison, the school children told me one day when I chided them for weakening its branches. "Don't believe that story," my uncle told me when that evening I inquired. "Long ago the Romans used the willow twigs for binding their vines, and the gypsies make their baskets of them in the spring." And then he went on to tell me that no part of the tree is without its uses, as the roots, spreading in all directions, held the soil in marshy districts. "Old Matthew," he continued, "gives a brew of the astringent leaves to the cattle, and, lastly, the silvery leaves add their ornamental gleam to the landscape. Never let an Englishman hear you call the willow a weed," he concluded. "His cricket bat is made of willow wood." That was the beginning of many talks about trees with my uncle, and these talks later led me to take a deep interest in all growing things and the history behind them.

School itself made me neither happy nor unhappy, but I learned many things besides what was taught from the books. I now could watch many more people, both young and old. I saw how teachers and children evaded issues and deceived each other. It was fun to sense these deceptions and sometimes to thwart them.

I was apart in temperament and spirit from the children of my own age. They were content with what was indoctrinated or told them and seemed never to want to discover things for themselves. They accepted the authority of grownups, but theirs was only a pretense of submission.

It soon became obvious that I saw things differently and knew things instinctively. I saw people not merely as physical bodies but as if each were set within a nebulous, egg-shaped covering of his own. This *surround,* as I called it for want of a better name, consisted of transparent changing colors or could become dense and heavy in character, for these coverings changed according to the variation in people's moods. I had always seen such *surrounds* encircling every plant, animal and person and therefore paid less attention to the actual body contained within. When I referred to these misty *surrounds,* no one knew what I meant, though it was very difficult for me to believe that others did not see these enveloping each living organism. From their tone and color, I could tell whether a person was ill or well, and this was equally true of the plants and animals. I saw how the animal natures responded to the changing seasons, and I knew when vitality was high or low in shrubs and trees. I was sure that the animals sensed the emanations of each other and of places, people and things. Rodents react to the presence of a hawk before they see its form, and all animals react to their enemies and friends by means of a similar mysterious instinct.

It was always hard for me to understand what my elders meant by the word "personality," because to me the secret of personality was revealed externally and physically through the blended lights of the nimbus-like covering, and it was from this that I caught impressions and knew how far from real were the pretended peace and amity of relationships. I was often accused of lying by both teachers and schoolmates — as I had been accused by my aunt — but still I clung to my own knowledge which existed for me beyond the reach of their perception. Reluctantly I became convinced that it was worse than useless to tell of such things, and I was again thrown back upon myself to live in a world where I intimately associated myself with the growth of trees, plants and all natural things.

Thus, in the early stages of my childhood I was forced to realize myself as being "different." Gradually I accepted the situation, learned the technique of deception and even learned to accept all the statements expressed by my elders, until eventually I almost won a reputation as an amenable and quiet child. Secretly I remained true to my own seeing and knowing. The impacts and reactions of thought and feeling of people as they met one another fascinated me, for it was clear to me that they were the victims of one another's envy and cupidity. I caught impressionistic but frightening glimpses of a huge and hideous conflict abroad over the world, created between people themselves and darkening all the bright clear light of life.

When I grew a little older, younger children in the school sought me in distress or need. I took them to the washroom, fought their battles, helped them with their lessons, and defended them against the older ones. They relied on me in a sweet and simple way and, though their demands often wearied me, my heart would never let me say "no" to their appeals. I understood a little that they played on my weakness in ways of their own, but this only intensified my sympathy, for I saw that, like myself, they were helpless in an adult world and restricted by it.

Because of the time I gave to the little ones, I was sometimes unable to complete my own lessons satisfactorily, but it was easier to take punishment than explain the cause of my failure. The only punishment that could really hurt was to bar me from games. Though I had bronchitis in the winter, I was usually fleet of foot, never tired, and managed to be the core of any new adventure, whether it was to explore the many caves in the neighborhood or to form the popular hurling matches. To be disciplined by being debarred from the school curriculum of games was usually cogent enough reason for keeping me lawful during school hours. When the day's tasks were over, I approached home with reluctance and did not feel right until I reached my room, that secret center of the free, exciting, more beautiful world that I recaptured when left to my own devices.

It was in my room, lying on my bed, that I had become aware of the vitality inherent in all light, color and space. In a beam of sunshine falling against a shadowed background I perceived globules of light that moved and wove in patterns and burst at intervals within the slanted brightness. I discovered that they floated in light and without light, swirling about one another, carrying color within themselves, expanding and bursting like bubbles and creating tiny rainbows of beauty as they burst. They were of different sizes and shapes within the field of their tiny dimensions, not quite round but rather ovate in form. I had to watch them intently follow their whirling dance — at times my eyes ached from the tension — , and then, as though the intensity of my concentration had enabled me to penetrate into some new dimension, I became aware of similar movement about me and heard a myriad of faint and sweetly ringing sounds.

Thus, from the beginning space has never been empty for me. There was both sound and movement in the "space" of every area, and I could discriminate among environments by the impressions of this tremendous "vitality" that I appear to gather otherwise than by means of my five senses.

Eventually these impressions of "thin" sound and infinitesimal particles moving and bursting in all spaces of the outer world shifted to the area of my own self. Mainly, it was not an impression of any outer activity entering into my person; it was rather as though my life were drawn out into it. I had a sense of being volatile within, of various inorganic movements occurring in different parts of my being but all synchronized with the rhythms of some larger vital activity. I experience an impression of "flowing" within me, and at the same time something moves out from me to an object, yet remains an individual part of myself. By means of an indescribable contact which takes place between the object and me, its "life" becomes clear. I *know* the nature of a tree or a flower or a rock, partly through the occurrence of this sensation. The process is instantaneous and timeless. It takes far longer to describe it than it takes to occur.

I can project a part of myself to distant places and into the presence of people I know, a process which began very early as a game to relieve weary days in bed during the long winters when I was often ill. It has since developed and is now a phase of my psychic capacity. Within the quiet of my own room, I could extend the nebulous me into the outer world. I gathered vitality from the atmosphere and drew strength to myself by breathing with my whole body. I have no delightful remembrances of food in those early days, perhaps because meals were stately functions where I had to sit still and where I had to eat what was given me, an ordeal always preceded and finished by prayer. Of course I did eat, but I remember better the sustaining vitality I absorbed from the earth.

I have already indicated that words sometimes have relatively little meaning for me. Naturally, I know what people say to me, not only from the words they utter but from a composite impression that I receive through intuitive perceptions. A conversation with anyone I know well is very apt to be a matter of short sentences exchanged back and forth. I like to listen, for I have learned through the years that it is necessary for people to *express* their difficulties, distresses, or desires, and I know in consequence how serviceable it is to be a good listener. I do not have to concentrate on words in order to follow a train of thought. In meeting a new person, I never really feel that the name matters. A name that identifies one and seems so important does not indicate a personality. Identity is contained in what I sense at a first meeting. A name becomes a strand in the cord or cable of relationship.

Many people have found it difficult to understand how I could have been happy in a world to which my nature was so alien and in which my associations, at home and at school, were so different in kind as to be unsympathetic. I lived most deeply in every moment. Looking back on it now, I know that inner freedom was the key to my happiness. I never conformed.

At home, I accepted my aunt's punishments without rancor, understanding that according to her codes she could not do otherwise than she did. When I came home late from school with a disheveled appearance and a torn frock and my aunt confronted me, I had already accepted the whole situation in my mind, and I went through the routine of talk and chastisement without fear, departing to my room when the ordeal was over. When supper-time arrived, she would often come to the door and call out, "Are you hungry, Eileen?" My answer would depend on the weather. If a storm were flying and pounding out of doors, I would answer an uncompromising "No." If the evening were fine and lovely, my poor aunt would probably get no answer at all, for I would have climbed through the window and would be out down by the river or roaming the countryside. Thus in either case I maintained a freedom.

❖ THREE

FIELD AND STREAM

If Sunday was a day of prayer and churchgoing, Saturday was a day of labor in anticipation of the holy day. It was then that the rudiments of housekeeping were taught me, and, if time allowed, my own garments put in an appearance in the late afternoon and evening to be mended or I was further instructed how to wash and iron them, knit my own stockings and crochet a lace for my own bed linen, which also had to be ironed smoothly and scalloped. A woman, my aunt counselled me, must not only be the mistress of the culinary arts and domestic accomplishments, but she must know how to use her fingers as well, for no matter what her station in life might be, she who can first serve proficiently will in turn make a good mistress.

With the coming of spring it was equally important to understand the earth's needs and prepare it for its seeding. Summer brought forth the flocks and flowers, and autumn supplied its own special tasks for everyone, however young. For then the flocks returned from the plains and meadows to the paddocks and barns to be counted and suitably housed before the winter, the hay and grain were taken from the fields, pigs, horses, dogs and goats were all as excited and busy in their way as were the human beings.

The pigs were especially delightful, and I want to reassure those who might despise a pig's friendship that he is a lovable animal and full of sporting instincts. He is of high quality and sagacity in all circumstances and is highly regarded by country people, not only for his food value but with a sense of awe, for, say they, he is the only animal who can *see* the wind.

The animals were not only friends but a constant source of wonder and delight. When the favorites disappeared, my uncle sagely advised that others, equally charming, would take their place. When I rebelled and grieved, he remarked that pain of mind was good for the soul, advising me that God had planted a spark of sorrow within the cycle of man's emotions to shape his character and strengthen his will. He added that grief in itself was an outlet for the emotions but unbecoming when indulged in too much, and he would halt me then and there to assure me that I was fast assuming the woebegone appearance of a scarecrow. In gentle measure, then, he taught me to look forward to the birth of another spring, other growing things and new loves to fill the emptiness; thus I grew to appreciate the cycle of change as it came and went with every season, as each of its kind grew, stayed for a while and passed on, making room for successors.

Thus gently, unconsciously even, I absorbed the greatest of life's lessons. Nature herself was ever in a state of change. My uncle would admonish me for tears.

"Life gives and takes away," he would explain. "Too-possessive love must always cause suffering." One day he would counsel, "I and you, too, will go our ways and cause others pain, but that is the way of the world. You must accept pain as both a repairing and building process, and as such it can be beneficial." A lot of words, then, without too much meaning, but in the adult years to come they served me well, teaching me to love in the moment and without expectation of return, to make everything a part of living rather than of oneself.

My uncle had other ways to divert me. One was to fish. His drolleries and general expression of amusement brought laughter instead of tears. His genuine mirth at my efforts to tread water up to my middle was fine training and the best way to enable me to overcome sorrow. Nor could I be less brave and patient in the swirling waters than he who coughed many a night through because he had insisted, in spite of his delicate health, that one was never too young to play his salmon and land him properly.

If it was not the season for fishing, then at the waning sunset we would set out on horseback — to see the rabbits grazing, he would tell me — and if we were overly late and ambled back through the woods under the white moonlight, my aunt made no allusion to our absence. With him, I could "pioneer" through rough thickets, over five-bar gates and stone walls. I think sometimes he locked the gates beforehand so that I had to jump! If I could clear the walls without disturbing a stone, he was proud of me, but praise had to be earned, and it had equally to be accepted in silence. Thus between us there remained an unbroken understanding that insisted on an economy of words. I divined his meanings from the look in his eyes, without explanation, and sometimes without even an external sign.

In the autumn we went together to the nightly roosts of the birds, for there, he taught me, was a fertile field for study. "Like the people of old," he would say, "they build themselves fortifications and lookouts on the high ground that they can better observe the countryside and their enemies, and flock together for safety."

To the little copse on a hillock behind the farm came not only crows but starlings, magpies and jays. These communal, nightly roosts were as clannish in their loves and squabbles as were the families of mill workers who lived a mile away on the banks of the River Boyne. Whole bird families trained their young in groups in the fields and meadows, and while this was exciting for me to watch it was a matter of deep concern for my uncle, for the birds did not always take toll of the insects, and often he was guilty of almost inaudible — but emphatic and blasphemous — comment about their depredations in the cornfields and orchards. Still, he was the first to forgive them, and if the hawks and owls moved too close he chased them out.

He taught me how to band the young birds. His interest in their flight and migration was a source of community chatter with him and his friends. The birds' struggle for existence was often as acute as man's, and so while my uncle said hard things about them in summer and promised to banish them all one day, when autumn and winter came he was the first to fill their trays.

It is amazing how the bird life affected both old and young alike. Long into the night, I listened to the old ones around the fire who predicted the weather from the movements of the birds and saw their sudden journeys as signs that foreboded good or ill to the community. The rookery was well-known to those interested in bird life, since there were many varieties of rooks — those who lived there all the year round, as well as those who came to visit.

The woods were sanctuary for scores of game birds and kept their nests well-hidden, and the deep thickets and hedges around provided security for the smaller ones. The brooks and ponds gave them keen satisfaction for their bathing, which is as much a bird's necessity and right as it is a man's. Their chatter and their songs enriched the life of the farm, and when they grouped together to migrate the old ones would shake their heads sadly and say, "We may not be here when they come back." But they often were there, listening for the whirring of the wings of the wild geese in the late night or early morning. Their conversational babble promised new life, and many a night I waited with these old ones to see the wild geese soaring high like a thin ribbon over the moon after their long nocturnal flight. My uncle told me how the birds made long flights by night rather than by day, so that they might not land in unfamiliar territory when the darkness came; with the dawn they could find the feeding grounds more easily.

Traveling faster than the seasons, these harbingers of changing time inspired my uncle and me to look beyond our horizons and, in fancy, follow the birds in their superior freedom.

Although the rookery was the source of a good deal of interest, there were also the preserves of pheasant and partridge, snipe and quail and various game birds whose feeding grounds were protected from raids of other birds and poachers. I cared less for them because I knew they would fall victims to the guns when the shooting season began, and I would not allow myself to become attached to them.

Toward the domestic fowl I was more or less indifferent, though it fell to my lot to look after one group of them — the turkeys. People describe them as domesticated, but for home-loving birds they had restless ways! Their roosts were placed higher than those of the ordinary fowl, but when night came they would be seized with a demon of excitement and leave their own secluded home to seek the trees and high chimneys. Often, with the dawn, I went in search of them. The gobbling of the cock birds revealed their presence, but not before some of the more timid hens had fallen prey to the foxes or had come to rest in a hardy poacher's stewpot.

For several seasons there was one fine cock bird who kept order. His raucous voice was hardly ever hushed. With spread, fan-like tail, head erect, his body bursting with arrogance, he strutted before a seemingly indifferent farmyard. His bronze feathers shone; from his bloated chest hung a beard of rich plumes and the skin on his neck glowed red and purple with affected rage, before which even the gander quailed. His legs were armed with pointed spurs, and although he was well equipped for battle, he avoided fighting, which was wise of him, for if he had given way to temptation, he would have been deposited in the enclosure to be forcibly fed for the Christmas season!

He and a goat — who I had raised on a bottle — liked each other and often went out together for walks. They were domesticated only in the most casual way, as I well knew, for I had chased them both through bracken and heather and escorted them back to the farm to save them from those who they had assaulted. I noted, at first with a certain indifference, the affection of the turkey cock for the young billy goat, but later on I turned it to my own personal advantage. One morning, at the paddock's edge, there was much noise apart from the usual cacophony. It was a day of the hunt meet, when the cattle, pigs and sheep — as well as the young bulls — usually sought quieter pasture than the paddock, which bustled with horses. The new note on this particular morning was supplied by a swerving and plunging horse and his feminine owner. The latter had been attacked by Billy the Goat, who rose up on his hind legs to defy horse and rider while the turkey cock interrupted the scene and claimed some attention for himself with strut and gobble. The horse, unaware of their intentions, pricked his ears and balanced on his hind legs. His lady called out to me to help her with the dreadful animals, especially with Billy the Goat, who gave as much offense by his odor as his horns. I drew them off and allowed her to pass by, for which service she graciously rewarded me with two half-crowns. I dreamt then of independence and saw that the alliance of the two friends could be profitable.

Many mornings from then on, the paddock gates were tightly closed, while Billy the Goat and the fine turkey cock, as well as myself, were not too far off in case help were needed. This operation helped my finances along. I saved my money within the house until my aunt found it and I was forced to confess the method of its accumulation. Warned that this form of "holdup" was likely to bring forth more punishment, I continued cautiously and buried my gains in a box at the bottom of the garden. Later on, during the autumn, one of the old keepers died, and I gave the money to his widow who had many children to feed.

When winter came and I had time for reckoning and dreaming, I would look into the bright light of the fire and breathe a prayer that I might be forgiven for my misdeeds the past year — and also that the turkey cock be preserved and the billy goat's horns grow stronger!

In those youngest years I had only one deep fear — the fear of God. My aunt "believed in God" in her unemotional way, and desperate, I suppose, at her own failure to reform to conventional patterns, she often assured me that He would someday punish me for my misdeeds. I truly accepted the fact that a day would come when a great Person or a great Force would strike me and I should be no more. Something in my nature went out, though in fear and trembling, to meet this threatening event. As time passed and nothing happened to support my aunt's threats, I became less fearful, and there developed in me a subtle sense of defeat; it was my childish egotism, no doubt needing attention and eager for the notice of the Almighty in whatever dramatic form it might be given.

For a long time the situation remained in suspense, until I began to consider how I might make Him appear. If He became angry enough, surely He would come and punish me. But no breaking of my aunt's rigid rules, no other disobediences or misdeeds provoked Him sufficiently. Then one day, in a rage over what I considered an unjust punishment, I tore a page or two out of His own book, the Bible, and hurled the book itself across the room against the farther wall. I crouched, half terrified, half eager, scarcely breathing, awaiting the great event of His appearance and His punishment. Surely He could not fail to respond to the challenge of such deliberate sacrilege. But time does not stand still, and after waiting for what seemed hours while still nothing happened, the acuteness of my anticipation dulled, my terror eased, I suffered further defeat, and life went on as before.

Yet not quite as before. For I knew in some inner part of my being that it was not God but I who had been defeated in that climactic hour of challenge, and in some way that I cannot now define, I caught my own first clear impression of the nature and meaning of Divinity, a Power too remote and majestic to notice me, my little rages and insults.

I have sometimes wondered if this early, intense desire to evoke Divinity was rooted in some vague impulse in my nature toward a realization of the unity of Life which I have since come to perceive. If so, I was too young for it. There was an immeasurable gap between Divinity as I imagined it and me, and though I had a deep and continuing desire to bridge that gap, I did not yet know how to cross it myself or how to make Divinity take notice of me.

Later, I began to observe problems in religion outside the ever-present God at home, whose only mission seemed to be to punish wrongdoing. At Sunday School, His image became equally vivid as one read from the Old Testament and memorized the Catechism.

At Day School, there were only three children of Protestant faith, including myself. Since, in Ireland, religion is taught in the schools, I absorbed the prayer and ritual of the Roman Catholic Church, whose music, ceremonies and rhythmic repetition of prayer impressed itself on me.

As a Protestant, I was expected to leave the schoolroom while the children prayed. This I did not always do, since it was comfortable to think of a God who could be approached by way of the Virgin, the Holy Saints and the kindly old parish priests. Within the Roman Catholic chapel there was a restful and comfortable feeling; the dim candlelight, the incense and the hushed silence as one approached the altar produced a feeling of tranquillity that no other atmosphere possessed for me. The chant of the elaborate mass created an emotion which I experienced neither at home nor in my own church, which was almost devoid of melody.

My peace of mind was usually short lived, for my classmates delighted in pointing out to me that I, a Protestant, was committing mortal sin by attending their chapel. Mortal sin was a term that I heard every day, and since — according to them — being a Protestant brought eternal damnation in its wake anyway, it soon lost its meaning for me, and I continued whenever possible to please myself in seeking the quiet atmosphere of their chapel.

This was not allowed to continue uninterrupted for long. When I asked my aunt's permission to attend my classmates' confirmation, she not only emphatically refused but expressed the hope that, as a good Protestant, I would conduct my devotions within her church. I compromised and watched the ceremony from the gallery, having received a little nod of encouragement from the parish priest.

In spite of my aunt, I continued to visit the chapel, which was close to school. I found its atmosphere more to my liking than that of the Presbyterian Church to which she belonged or the Episcopal Church to which I went three times on Sundays with my uncle.

The effect of absorbing so many aspects of religion at one time was often overwhelming. The fearsome and forbidding interpretation of the continually wrathful, Avenging God of the Old Testament produced a period of awful nightmares. Within easy reach of school was the consoling presence of the beautiful Virgin and the Little Child. It was therefore difficult, under these circumstances, for me to keep my promise to my aunt and stay away from the little chapel.

❖ FOUR

THE SHAPE OF LIFE

My aunt's house was the place where I dwelt and took my meals, where certain misdemeanors were committed by me and where I was duly punished. I had very little sense of belonging to the community, and if the house itself had some day folded up and disappeared, I should have been astonished and curious about what had happened to it, but I should not have suffered any devastating bereavement on account of the event.

In my companionship with the animals and growing things about the farm — as well as with "The Children" — I was happy, and if nobody paid much attention to what I said, except to correct me, it mattered very little, for I was not acutely dependent on that side of my life. At school I had now learned to keep my own counsel, and being less strange to my companions in consequence, I became better liked in a general way. Then something happened that caused me to be deeply perplexed.

I was sitting one evening on the porch, lazily turning the pages of a schoolbook, when I looked up suddenly and saw my Aunt Leone, a favorite aunt, coming up the path toward the house. She was carrying a baby. I had not seen my aunt very often, but I was fond of her. Her house was some twenty miles distant from us, and I knew that the aunt with whom I lived was devoted to Leone and had recently been worried about her, for she had not been well for some months. Not having seen her for a long time, I was happy at her arriving without invitation. She looked tired and very ill, and as I went to reach out and greet her, she said to me — *and I shall always be sure she said this —*, "I am going away now and must take the baby with me."

I waited for no more but flew into the house to fetch my aunt. She was astonished as I strove to drag her out of her chair to come and help Leone, at the mention of whose name she hurried to the door. But Aunt Leone was gone. I went into the garden and down the lane in search of her, but she had disappeared completely.

When I returned to the house, my aunt questioned me closely, asking about every detail of Leone's appearance, how she was dressed, and what she said. I described everything to her minutely, but I was most keenly interested in the baby — the little bundle that Aunt Leone had carried close to her breast — , and I wanted to ask questions too. My aunt upbraided me instead of answering: I had imagined the whole scene; it was cruel of me to play such a trick on her. She put me through an examination concerning what I had heard in recent conversations about my Aunt Leone. I assured her that I had heard nothing, and in this I was completely honest, but she would not believe me. She accused me of concocting the story and declared that she must punish me severely.

I took my punishment. That night I cried myself to sleep and in the morning awoke with an aching head, my body as heavy as a stone. The scene of Leone's visit the day before was crystal clear in my mind, and I knew I had not invented the story. I wept again at my aunt's accusations and refusal to believe me as much as at the injustice of the severe punishment I had received. That day I was too ill to go to school, and in the afternoon wandered into the garden, still suffering a sense of deep injustice that had been done me. There was born in me a cold hatred of my aunt. I longed to hurt her as she had hurt me and wished to avenge myself for all she had made me suffer.

Strolling down to the pond in the paddock I stopped to watch the ducks floating in the cool water. Dipping here and there, the baby ducklings swam in circles, 'round and 'round, talking to themselves, and suddenly I knew that here was the means to my revenge. My aunt took pride in raising her ducks and would be hurt if any harm came to them. Bending over the edge of the pond, I caught each small duckling as it came floating by and held each one under water, one after another, until I had drowned the entire brood. I laid them in a row on the grass beside me, and as I contemplated them I became filled with a terrible dread of the wrath to come. I felt now that God Himself might come to punish me for this, and I remained rooted to the spot, frozen with fear, awaiting the force of His anger. The very intensity of my fear created a state of suspended quietness in which I seemed scarcely to breathe, yet I was alert and waiting, anticipating the final overwhelming disaster.

In this condition I gazed at the little bodies lying on the grass, half hoping that somehow they might still be alive. The little dead bodies were quiet, but a strange movement was occurring all about them. A gray, smoke-like substance rose up from each small form. This nebulous, fluid stuff wove and curled as it rose in winding spiral curves, and I saw it take new shape as it moved out and away from the quiet forms. As I watched the spectacle, fear gave way to amazement. I became almost joyful, for I thought the ducklings were coming alive again, and I waited in tense expectancy.

I do not know how long I remained gripped in fearful fascination, but it was thus that my uncle found me. There was no hint of anger in his voice as he said, "You had better come with me and see your aunt." When we found her he said quietly, "You had better go to the pond and see what has happened to your young ducks." Startled but restrained, she looked at my uncle and then at me and went to the pond, while he and I awaited her return.

Strangely enough, for the first time in my experience, she did not punish me with a thrashing. Instead, she told me coldly that it would no longer be possible for me to remain with her; I was such a wicked and undisciplined child that I would have to be sent away from home. I was suddenly elated at hearing that I should be sent away, even though I did not know where, and when my aunt assured me that God would surely punish me, I didn't believe it.

"Go to your room and don't let me see you again tonight," she said, "and ask God to forgive you."

I went to my room without any supper, but I did not care about the food or anything else. I was filled with a happy relief that I should be leaving my aunt very soon.

Later that evening my aunt appeared in my room and woke me. In a quiet mood she sat down beside me on the bed. She told me she had just had word of my Aunt Leone's death while giving birth to a baby, and that the little one had also died.

"Don't ever again speak of things that you *see* like that; they might *again* come true," she said. Then she left as abruptly as she had come.

During the days that followed, I was almost obsessed with vague thoughts and wonder about the mysteries of birth and death. I had seen the spiral breath of the ducks escape from their inert forms, and now I had learned that a human baby is also born of its mother. I wondered if all creatures escaped life as the ducks had escaped. Had Aunt Leone? Had the baby? I had to kill something else and see what followed, in order to solve this problem of the rhythm of unending life.

For weeks, then, birds and little rabbits became the victims of my need for knowledge. Then I suffered revulsion against death — and against myself for all the killing I had done. A startling truth had flashed into my mind. In killing a thing I simply changed its form, but I had no right to change it. A new sympathy had been born in me. I would not go with my uncle when he went out to hunt. A mouse caught in a trap made me suffer. Rage filled me when I thought of those who killed living creatures, and I even turned against the dogs for their killing of little animals. I could not tolerate the sight of a cat stalking a bird. At night I shed tears for all the living things that were killed daily, and I wept in bitter penitence for the ducklings and other things that I had killed.

My preoccupation with birth and death led me to ask many questions about them both. I could get no satisfactory response at home; I was still too young to understand these things fully, they told me. I was too wise to ask questions at school, for I knew that my schoolmates were as ignorant as I. I went to the old people around the farm, but they would tell me little. I told them of my own experiences to draw them out, but they only crossed themselves or shook their heads. One old woman assured me that I had been bewitched by the fairies that lived in the valleys and glens, and she told me in all seriousness that, because this was so, I had been made to see things that the fairy people saw but that no Christian creature ever beheld. It was this suggestion that finally diverted me from my obsession with life and death.

Although I had heard them spoken of, I knew little about fairies at that time. I had been told that clans of leprechauns lived in the valley underneath the lonely thorn trees, near springs of water that bubbled out of the earth, and I made up my mind to find out and see for myself. Every morning and every evening I sought them in wood and glen, but I never found the little people. For while I waited so quietly for them to appear, I began to be aware of new, faint sounds and areas of light around me and throughout the wood.

At first I thought that these were fairy manifestations, but as fascination with the lights and sounds increased I forgot the little people and began to understand that everything has its own quality of light, its own song and sound. With my back to a stone or a tree, I could hear their faint inflections and feel them vibrate through my body. With my head pillowed on the earth, I could hear within the ground the gentle movements of growing things that sprang from its strength. I began to distinguish between the song of the grass and the song of the insects under the earth. Each tree and even its tiniest leaf had a protective mantle that seemed to breathe and move very gently, and I knew that these little gossamer shields corresponded to those that I had always seen about people — cradles, in which every animate creature and growing thing breathed and was gently sustained while it found health and protection and the means of growth. Thus I came to know that all things live both within and from without and that the injury or destruction of either the inner or the outer form would affect the other.

Trees, shrubs and flowers drew nourishment, air and color from the dancing spherical bodies of light that filled all space. I had been familiar with these tiny globes for a long time, but I now discovered that they contained a color-stuff which was absorbed by everything living. At midday, I saw tiny globules drawn away from the flowers by the intense heat of the sun, but at dawn and at twilight the light-substance of the little spheres danced swiftly toward the outer manifestations of all living forms. Theirs was a steady affinity between them, a lightness of interplay akin to laughter.

In the darkness, I saw the globules intensified. They were absorbed by the flowers with a new intensity. The perfume of the blossoms became stronger and their petals more vigorous. The overblown rose revived for a moment, and drooping plants lifted their leaves again until the night air recharged all living things with new vitality.

In the moonlight the alabaster-like globules moved with renewed rhythm. The influence of the moon's rays was different from those of the sun. The little spheres grew seemingly stronger; the blue tones turned to violet and purple, matching the night. I, too, drew conscious strength from the moon. Under its magnetic light, I threw off my clothes and allowed its rays to flow into my body. I moved to the rhythmic melody of darkness and moonlight. When I shared my thoughts about these things with "The Children," they understood and sagely nodded their heads.

❖ FIVE

ROMANY, SCHOOL AND HOME

It was mid-spring and the country lanes were sweet with perfume when the gypsies arrived with their beribboned caravans and fine horses.

I had seen them before, but this time my uncle offered no objection to my going along when he went to show them where they could camp.

They came every year and stayed about three weeks, during which time the men worked for him and the neighbors. Particularly fine were the baskets of purple osier which they made for the women to hold their bleached linen. New cradles were made for the babies and new toys and bats for the children, gates and arbors were mended, reapers and knives were sharpened and ploughshares ground, the copper kettles and iron pots were soldered and vessels of new tin were made for the farmers' wives. All day long the men worked, their dark faces and downcast eyes aloof and alien. But there was fire in their swift, oblique glances when they looked up from their work. I noted the full, gay skirts, bright kerchiefs and gleaming bracelets of the women — and earrings, which even some of the men wore. While the men were busy about the farm, the young women went around the countryside selling their unguent and fine lace. They carried their solemn, gypsy babies — silent infants who never cried but looked out at the world with unblinking, wide, black eyes.

The morning after the gypsies arrived, before the household was fully awake, I slipped away to the camp. Breakfast was already cooking over a bright fire. They barely looked up as I approached, but one very old woman who I had not noticed the night before addressed me and bade me sit down. I instinctively liked her, even though she was dressed in heavy, dark clothing that was unkempt and not too clean. I had only time to inspect her gravely when my visit came to an abrupt end, for my uncle appeared and took me home, warning me not to make a nuisance of myself by visiting the camp on any pretext.

In the evening I asked his permission to go again. He relented, and I returned to the camp with the idea of seeing more of the old woman. It was obvious that all the others regarded her with respect. The accent of command in her voice brought them all to a strained attention. Her figure was still like a bundle of rags, but her deeply furrowed face was kind, and her dark eyes were merry and young. She welcomed me and told me she was happy that I liked to visit her.

Often thereafter I went to the camp in the evening. The families gathered around the fire, the men on the ground resting and sometimes singing together. When I arrived, they would move to make room for me. It was easy to talk with the old woman, and in time I had told her all that had happened to me and everything I thought and felt. She listened with interest to all I had to say and even understood about "The Children."

"Do not be unhappy if others do not believe you," she said. "It is not given to everyone to know and see such things. Not all of my own people can 'see' and 'hear,' though we are born of a mighty race to whom the good God of Beauty and Wisdom gave direct knowledge. Years ago, in the dim past, our people talked with the tongues of prophets. We have been wandering over the face of the earth longer than man can remember, and some have forgotten the ways of our fathers. The things you tell me are not strange to me. Ever since I could walk and talk, I have seen and heard things beyond man's understanding, for I was born with the 'seeing eye' and have the power to work charms and to heal."

I visited the old woman whenever I could slip away from the house. Sometimes she allowed me to accompany her when she went out to reconnoiter, and I noted how, with unerring eye, she chose the most prosperous farms and cottages for her calls.

Together we went to the fields to gather herbs for seasoning or the ingredients for her potions and ointments. She taught me strange and beautiful names for the flowers and told me legends of how these names came to be given. She would speak of her own childhood in the east, and of her travels all over Europe.

"You may not believe it," she told me, "but I once had great beauty which brought privileges and presents to my people wherever we wandered. Look here," she said, and putting her hand inside her jacket she pulled out a beautiful *ungaro* necklace made of Hungarian coins. "This I especially prize. It has been handed down in my family from mother to daughter and holds mystic power of blessing for the owner."

Although I loved to wander with her by day to gather leaves and roots for her mysterious brews, I waited with impatience for the night, when, unknown to the household, I would cross the garden and go to the camp to take my place beside the old woman at the fire. There in the wavering light the men played wild songs on violins which they made themselves. The women joined in, sometimes rising hastily, as though impelled by the staccato notes of the music, to break into a dance. This atmosphere, the music and the night moved me deeply.

Conscious as I was then of my aunt's threat of sending me away, I would beg the old woman to take me with her, but she would shake her bead and say, "No, you must not think of it," and when she said that, I was sad and knew I had no hope of going with her.

One night, from the drawer of a black box which contained strange coins and amulets, the woman brought out a pack of tarot cards, greasy and frayed, and began to tell me the meaning of the symbols that they bore. An old man looked up in protest, but she told him, "This is a knowing one that has come amongst us," and he made no further objection. She taught me how to lay out the cards and how to read them, while she drew sand pictures and made mysterious signs, and later still she showed me how to "compose" the pictures and how to read their meaning. But she warned me never to tell my uncle what she had shown me, for if he knew it he might no longer be friendly to her people.

One evening the old woman told me, "Tomorrow night there will be a wedding, and I want you to be there." I lived through the day with an air of anticipation. When I reached the camp, women were gaily dressed and were cooking over the fire. Men were drinking from goblets, and an old man was playing softly. The old woman was animated as I had not before seen her; she darted to and from the caravan carrying brightly colored garments in preparation for the ceremony. The bride was young and solemn. Over a dark skirt she wore a brilliant red shawl knotted to leave one shoulder bare. Her black hair draped her long neck and shoulders, and she wore no jewels. Others, unknown to me, came out of the dark, flamboyant and joyful. No one seemed aware of my presence. Kneeling there, my knees pressed to the wet earth, my eyes followed the old woman as she arranged colored drinking vessels and platters on the table, upon which she also placed a small dagger.

When the table was set, they all gathered around and drank solemnly. New kindling was prepared and added to the fire. Caught in the tension of the scene, I had no idea of the passage of time until I saw the old woman reach for a piece of linen to bind the wrists of the boy and girl, and the old man took the dagger from the table. The music, the night, the ceremony and the sight of blood produced in me a sense of terror and unreality. I got up and ran swiftly home.

Next morning when I went to see them they were breaking camp and going away. I was deeply sorry to lose the old woman. I had an odd feeling I should never see her again, but all she had shown me and told me remained alive in my mind and blossomed into a new enthusiasm for a herb garden. The little piece of ground that my uncle had set aside for my garden became filled with strange herbs and weeds. He shrugged his shoulders and ridiculed my collection, but, recalling all that the old woman had told me, I regarded them all as treasures and was rewarded for my care of them. Every one of them had a personality of its own. I watched closely the struggles which went on among the growing things in the garden and had clear intimations of their loves, struggles and joys.

My aunt had promised my departure, but time passed and nothing happened. Still, I was fated for the event. My teacher noted my general lassitude, frequent headaches and coughing in class. She drew my aunt's attention to my rundown physical condition — which I tried hard to conceal at home—, but not in time to save me from a collapse and a procession of illnesses which kept me in bed for several months. I developed an incipient tuberculosis, an inheritance to which most members of my mother's family had been susceptible.

When I had recovered sufficiently my aunt decided that I must now go away to boarding school. She felt unable to control my habit of running out-of-doors in all weather, day and night, inadequately clothed. Besides, she felt that my general education would be more profitably assured if I were in a different environment.

Although the idea of going away to school pleased me, the thought of leaving my room, the garden and the countryside made me quite sad. I knew that I was being separated from a very precious part of my life that I should never know again. Most of all I regretted leaving my uncle. He had not been well for some months, and I knew deep within me that our daily, happy companionship was ended forever. I wondered vaguely about school in a city where I should be confined indoors for many hours of each day. I shuddered at the prospect of living in a place where there was no garden. I had to be freely related to growing things; only then did I feel complete and secure. So I left my aunt's house with mixed feelings, though I parted from her without regret.

The new school made no great appeal to me. It was a three-storied Regency building in old Dublin Square. The principal was a shadowy creature who had little to say and who did not impress me when I was taken to her on my arrival. Her two sisters were present, dressed in black and speaking in whispers, and it appeared that they had charge of running the establishment. They seemed to me to be gentle enough and none too vital.

There were sixty girls in the school, ranging from ten to sixteen years of age. It was strictly a Protestant establishment, chosen by my aunt in the hope that I might there forget the Roman Catholic teachings in which I had shown a "dangerous" interest. I shared a dormitory with five girls, all of them older than I. I was happy that they accepted me, and I saw that I, in turn, should have no trouble liking them. They found me agreeable but reckless and always ready to enter into the little pranks that would tend to enliven an hour, even though discipline might suffer.

I was full of curiosity and passionately eager to learn, especially languages and music. Yet it was with the teachers of these subjects that I had my troubles. The teaching methods of those times were even worse than the methods of today, but in addition

I undoubtedly had my own peculiarities as a student. I could never learn a thing by repeating it by rote. Strings of verbs meant nothing to me. I had to use them in the creation of some kind of form before they would take on any significance. If I could write and rewrite a thing I could absorb it. There seemed to be some visual necessity in the process for me. I made my pleas to be allowed to learn in my own way, but the suggestion was attributed to stubbornness, and a feud developed between the teacher and myself until, finally, it became difficult for me to study at all.

I had always liked music until I began to study seriously. I was accused of singing off-key, and when I was requested to sing or play a scale I attempted to insert additional half-tones which did not belong. I was repeatedly reprimanded for my failures, and when I tried to explain to my instructor that I heard the additional tones she was indignant and sarcastic, suggesting that perhaps I had a new theory of music to expound. Again and again she would say, "Listen to this." She would play the scale over and over and then state with emphasis, "There are no other tones to be heard." As she played those never-ending scales, I was slowly defeated. I heard many other tones, and I felt with a kind of sad loyalty that there should be a place for them on the piano keyboard.

Such blame and criticism affected all of my relations at the school, and the time came at last when I could fight no longer against the general misunderstandings and accusations. I was filled with regrets over my failure to adjust myself to the school. I knew that I was conscientiously doing my best, but no one would believe me. The collapse of my health followed in the wake of my despair, and I had to be taken home.

Pneumonia developed, and again I was weak and sickly for many months, but this return to my aunt's house was a release from the distresses of school. One day while I was recovering, I heard the doctor telling my aunt that it was a miracle that I had not died, for he said I had shown no will to live. I knew he was right. I was exhausted in a world that did not understand or believe me.

The doctor attending me had also visited my uncle, who had visibly aged. Then suddenly, one day my aunt called me to my uncle's room. She was upset in a way I had never seen before. I entered my uncle's room and stood looking at him. He lay very still, scarcely breathing, and I knew that he was dying. Once again the fascination of death possessed me. He tried to speak, but no words came. I touched his hands gently. They were cold. I became absorbed by memories of our happy times together, and though I cannot say that I was emotionally upset I felt terribly empty and hurt, as though a hole had been made in my head and my brain was slipping away. How long I remained in the grip of this sensation I do not know.

The evening was closing in. That day no sun had emerged from the gray clouds; no evening glow came out to lighten the sky. I looked at my aunt searchingly. How did she feel now that she would be alone? I gathered that she had often been very lonely in the past. A great part of my uncle's life had been spent in India. Their children had been sent to boarding school at an early age and had left home early to go to the Continent and the Far East. But this must surely be different.

With a look of intense fatigue, she seated herself near his bed, her hands clasped on her knees, her eyes closed. One felt that her lungs had closed, too; she was so stiff and inwardly withdrawn. It was as though death had taken hold of a part of her.

There was no telephone to bring immediate help from her brothers and the outside world. Not quite knowing what to do, I reasoned that I could best help her by fetching old Matthew, who had worked side by side with my uncle for many years and who had also been with him in India in the past. Matthew had been in despair over my uncle's failing health and had implored my aunt every night before he went home, "Let me stay with him this night," but she had always shaken her head. Now I felt I could best serve by fetching old Matthew. With the evening's end all the laborers had left, and it seemed to me that there would be so terribly much to do, and only Matthew would understand.

I raced across the fields, for the road was the long way around. Candle in hand, old Matthew opened the door himself and peered out. I told him the sad news and begged him to hurry back to the farmhouse with me. "Has she sent for me?" he demanded. I answered, "No, but she is alone, and you were his friend." "You know," he told me, "Your aunt is a strong-minded woman and likes to manage her own affairs, but I'll come."

Staggering through the dark, we made our way to the foot of the hill where a brook divided the road and fields. Old Matthew set out carefully to walk the bridge, which was no more than a plank of wood that spanned the water. He wobbled precariously and fell backward into the rushing stream, which was swollen with autumn rains. He had a grim struggle to get on his short and stubby legs to find a footing and pull himself out. It was impossible to choke back my laughter; nor could I banish the irresistibly comic figure of Matthew as I followed him home to change. In his fury he spat words of abuse at me, finally pronouncing that I was devil's spawn anyway and that all my life would not be long enough to pray for forgiveness for my lack of consideration on this sad night.

Once more we set forth, but this time Matthew's rage would not permit him to navigate the plank on his two feet. Armed with a candle and a box of matches he got down on all fours and inched his way across, proceeding very slowly due to the countless times he had to stop and relight the candle, which he pushed in front of him in order to inspect the plank more thoroughly. By the time he had struggled to his feet on the other side his temper was at such heat that I was forced to follow at a distance, my body still rocking with irrepressible laughter, while he admonished that, on such an occasion, I should truly be ashamed of myself.

The lamps were lit when we returned, and outwardly the house seemed the same. Others had arrived, but my aunt looked up at Matthew gratefully. Perhaps now she would need me a little more. I was suddenly seized with a passionate longing to be a comfort to her, and in anguish of anticipation I approached her, hoping for a change then and there, but she turned away from me. The long, wearisome night without my uncle's presence had begun. The morning would bring the mourning relatives.

During the days that immediately followed my uncle's death, events had no meaning for me. I was filled with a deep, nameless pain. Only with his loss did I know how vastly important to my life he had been. It was he who had made it bearable at all, as he so often interpreted my needs and wishes to my aunt when I could not. Now there was literally no one to talk with or consult. My body was limp and heavy with a sadness that no one within the farmhouse could understand. For once the wild passion to tell all to the night failed to rouse me. The kind of grief I felt was a hard and terrible thing without words, with which only time itself can compromise.

I did not go near my uncle's room after he died. From what I knew of death I was sure that he was not there anymore. So surely did I believe this that on the day of his funeral I went to the garden where he used to sit in the sun and spoke aloud to him, telling him that I understood why he had gone away. It did not occur to me to doubt that he had heard me. When the time came to go to the cemetery, I refused to leave the house. On the following Sunday I was given a wreath of flowers to place on his grave. I carried them to the churchyard, but the idea that his body should want them seemed incongruous, and I hid them out of sight behind the chuchyard wall.

A few weeks later, sitting in my room in the twilight, feeling restless and unhappy, I saw my dear uncle clearly standing before me. I had not been out-of-doors that day because my chest was troubling me. I was waiting for the lamps to be brought in and the curtains drawn across the evening light when the door opened quietly, and there, by the lamplight from the hall, I saw him standing. I was surprised at his appearance of health, for before his death he had seemed feeble and worn. Now he appeared young, erect and strong. I was overjoyed at seeing him, and he showed that he was happy to see me. He asked that I should obey my aunt's wishes whenever possible. He gave me to understand that he realized the difficulties of my present life with her, and that in two years I should be free and would go to study in London. Then, before I had time to ask any questions, the door closed quietly and he was gone.

My impulse was to run after him, but I found myself rooted to the spot, and gradually it dawned on me that he had gone and I could not reach him. I collapsed in my chair and, on recovering, tried to understand what had happened. When the lamps were lit and the night came on I experienced a new peace, for I understood definitely, for the first time, that death is truly a "coming alive" again in some place that lies beyond my ordinary seeing. My uncle never visited me again. Nevertheless, I continued to believe that he remained close to me and would be able to hear when I spoke to him.

My uncle had expressed a wish that I should be confirmed in the Episcopal Church, and I was being prepared for this before his death. I had looked forward to the ceremony ever since I had watched the confirmation service in the Roman Catholic Church. Then, I had been disappointed that the children had grasped very little of the meaning of the Sacrament they had received. Thus I had a feeling that I had to experience it myself in order to understand it completely. I was surprised that the children had not been stirred by the mystery of the confirmation services, and that their greatest pleasure had been derived from their dresses and filmy veils.

The morning came to find me full of expectancy. I reread the Catechism to be sure that I understood the importance of that in which I was about to participate. With a half-dozen others I knelt by the communion rail, hopeful that at last I should be transformed into a more grave and responsible being. Had I not looked into the face of the Bishop it might have been different, but I did! He looked insensitive. I could not conceive that this coarse, red-faced and softly fat man could be the means of bringing me that deep, awesome experience for which I hoped. Watching out of the corner of my eye the hands that gave grudging benediction, I began to dread the moment when he would move up the line of children and bless me. The memory of the Catholic confirmation I had witnessed flashed into my mind, and I remembered the kind, Catholic prelate placing gentle hands on the heads of my schoolmates. Here was neither beauty nor kindliness. The service was hurried, perfunctory and cold. I left the church depressed by the knowledge that my confirmation had not changed anything in my life.

That night I spoke aloud to my uncle, hoping that he would understand that the devil and all his works and the lusts of the flesh were beyond my comprehension. Later, I asked my aunt why the confirmation service had brought me no change of spirit, to which she answered simply, "I suppose you hardened your heart."

After recovering from the disappontment of my confirmation I looked forward to my first communion, where I hoped I would still experience that unfolding within myself which I had missed at the previous ceremony.

The whispered words, accompanied by the participation in the ritual of the communion, brought me no sense of peace. I left the communion rail thinking that the minister, whom I knew well, was on the verge of a nervous breakdown and hardly an adequate representative of God's grace on earth. I departed feeling that, whatever the Divine Impulse contained, it was not to blame for the perfunctory and empty interpretation of His words and works.

After my first communion I tried to develop a different attitude toward churchgoing, but without much success. I listened to — and watched with critical attention — the preachings of the padre, as we called him, and was especially amused in noting how often he repeated the same sermons.

The nobility of the countryside came to church and sat in galleries, far removed from the crowd below. They paid special prices for their seats, and these were marked in gold with their names. I awaited the moment when the baronet, looking down from his height, would count his retinue of servants in the pews reserved for them, and I knew that if one of them had dared to miss a service, he would be severely reprimanded. Then the baronet would run his finger around the hymn books and examine his chamois glove in search of dust. If and when he found it, it was bad for the verger, who — poor man — never could have a chance to listen to the service without interruption. He was kept too busy watching the rise and fall of the thermometer, for more important than the service was that the temperature of the church should be agreeable. Often the stately lord of the manor arrived early in search of trouble, and when he found it he had been known to interrupt the bell-ringer and abuse him with blasphemous words. I, too, had been threatened with punishment for giggling, not listening with wrapt attention or if, on leaving the church, I had not curtsied suitably when the nobility passed.

Our family pew was in the rear of the church, and I had full view of the community that came to worship. The prosperous middle class sat in front in their stiff Sunday garments and the poorer ones behind them in their faded black. Sometimes I wished that one more daring than the rest would come to service in a vivid shawl or don some bold garment for the occasion. And most of all I wondered if the dull monotony of this Sunday habit gave pleasure or did any good. There were moments when I had an unholy wish that the wrathful God of the Old Testament might come and manifest His presence to a bored and dozing congregation. How startled and fearful they would have been! This, then, was the method of my *devoir* each Sunday morning when I was forced to attend these dull and sleepy services.

Later that spring, life was interrupted by the homecoming of my cousin, Ann, my aunt's daughter. I had never given thought to her, nor to any of my cousins who were grown up and came home at intervals. Now my aunt told me that the doctor had ordered Ann to give up her work and take a long rest. I was turned out of my room, which contained all the secrets of my life, and was given another upstairs that had been my uncle's study. It was a pleasant, sunny room, and the roses peeped in at the windows, but I could not slip out from there into the garden or into the farther fields. When Ann arrived it was a happy day for my aunt, but not for me. Ann had been undergoing cures abroad for two or three years — which accounts for my not having seen her for a long time — , but now my aunt, realizing that her daughter's condition was hopeless, had brought her home.

My cousin died suddenly, in the autumn. Hers was the second death I had known intimately, but it touched me very little. I asked permission to visit her room. Tiptoeing in, I remained quiet, lost in contemplative wonder about the place to which Ann might have gone. Again I perceived a gray substance rising from the body. When I entered the room it was already gathering itself into slow movement, a spiral shape that finally disappeared. I remembered the emanation that rose from the little drowned ducks, and it interested me to discern that, with a human body, this process of separation took hours longer than it had taken with them.

While I had been able to avoid going to my uncle's funeral, I was not able to avoid Ann's. I had the same dread of the lugubrious ceremonies. At the cemetery I listened to the minister without interest, and when I looked down into the grave and watched them lower the coffin, my head swam and I felt suddenly ill. I caught my aunt's arm and begged her to let me go home.

A sudden sense of indignation overwhelmed me at all this conventional but useless ceremony. I knew that in the animal world death comes as a clean, natural departure of the life-stuff from the body. The rhythmic change which I had watched again and again with many living creatures gave no sense of finality but rather a sense of continuity and movement toward fresh adventures of living. Close to the animal and plant worlds, I had come to understand that neither birth nor death is a tragic event for any living creatures excepting the human. I knew both processes of change to be equally creative, and I wondered — since the perfect balance of the universe is maintained by Infinite Direction — why man alone, of all living creatures, fears for his place in the scheme of Eternity?

❖ SIX

THE END OF CHILDHOOD

When I had completely recovered, I went back to school in Dublin, where everyone seemed glad to see me, and even the teachers were more kind in their attitudes. They still found me incorrigible, but the doctor had declared that this was due to overwork and cramming, and I was not required to carry the whole program, which made me the envy of all my schoolmates.

Accompanied by two teachers who conducted the promenade, we went out in the afternoons, walking two-by-two in our dark uniforms in what was known as a "crocodile." The taller girls marched in front, the smaller ones behind, and though I was fairly tall I often contrived to walk with one of the smaller girls near the end of the line. This was a strategic position. There were several clandestine romances in progress between the older girls and the boys of a nearby school, and I was delegated to pass notes from our group to the boys' waiting scout. I enjoyed approval for my success in this undertaking.

Contact or communication between schoolboys and girls was absolutely prohibited in Ireland; yet as soon as a girl left school she was expected to marry and settle down, for there was little chance for any professional career for women in those days. The strained and repressed attitude toward normal companionship between growing boys and girls was the cause of many hysterical outbreaks and constant secret maneuvering. Only at church were the boys and girls ever together under one roof, and it was inevitable that at the morning and evening services on Sunday they should make the most of their proximity, as far as glances and hidden gestures could go.

It was at church that I became aware of a tall, good-looking young man who watched me on successive Sundays. When I glanced at him he smiled, and I smiled back. Some time later, one of the older girls took me aside with a mysterious air and confided to me that several of our schoolmates had a way of escaping at night to keep secret meetings with the boys, and now she had been asked to bring me along to meet someone who wanted to know me. I was thrilled at the prospect of the clandestine adventure, and when the evening came I went along with her.

I was delighted to find that the boy who wanted to meet me was my admirer from church. He was an Argentine and older than the others, for he was studying medicine at Trinity. On his side, he was surprised to find me so young; he had supposed that I was older.

At our second meeting we were happy to be together again. We walked into the park and sat down on a bench, and he took hold of my hands and explained to me quite seriously what the disastrous outcome of such meetings as these might be. A medical student almost twice my age, he had a keen sense of his responsibility. He advised me not to indulge in such escapades, and I knew to my deep regret that I should not see my handsome friend again.

I hurried to the place where I was to meet my school chum, but she was not there, and I sped back to the dormitory and found that she had already arrived. The other girls were grouped about her bed, and she was weeping heartbrokenly. All I could gather was that "something terrible has happened." I had a premonition that the terrible something was of the nature of the "tragic consequences" about which my Argentine friend had just warned me.

Next morning, when the principal sent for me, I found the unfortunate girl already in the office. Frightened into panic by her unhappy experience, she had gone to the head of the school, confessed what had occurred and exposed the whole system by which the girls left the school at night. I had accompanied her, so my part in the whole sorry business was serious and grave. I was forced to tell all that I knew, and I confessed my share in disgracing the good name of the school.

Thus it occurred that I was expelled from school. My aunt received me coldly. During the drive to the house neither of us spoke, and when we reached home I was sent to my room. I would receive my supper there, she told me, and when I had finished it I was to come downstairs and give her an explanation of my conduct. When the time came, I did not beat about the bush but told her everything that had happened, including my dark young friend's explanation of sex and his warning that a girl ran risks who went out into the world alone without this knowledge. My aunt upbraided me for my "sinful and venial behavior," and our interview ended with a command and a threat: "Now go to bed, and by morning I shall have decided what to do with you. I shall have to tell you about your parents, whose tragedy must not be allowed to repeat itself in your life."

Next morning, with a cold and distant air and without any word of explanation, she handed me the photograph of a young woman whom I recognized as the "Anna" belonging to "Anthony." My aunt said, "This was your mother at the time of her marriage. When she died, I prayed that you might die, too, and be spared living, for your inheritance was bad. Your mother was the youngest child of a family of thirteen. I was the oldest, and she was like my own child. Your grandmother's health failed after your mother's birth, so for a time I became responsible for the care of the family, especially for the care of the babe. I loved her. She was unlike the other children of the family; she had an independent and wayward nature like you. She did not fit into family ways very well but was too fond of the pleasant and artistic things.

"Your grandmother, a Frenchwoman, loved this last child very dearly and arranged for her to be educated abroad, though this was bitterly opposed by other members of the family. Your mother was educated in Belgium and later went to visit our mother's relatives and friends in France and Algiers. On one of these visits to Algiers, she met a young Spaniard and later entered into correspondence with him.

"When it was discovered that she was taking his attentions our parents forbade the correspondence. He was a Catholic who had neither position nor money. Your mother had been strictly raised in the Presbyterian Church, and our parents would never permit her to marry anyone who was not of like faith. They already had hopes that she would marry a young clergyman of her own church who was devoted to her. She even seemed to conform to their point of view, to give up the Spaniard and to accept the situation, and preparations for the marriage proceeded in the family. Then, on the eve of the ceremony she disappeared, without leaving any word of explanation or indicating her destination.

"I was convinced that she had gone to her Spaniard. I had never been wholly deceived into believing that she had given him up. Our parents spent many anxious days in trying to discover her whereabouts, without success. Then came a letter telling them only that she was in Paris, where she had gone in order to marry. The family, outraged by your mother's disgraceful action in turning from them to marry a stranger, forbade her communication with any member of our family, and no more was heard of her for some months.

"Then a letter came to tell us that she was to have a child. She was unhappy and afraid to be alone and asked permission to return and have her baby in her old home. Her parents would not receive her, but I, who had been recently married, wrote to her to come to me.

"She came with her husband. From the first I did not like him. He bitterly resented the family's attitude toward him, but he had no right to be resentful — he, a Roman Catholic who had neither position nor money. There could be no peace between us. I could not bear to have him in the house. He found a position as secretary to a cabinet minister, and it took him away from my home. Later, as soon as he had enough money, he took a little cottage not far from us, and there your mother went to live until you were born.

"During all this time before your birth, your mother was very unhappy because her parents still refused to see her. Under the circumstances, I gave her all the love I had, but this was not enough to bring her peace, and she became sick with grief. Your father was moody and resentful, and he often became irritable with her; though I sometimes felt sorry for them both, I could never forgive him for having taken your mother away from her family and her church. The time came when he was bitterly jealous of my fondness of your mother and my influence with her.

"You were born to her with great difficulty. She hoped that your coming would bring about that reconciliation with the family for which she longed. But I told her, when she was up again, that our mother and father would not forgive her. I knew that for them the barriers of religion could never be dropped. Your father could never be accepted into our family.

"The next day I saw your mother's body being carried to her home. She had been unable to bear the family's rejection of her and, in grief and despair, had drowned herself. After that I could never bear to see your father again. I insisted that you must be brought up in our religion, though later I gave in to your uncle and permitted you to become a member of the church to which he belonged. Your father wished to take you away and have you brought up by his sister, but this our family would not allow. Then, six weeks after your mother's death, your father shot himself in his employer's office. Later, I had your name changed, and you were baptized within the Episcopal Church.

"I've told you the story of your parents' unhappiness to show you how easy it might be for the child of two such temperaments to sin. The laws of God cannot be set aside. Don't ever forget the blood — their blood — that flows in your veins. I have often prayed that this heritage might not show itself in your behavior, but already you show a tendency toward waywardness. You are like your mother, wayward and headstrong. Never forget that she gave way to the desires of the flesh with a foreigner and a Catholic who had nothing to offer her and was in no way her equal. Beware that your own inclinations are not the cloak for a desire to fall away from spiritual ways. The lust that overcame your mother ended in shame and disgrace for our family. Unless you can turn to God and our Church and away from sin, you can never seek redemption. I feel that it is not possible to send you to school again. If you remain at home, you can attend school in a nearby town, and, under my personal supervision, perhaps you will learn in time to conduct yourself properly."

The tragedy of my parents' lives — and deaths — failed to bring home to me the moral that my aunt had intended the story to point out. I saw only the injustice and intolerance of the family, which had really caused their deaths, for sympathy and understanding might easily have helped them to live and adjust to all difficulties.

I could discover no sin in the love and marriage of my parents. And since I already took neither the Protestant nor the Roman

Catholic religions too seriously, I failed to see my mother's marriage to a Catholic as a crime.

This revelation of my parent's history did not make them any more real to me than they had been before. What remained with me as a final result of this interview was an intense coldness towards my aunt's intolerance. She had that day put up an even greater barrier between us than had existed before, and I knew that there was little hope of our ever understanding each other.

In my dejection I sought out "The Children." I hoped that, as I had returned, we might recapture our former happy intimacy. But to my disappointment, they came less often, and at last they went away as suddenly as they had come.

For some time I remained at home with my aunt, attending school. Everywhere in Ireland, religion and politics were constant sources of argument and conflict, sentiment and emotion. The history of Ireland was an ever-living thing which did not begin and end with the textbooks. On Sunday mornings after Mass was over, political meetings were held in the National School. The country people from far and near attended, full of fire and enthusiasm, and I often went there instead of going to church.

Men of position and standing — like Joe Devlin, John Redmond and William O'Brien — sometimes came to address these meetings. Their oratory was superb, begotten of struggle, and I was deeply stirred by their language, full of color and warmth. I loved the sincerity and fervor of these Home Rule leaders, but the violent tactics of a Jim Larkin, driving the horses and cattle off the estates of the landowners or causing them to be maimed, alienated my sympathies from the Home Rule cause. When my aunt discovered my interest in politics, we had many altercations. She had been raised a Conservative, and even here we failed to find a meeting ground.

During this time I was neither happy nor unhappy. I conformed to routine at home as far as I was able and curbed my adventurous impulses, and in a measure I succeeded. I hardly ever needed companionship, because by this time I had become introspective and deeply attuned to an interior life which had its own meaning and reality for me — so much so that I no longer thought of winning understanding of it from others.

At the age of fifteen I had another serious breakdown in health and again spent the winter in bed. The latent tuberculosis became active. In the spring the doctor said I could make no permanent recovery in the damp Irish climate, and he advised my aunt to send me to the South of England, which she arranged to do.

I was inwardly excited at the prospect. What my aunt might feel at my departure never entered my mind, so little emotion or sympathy did she ever show me. To say good-bye to the farm people was a simple business. But for days before leaving I spent my time bidding farewell to the trees, the flowers and the brooks, and to all the hidden places in the woods where "The Children" and I had spent so many happy hours.

The night before I left home I felt a clear, strong conviction that I should never again be as happy as I had been here, that I should never again see these precious things with the same eyes. I wept for all the bushes and blossoms and birds that I loved, and a cold, premonitory discomfort possessed me. I should have been glad in that moment not to be going, but I managed to accept and face quietly the inner knowledge that never again would this kind of childish peace be possible for me.

I bade my aunt a formal good-bye. She admonished me to curb my temperament, to be obedient and to attend church regularly. Then, a cousin — her son, whom I had rarely met or seen — drove me to the boat. He told me, on the way, that I was very much like my mother, and he promised to send me pictures of her. He mentioned also how deeply hurt my aunt had been when this child sister had left her and attempted to live independently of her family. He spoke about my father, of his family background in Spain and of his tragic death. With a sympathetic understanding that my aunt had not shown, he indicated something of my father's sensitivity and intense nature and made it possible for me to realize his tragic bewilderment and grief at my mother's untimely death.

The tiny mist of sorrow that departure from the well-known scene had brought was lifting from my mind before the boat pulled away from the Irish shore. It seemed that the lapping waves were telling me the story of a changeling — which was what Old Matt had once called me — who had come into their possession to be beckoned away in search of an inner world whose long white road, with many shadows, was over there. Along that beckoning road it was I who was setting out, alone but never lonely.

There was a kind of finality for me in this experience of Ireland. I was finished with a way of life that could never be recovered. I turned my face and my mind toward England and an uncertain — but, I hoped, adventurous — future.

❖ SEVEN

LONDON AND MARRIAGE

My arrival in London excited me, and at once I gave my heart to that great city. I went to stay at the home of a distant cousin and here found myself in adult society where, for the first time in my life, I was treated as a mature person, and what I said was considered worthy of attention. As I could not enroll at boarding school before the autumn it was arranged that I should attend a school in London with the young daughter of the family. However, I did not continue long, as it was agreed by everyone that I was gaining little and was mentally "too mature" — an idea I adopted with alacrity.

One night shortly after, a dinner party was given to celebrate the engagement of another daughter of the family. I was seated beside a dark, charming and very amusing older man who asked me many questions about myself and my impressions of London. He laughed at the idea of a girl with my grown-up attitude towards life going to boarding school. By the end of the evening I secretly began to agree with him and spent a good part of the night dreaming up ways and means by which I could avoid school and convince my aunt that I was right. Everyone was so busy with plans for the wedding that, when Clive inquired if he might take me on a tour of the museums and cathedrals, no one raised any objections. He took me to the Tower of London, the Houses of Parliament and all the cathedrals, until I complained that I was stifled by buildings and asked if there were parks, gardens and animals to be seen. Thereafter he found a great deal of time to take me to explore the city, to lunch in the park and for long walks in Regents Park and Kew Gardens.

I accepted this delightful state of affairs and secretly hoped that, when the household settled down again after the wedding, it might not end. Everyone teased me good-naturedly about the way in which I had taken possession of Clive. He became the confidant of my misgivings that this pleasant way would cease abruptly when I departed to boarding school, to which he always replied, "Don't worry. When the time comes, we'll find a way out." The reply, though vague, was very comforting, and as I was always glad enough to live in the present I put the thoughts of school in the autumn out of my mind.

The wedding of my hostess' daughter made a deep, emotional impression on me because I had been taught to regard matrimony as a most sacred ceremony. I became so interested that I took the Prayer Book to bed with me in order that I might learn by heart the ritual of the marriage sacrament.

When the day came I was in a much more exalted frame of mind than the bride, for I was certain that I was going to take part in some mysterious and mystic rite. The anticipation of the experience had become so overwhelming for me that I began to fear that the bride, too, would be likewise affected and perhaps be unable to participate. My fears, however, were entirely unfounded, and I was almost disappointed to see her appear in a gay and laughing mood.

After the ceremony, I regarded the bride and groom intently. My hopes that the lofty and impressive meaning of the service would have caused some outward and visible transformation were dashed. My thoughts of wedlock were archaic, poetical and entirely mystical, as though I were attending something that happened long ago, the memory of which almost overcame me. Perhaps I was unconsciously remembering the weird and tense atmosphere and the music of the night when the gypsy boy and girl pledged their union.

That summer I was completely happy and jealous of every moment that I had to sleep. Every day took on the brightness of sunlight against a thundercloud, the latter to which I now likened my childhood. From this new and rosy perspective of complete emancipation, I was brought back to reality by the dismay of my hostess when I confided to her that Clive had asked me to marry him. She communicated with my aunt immediately. The atmosphere of the house became strained, for my poor cousin felt that my aunt would most certainly never approve of my marriage and would, moreover, blame her for allowing me so much freedom.

Clive arranged for me to move to the house of one of his friends. Once there, it was easy for me to agree that he should apply for a special license so that we could be married at the earliest possible moment. In the meantime, my aunt had sent her son to London to forbid the marriage and take me back to Ireland, but when he met Clive they became fast friends, and he advised my aunt that the ceremony should take place. She coldly acquiesced.

We left London for Paris on our wedding trip. The excitement of the morning gave way when I found myself alone with my husband — calm, remote, even impatient — as he rang for the waiter to bring him a drink. He suddenly seemed to become a stranger. "Thank heaven all that fuss is over," he laughingly remarked, and he settled himself down complacently in his corner seat.

All at once I felt hollow and looked within myself for that place where romance had bloomed so cheerfully before the morning ceremony. Instead of the usual adventure and excitement that had marked every other morning, now I was married. I felt a little sick. I beguiled my mind to let me escape from the thought that I now belonged to this contented male who from now on would possess my life, and from whom no flow of warm words would come to end the feeling that I had exchanged my freedom for something I really did not understand. But my heart would give my tongue no aid.

Then I found my thoughts were rounding out the figure of a woman, older than I, but who bore a striking resemblance to me. With a guilty start I woke from what seemed like a dream to hear her say, "You cannot speak to him of love; you do not know its meaning." I looked at my husband. Had he seen her or heard the words? Had I dared to sleep, even to dream? I reached to touch his hand in contrition. He smiled at me and looked out again at the passing landscape.

It was only then that I began to think seriously about the consequences of the vows I had taken that morning. I had faced the service with a feeling of emptiness akin to defeat, which I combated with indrawn breath. This kept me steady and eventually produced enough tranquillity for me to gather conviction that everything I had promised to do I would carry out. Now here I was about to move into a new world. I felt completely lonely, and, if I could have had any choice at that moment, I would have returned to test the measure of my aunt's severity rather than continue on a journey with somebody who had suddenly become a stranger.

Before the honeymoon was ended my husband's perplexity with all my moods was intensified when I announced to him that I was not prepared to be an appendage, but that this marriage must allow me freedom to work and live my own life. More than anything else, it seemed vitally necessary that he should see my need for independence, which meant that I must now work to maintain myself. No wholehearted desire consumed me to surround myself with a husband's loving care.

With such an attitude on my part, it can be readily understood that my new relationship caused my imagination to work overtime. Here I was involved in one of the most powerful human urges, in which I had to live in a new intimacy with another human being, and could find nothing to overcome my inner resistance and my reluctance to investigate this new life which I had entered thoughtlessly. Immediately faced with problems of my own status as an individual — and the problems of reproduction and spiritual sustenance marriage needs if it is to succeed — it was difficult to accept my new and changed state. From the Old Testament I had clearly gathered that a husband must be regarded as a master, and I believe my arrival at this conclusion had much to do with my resistance to marriage. Morally, I was ready to accept the Biblical pattern, but with almost prophetic eyes I saw the future as a struggle for the right to my own independence.

On our return to London we settled into a newly built house, lichen gray and beautiful, and as I had been well-trained in the rudiments of good housekeeping, I was eager to display my wifely talents. However, my husband informed me that if he had wanted a housekeeper he would have secured one, and he pointed out that he was supplying me with maids to do the work. Furthermore, he expected that I should always be ready to give him company; be vivacious as when we first met; be well-dressed, presentable, entertaining, and a charming hostess to his friends. I was disappointed that he had very little interest in my personal wishes, but I was rapidly finding out that, having gotten over the initial days of getting acquainted with each other's weaknesses and idiosyncrasies, I had exchanged one form of discipline for another. He also told me, with a cold and definite air, that I must positively give up my *seeing* and *sensing*. But this I was unable to do, for it occurred anyway!

When, after four months of marriage, I found that I was going to have a child, I began to change temperamentally — to live two lives. I was always gracious to my husband and his friends, but I escaped as soon as I could into a privacy where the unborn child and I lived a life apart. Giving birth to my child was something that I felt I understood, for I had often helped the young of the animals to be born. Now I could identify myself completely with this miracle of life, and I knew that I should give birth to a male child, healthy and strong. I had a wish that he might come into the world when I was alone, in the open, under the stars. I was an animal about to bear her young, a vessel through which the natural currents of life were flowing like a torrent. Whenever I could, I threw off my clothes and crept into the little garden to lie under the stars. I was exalted and living again in the rhythm of natural things. I walked in color, in which my child was also bathed. I stayed away from people as much as possible, sought the woods and open fields and was close to the living earth.

My husband was not as interested as I was in the arrival of the child. I learned that he had returned at this time to a mistress of his bachelor days. Indignant at the news, I felt deserted, but my mystical acceptance of marriage held me to my vows: "Whom God has joined together. ... I was lonely, and my loneliness drove me to a closer identification with the child I was carrying.

At last my son came — came quickly, a little before he was expected. And so I was able to bear him alone, as I had wished. I had no fear, either for him or for myself. My husband had seen to it that everything possible was furnished and done for me during my pregnancy, and I was grateful to him for all that. Now, however, with my son in my arms, I deliberately alienated myself from his father. It mattered little to me what Clive did. I was glad to be alone with my child and to be excused from entertaining Clive's friends. Isolated with the baby, I lived in a state of bliss bordering on exaltation, and this condition of ecstasy frightened my husband. When I explained to him that I was living as I had lived as a child, in intimate relation to the rhythm of all growing things, he became more worried and begged me not to speak thus, since no one would or could understand.

My son developed in loveliness and, in spite of difficulties, life moved fairly easily in the household. When my baby was five months old, I had him out in the perambulator one day when he became fractious and irritable. I stopped to change his position and, in doing so, shook him impatiently. As I put him back in the carriage I heard a faint sigh over my shoulder, my name was uttered distinctly and a cold, admonishing voice warned me that I must not lose my temper with the child, for he would not be with me much longer. Frightened, I turned in the direction of the voice, but no one was visible. It was a voice I did not know. I was alarmed and upset at the threat contained in its warning words, but my son throve and grew, and I began to suspect that I had been a victim of my own too-vivid imagination.

My second child was born the next year. The wide-eyed baby came quietly, and with this child I had no such intense feeling, either during pregnancy or at his birth, as I had had with my first son. Strangely, too, I had a vague impression that he would not live long, and the threat that had been made concerning my older child returned to my mind and grew in intensity. My anxiety about the babies affected my own health and worried me constantly, and I finally mentioned it to my husband.

He tried to be sympathetic, but it was hard for him to understand me or accept my fears. He called a doctor who gave me a tonic, recommended taking up some outside interest that would divert my mind from the children and myself and suggested a change of climate. But I knew that I was not ill in a way that a change of climate would cure, and I could not accept the idea of leaving my sons, even for a short time. However, I followed his recommendation about directing my energies beyond the house and the children.

I joined a series of clubs, literary and otherwise, and attempted to interest myself in social affairs, but it seemed futile and a waste of time. There was also developing in me a deep suspicion that marriage would not much longer occupy the whole of my life. The need for independence was growing in me. I knew very surely, though without any perception of why or how, that outside in the world a change that would involve me was in the process of developing. I was already aware that it was not necessary for me to take physical steps in order to have things happen to me. All that I or anyone had to do was to realize and give voice to a deep need, with faith and conviction, and in its own good time and measure the Vital Breath would do the rest.

Then one day my first boy, who was now two years old, fell ill suddenly. At first the doctors were unable to diagnose his complaint. They hinted at infantile paralysis, and in a few days brain fever developed. Within a week he was dead, and the doctors decided that meningitis had been the cause. Some months later the second boy died of the same disease.

I was childless. Shocked by the loss of my two sons, my fortitude left me. I could not grieve for them in conventional ways for I knew that death was not an end but led to other states of being. I had seen the nebulous life of my older boy weave and wind away from his body while I held him in my arms. As though unseen fingers wove a silken thread, the floating emanation curled and wove rhythmically until it disappeared beyond the reach of my vision.

I suffered deeply at the death of my sons and was unable to understand why they should have been born, only to die. Many times now I had been able to see this filmy life-force escape from the bodies of those who died, and I began to search for a method by which I could follow these moving energies into the future state that existed for them beyond my vision, beyond my understanding. While the intensity of my desire did not carry me as far as I wanted to go, I did begin to realize a more subtle dimension around me.

Again, as in my childhood, I saw the streams of color and light blending and interchanging their forces and growing from beams into slowly curving spherical forms that reached into space. I began more readily to feel and sense the thoughts of people as forms of light that moved to their destinies, impacting and dissipating according to their natures and the force with which they had been projected. I came to know that thoughts are dimensional things which become clothed with form and life as they are born.

Thus the drama of vision went on for many weeks and "exalted" me in body and mind. Its force passed through me like a series of slight electric charges.

In a relaxed and passive state one day, looking before me, I saw the shadowy replica of myself as in a three-dimensional mirror. Never before had I had such a setback. Was I actually the person that I now saw myself to be? I knew that it was I outwardly, yet it did not tally with my inner sense of myself. I rose and tried to approach that other self, and as I did so it lost its outline, drew back toward me and fell into place as my own protective surrounding. I was curious rather than frightened, and I later came to know that such projections are not uncommon occurrences. They take place at times when the objective mind is completely relaxed. In time I came to understand that, in everyone's case, in states of sleep, intoxication, or illness, the protective envelope separates and moves out from the physical body. I learned of the positive importance of the *surround* as protection for the physical body, receiving and condensing the impacts of sound, light and movement and diminishing their violence.

I learned to use this capacity to divide consciousness, finding that I could make this protective covering into a mirror in which I could see myself at any time. Whenever I wished to assure myself that my appearance was as I wished, I needed never look in a mirror; rather, I viewed myself by means of this projection.

I knew that all of this had some deep significance, but I did not then penetrate to its inner meaning. I needed to find someone who understood what was happening and searched in scientific and religious books in the hope of finding some hint of explanation.

During this time I faced the routine of domestic life with difficulty. When my husband suggested that I should go home for a visit, I agreed in the hope that there I should find peace — that the woods and little haunts of my childhood would heal me in mind and spirit.

My aunt's cold greeting, as she opened the door on my arrival, chilled me to the core. She appeared older and more frail, but her grim determination to rule and be obeyed was more rigid than before. She disapproved of my leaving my husband, even temporarily, intimating that my place was beside him in my own household.

Though I had my old room and was welcomed by the people who knew me, when I sought my secret places in the countryside, changes had occurred, and I did not find the flow of peace that I had hoped for. I realized that this journey back to Ireland was an abortive attempt to escape from the problems of my married life and would not solve them. There was nothing to be gained by staying longer than a few days, so I started back to London and my husband, stopping on the way in Dublin.

When I had been in Dublin previously, I had been interested in the Abbey Theatre, and I now began to think seriously of acting as a career. I had always regarded actors with wonder and awe, as individuals greatly gifted and set apart. After seeking advice from them I found that nearly all were hard-working people, interested in themselves and a way of life that contained more than glamour. I also came to realize the tremendous amount of time and routine training that the profession demanded, and a career as an actress became less attractive to me. All through my life I have had an aversion to beginning any new process by conventional training, preferring to work first at things myself until the awkward stages are over. I know immediately whether I can or cannot do a thing. If I can do it, I know that I must do it my own way; if not, I leave it alone.

I did not remain long in Dublin but returned to London in a better frame of mind. Going home had helped to clarify my vision. I was now ready to face issues and find some means for either making a success of — or terminating altogether — my marriage. I really wanted to find something that would be an expression of myself and would give some value and meaning to life.

I appealed to my mother-in-law, who was always sympathetic with me, but she, far from seeing my point of view, told me that my first duty was to my husband and home and that my job at that moment was to have another child. She made me see that the loss of our two sons had been as great a sorrow and distress to my husband as it was to me. Up to that time I had selfishly thought of the children as wholly mine, and that Clive had suffered through losing them had barely occurred to me.

I took up our life together again, and in time I bore another son. This baby died a few hours after birth. My recovery was rapid, and I scarcely realized at the time that I had suffered another tragic loss. I had borne this child as a duty, and I experienced no intense emotion over either its birth or its almost immediate death.

After this, I tried to interest myself in social service and nursing in the East End of London and again attempted to employ my energies in civic and charitable affairs. But all of this activity, though it used my physical strength, gave me no inner satisfaction. I then went to the other extreme and got myself a role in a musical comedy. I would have liked to remain long enough to accomplish something, but my husband and his family were displeased and insisted on my giving it up. Clive now more often reminded me that I had obligations to him and pointed out that there were many delightful ways for a wife to pass the time and still remain home, attractive and responsive to her husband. These were my first unsuccessful attempts to free myself from the individual and economic bondage that a house and a husband represented to me.

Relatively idle at home again, the inner world opened to me without any seeking or effort on my part. I was simply the victim of my own hypersensitivity. I hesitate to indicate the state in which I then lived, for I suspect that most people would consider it a state of unbalance. Nevertheless, this period did contain much supernormal sensing, more deep and more intense than any I have since experienced, except in times of serious illness. Difficult as it may be to accept, the fact is that I found myself *seeing* more easily and clearly through my fingertips and the nape of my neck than through my eyes, and *hearing* and *knowing*, for instance, came through my feet and knees. Sound was a current that flowed through me and vibrated intensely through the bony structure. Auditory sensing came more often, matching the clairvoyant knowledge that occurs without the use of my eyes. When I lay down to rest, confused by these experiences, I would suffer a feeling of nausea and lightness, and above me I would see myself as clearly as though I were looking at someone else. I believe that this was the beginning of the conscious projections which I was later able to use in controlled telepathic experiments.

Subsequently, my husband told me that during this period I had short spells of amnesia, in which I described traveling and seeing people in distant places. He had a constant dread that these experiences were symptoms of progressive mental upset and, at his suggestion, I had several interviews with physicians and psychiatrists. They plunged me more deeply into bewilderment until it finally occurred to me that, if I was to become capable of living a normal life, I had to learn the way to do it for myself. I knew at once that the correct antidote for my unhappy state would be work that interested me and kept me busy every moment of the day.

One day at luncheon a friend told me she was opening a catering establishment with some capital which her husband had left her at his death. She asked me to join her in the venture, and I literally jumped at the opportunity to absorb my energies and fill my life with outside interests.

I threw myself wholeheartedly into the new project. I had been well-trained in the fundamentals of this type of activity, and I was happy to find that I thrived on work and responsibility. My partner complimented me on my own special ability to make people feel welcome and at home so that they became expansive in their spending. As the business flourished my health improved, for the natural tiredness resulting from hard work gave my mind less chance to separate into its two parts and prevented me from indulging in self-analysis.

Then came news that my aunt was dangerously ill. I was not asked to do so, but I felt the need to go back and see her. When I arrived, my relatives met me with frigid greetings and were reluctant to let me see her for long lest my presence should weaken her. I slipped into her room quietly, where she lay in a semiconscious state. She opened her eyes and turned them to me for a moment — I believe she recognized me, for she regarded me with a cold and hard expression — then closed them again. I left the room realizing that she was going out of this life in the same hard, unrelenting manner in which she had lived. Thus my relations with my aunt were finally ended.

I saw no reason for staying through the dreary funeral ceremonies, so I announced my immediate departure. I knew that the family would be relieved to have me go, yet they did not hesitate to express disapproval of my unconventional behavior in leaving before the end.

Out-of-doors, in the dark, I stood and tried to recapture the happy sensations I had experienced there in my childhood, but the dream of childhood was over. That phase of my life was ended forever. I knew suddenly at that moment that I was free and alone. From that time on, however difficult life might become, I knew that I would be able to meet it before it came upon me, by some intimation or foreknowledge of what was in store for me.

The First World War broke out almost immediately after my return to London. My husband, who had trained yearly with the Territorials, was immediately detailed for duty abroad. In the emotional upheaval of the coming of the war and his departure for the front, I was remorseful for my inadequacies in our married life. When finally the train bore him away from me, I found myself within a vortex of sadness. Women of all ages had come to see their men depart for France. Only she who has stood in such a crowd and watched her man melt into the gray, shadowy army of human beings going to war knows how empty life can become in such a moment.

There was a deep flooding of feeling as I walked away. Everything which had been so real a moment ago when he was still there now melted into the nebulous past, but beneath it all was the knowledge that the independence I had craved was now mine; it was time to be alone, time to think and to feel and to realize what it was I wanted to be. All I knew was that I wanted to work. I gave myself over to labor with hands, brain and feelings, for almost at once the common danger of the war was brought home to every household, and people of all classes — at home, in the factories, in the hospitals and on the battlefield — were welded together by tragedy as the dead and wounded began pouring back almost as soon as the battle had begun.

Work was good and gave me a wholehearted desire to be intelligent and helpful when my husband returned. War had its sobering effect, and as the daily strain and the horror mounted,

I grew to understand that there could be no real independence of mind or character if innate selflessness and goodness did not prevail. My own sense of security had to be established in the blood and being of myself before it could happen in the external world of human effort.

Several months later my husband returned to London to transfer from one regiment to another. This meant that he would be in England for a training period. The sacrifices that the men were making in the war had moved me deeply, and, with more maturity, I knew that I had a great deal to make up to him for the unsatisfactory nature of our marriage. Conscientiously during this time I turned my thoughts toward making him happy. The instinctive drive toward work was satisfied, and I accepted my biological role without too much concern with my own individuality. In these months the evolution of love and human companionship wrought its own emotional rapport and brought me closer to the significantly mystic and spiritual understanding of the marriage bond for which I had earlier looked. The outward-flowing stream of my energies was now directed toward building a permanent relationship, founding a family and being a satisfactory wife and mother. I was very happy when my daughter was born, but after her birth I was very ill. My lungs had again become affected, and it was quite a while before I was able to regain my lost vitality.

While I was in this happy frame of mind, my mother-in-law came to visit me one day. I could see that she was very nervous, and I inquired as to the cause. Reluctantly she told me that she had been quarreling with my husband over his recent behavior, and she felt it was her duty to let me know that he had been living with another woman. Rather than have the news reach me from any other source, she had volunteered it herself. She was worried over my health and begged me to pull myself together and get well as quickly as possible so that he would have no further excuse for his neglect of me.

At first my pride was hurt, but that feeling quickly passed. My husband's family took his infidelity more seriously to heart, but I only wished that he had the courage to tell me himself. The ease with which I accepted the change in my outlook bothered me for a while, but I never doubted that I had realized the spiritual significance of marriage, and that now, as such, it was ended for me. Far from being unhappy, my mind leaped ahead to contemplate the days when I would once again find myself free. There was adventure in looking ahead to a future which would be occupied with bringing up my daughter and making a career of my own. Having once reached this solution, I wanted to be up and away long before my strength had returned.

The brittle existence that one leads in war — and the day's casualties — make one's own small pattern of change too insignificant to assume importance. The heartache that death brings to everyone makes one's own sorrow lesser. It was therefore easy to take the steps that had to be achieved in order to gain that freedom I had always envisioned. A part of me had always known that I would, unaided, weave a pattern of life that would subjectively fulfill me. I accepted the road ahead and saw with clarity how definitely the way was shaping.

❖ EIGHT

WAR YEARS

The success that I had as a partner in my friend's business led me to the decision to open a restaurant of my own. It grew rapidly and kept me busy — much too busy to have time to spoil my child. I could only give her physical care and attention. This was evidently very good for her, however, since she grew up a healthy and contented little girl.

Both my husband and his family came to see me on various pretexts. That I threw myself so vigorously into active work when I might have "protected" my marriage seemed to them to offer proof of my strained mental state. They could not understand that hard work was saving me from the very condition with which they charged me. However, since business continued to prosper, any anxiety about my mental state lost its justification.

Finally, when I made up my mind to get a divorce, only my mother-in-law inquired whether another man was the true reason, but there was no one else. I wanted to be free — free to work, to find my own pattern of life.

My business was successful enough to warrant moving to larger quarters, but before I could make new plans it was obvious that the war had made it necessary for everyone to serve the country in some capacity. Most women volunteered their free time to drive trucks and ambulances between the stations and hospitals. I took part in this work for a short while but suffered a severe attack of rheumatic fever which the doctor ascribed to overwork. When I had recovered sufficiently, I opened a hostel in central London that would combine the atmosphere and appurtenances of home and club for wounded soldiers from overseas.

Friends, troubled by the state of my health, attempted to dissuade me from the undertaking, but opposition made me determined to make my venture a success. Besides, the growing need for organized effort, coupled with my new independence and financial freedom, helped me to carry out my plans and sustain the club. I hated war and had no false sentimentality about its brutal cruelty and folly. I could never find any warrant for wholesale killing, and it had always seemed to me that some means should be devised for holding economic and peace conferences *before* instead of *after* the conflict and carnage. However, I could devote myself with enthusiasm to helping the victims of battle back again to health and a normal way of life.

During the war years I took time to understand the psychological disturbances of the wounded men as well as those of the civilians with whom I worked. The pattern of all such disturbances had a familiarity. A great deal of the revealed instability had begun between children and parents in the early and formative years. I learned that the assets of marriage are best maintained when friendship is first established within the association, for marriage demands not only daily adjustments but, more importantly, a continual putting aside of one's "official" personality in order to be at all times one's own self.

Marriage offers continual creative impulse, but each must move into the other's new area of interest. During that time, however, the English husband was still on the defensive and felt that to relax and allow a wife too many interests beyond himself was a poor reflection on his own superior role.

It also became obvious that men have strong desires to remain children themselves and often become envious of the legitimate dependents of their own wives and families. Perhaps this is one reason why the world — as well as families — finds itself so bitterly divided over who should rule; this agony will continue as long as man is busy maintaining his official idea of himself and of his position. These pretenses often become more important than the impulse to live creatively, and if such pretenses are insisted upon, neurotic behavior results.

At that time I found that my responsiveness to people — and my own gift for living in the moment — made me an unwilling but dutiful recipient of my friends' tales of their economic and physical marriage problems. Often I found that the children of such parents were condemned to be problem children through no fault of their own: they had to live side by side in immaturity with problem parents. The opportunity to examine cases of mental conflict matured and clarified my own impulse toward health and happiness. Successful functioning of my own life became more important in order deal with the problems of others which each day brought forth. From every day's difficulties I learned that the growth of one's own self-respect is important, not only in marriage but in all relationships. Growth and usefulness, which are self-respect, led me to further study of myself in the hope that I might become acceptable in a world where the process of giving of one's best was obviously so sorely needed.

The supervision of the hostel took a good deal of time but still did not absorb all my energies, for in my "relaxed" moments I found that my interior world had fewer boundaries. I saw fragments of episodes in the lives of people whom I knew: scenes flashed before me like pictures on a dark screen. This wider and unsought vision into people's lives disturbed me, especially when I began to see events occurring in the lives of many of my friends before they actually happened. A tiny screen, containing images, places and events of which I knew nothing, would sometimes interrupt my normal vision. A few days later, or perhaps months later, I would meet and recognize someone who had played a part in these episodes. Sometimes the picture of a fire, an explosion, an accident or even some trivial event would flash before me, and the next day I would read about the happening in the newspaper, or somebody might describe it.

For days I lived subjectively and happily in a world of inner experience. Then the influence of temperament and heredity would take over and demand a different kind of life. Gray days of war, with the emotions they involved, made it a time of tension in which one had to live expansively to achieve the capacity for strength. The ability to share and serve was the qualifying action that guided the day. War, then, shaped one's life and one accepted all its experiences as inevitable.

Among the officers in my hostel there was one to whom I was immediately attracted. He was artistic and sensitive and very good looking. He had not been in the firing line. When the other men spoke of their war experiences, he would shudder and say, "I wish you fellows wouldn't be so bloodthirsty." He confessed to me one day that he had gone into the army because it was the only decent thing to do, but that he dreaded the grim experience.

He had never been robust, but, as his health improved and the time for his departure approached, he turned to me more and more for companionship and sympathy. I was very fond of him and I responded to his need for mothering.

One day he told me that his regiment would be leaving for the front very soon. "I can't go away and face what I have to face," he said, "unless you marry me." I was not deeply in love with him, nor was I very much interested in marrying again, but I had then a horrible premonition that he would not return. It seemed a little thing, therefore, to marry him and give him the brief time of happiness that he asked for.

We were quietly married. It was very easy to build a picture of the gay and happy life that would be ours when he returned. Aboard the train at Victoria Station, he was full of courage and dreams of our happy future. A few weeks later I suddenly "knew" that my young husband was going through hours of terrible suffering and fear. In order to find release from the depression of what I was feeling, I gathered several friends together and went out to dine. That evening, in the crowded dining room of the Savoy, I had a vision of my husband dying. For a moment I lost all sense of my own identity and was caught in the shattering concussion of a terrible explosion. I saw my gentle, golden-haired husband blown to pieces. I floated out on a sea of terrific sound. When I came to myself, I knew that my husband had been killed.

Two days later, my husband was reported missing, and subsequently word came from the War Office that he was listed as dead. His brother officers wrote that he had gone out on a wire-cutting expedition and never returned. Years later, when the war was ended and done, I saw his name on the Menin Gate Memorial at Ypres. More intimately than the men who had been near him, I knew the manner in which he had died.

Again I was troubled by the realization that coming events could register themselves beforehand in some part of my consciousness, whether I wished it or not. Again I sought to prevent this invasion of external happenings from tearing my nervous system to shreds. I prayed that I might find a way to shut out these unwanted experiences. Almost unwillingly, I had to accept the fact that I had two separate selves, and in this difficult time I stumbled on the technique of autosuggestion, though I did not then know it by that name. If I relaxed, the extraneous impressions would rush in, but if I made a conscious appeal to my "other self," the invasions would diminish, and this method of self-protection became a regular exercise. As I became convinced of the success of the process, I began to use it to protect myself against illness and for the correct handling of human relationships. Thus I developed, without knowing precisely what I was doing, a system of self-suggestion. I succeeded so completely in shutting out my visions of external happenings that I soon began to wonder if I had lost the capacity for perceiving them. Yet I had only to allow myself to drop back into a relaxed and passive state for the external and internal events to return and invade my consciousness again.

A growing ability to control the partitions of the mind made it possible for me to carry on my business and personal lives with what seemed to my friends to be a new sense of security and confidence, and I found it unnecessary to refer to the difficulties and perplexities which arose out of the interplay of my other selves. Thus, I was sometimes accused of being hard or indifferent. This was not so. The fact was that I had acquired a swiftness and acuteness of perception, so that events came and went and life experiences played themselves out at a fantastic pace. I came to accept what was "normal" for me. I sensed that my perceptions had significance beyond my understanding. My problem at the moment was in grasping the interrelational working of patterns of my mind so that my life might not be disordered, but that I should learn to work consciously and creatively. I gradually controlled my visions by permitting their manifestation only during a time set aside for practice and contemplation.

As my new assurance developed, the events which I witnessed continued to cover a wide range of subjects. These were seldom connected with my own personal life, but were often related to happenings — past or future — in the lives of others. I would hear snatches of conversation which had no meaning for me, but a few days later I might find myself in a room with several people, and to my amazement I would hear again the identical conversation. Sometimes I would hear the names of people or places unknown to me, and days or months later these names would crop up again through some unforeseen meeting or some other definite association which I was newly concerned.

Other experiences occurred. Within a few days of each other, two close friends wrote to me; one was living some three hundred miles away, the other not more than twenty miles. Both inquired as to whether I was ill or needed help, for they had both been aware of my presence in their houses and were disturbed by these strange appearances. I did not need help and at that time I had no immediate explanation which would account for their experiences. I assumed I had been thinking of both of them while in a passive state and some aspect of my consciousness had reached out to them. It was not until much later, when I came to understand the mechanics of clairvoyant perception and telepathic communication, that I discovered my ability to at times project myself into the presence of a person whom I might wish to reach or with whom I had a warm feeling of sympathy.

These psychic developments had their physical effects and counterparts. I was conscious of an increasing pressure behind the forehead, and at the same time I had a feeling of a channel being gently opened up from a point between the eyes to the cerebellum. The process was neither painful nor unpleasant. I also became aware about this time that images registered behind my forehead. Beginning at this point, the images appeared to move out and beyond into space. I used to compare the process to a kind of mental magic lantern, with the lens for the projection of the pictures located behind the forehead.

Thus, as I struggled towards comprehension, I came to know that consciousness was a vaster wonder than most people realized. While a ribbon of it guided the mechanics of sensory experience and conscious thought, there were vast untapped realms in which all aspects of life were linked and related to the vastness of the Universal Scheme, in which each individual plays his part. I realized that the human being is not nearly as self-important in the existence and evolution of the Universe as he likes to believe but is at the same time more responsible than he is willing to accept. I saw man as a channel through which the Primary Force and Intelligence of the World works toward its own fulfillment — an incident, but an important one, in the larger scheme of things. I was able to conceive of the Life of the Universe as a process in evolution in which the place of man, though at present of minor importance, is potentially one of greatness. I caught a conception of consciousness as infinitely greater than brain or mind.

Another spell of illness made it impossible for me to work with as great intensity as I had done in the preceding months. Finally I was forced to dispose of the club and seek rest and recuperation for a few months. It was then that I heard that one of my friends was wounded and seriously ill in a hospital not far from the town. I found him not only seriously ill but very depressed. His fiancée had just broken their engagement, and to make matters worse, he had been informed by the doctors that the amputation of one foot might be necessary. Here was something I could do to help. I fell into the habit of seeing him often until he began to depend upon my visits and gradually to stress the necessity of seeing me more and more. I was glad of the companionship then; anything that had a basis of reality or a feeling of lasting, even for a short time, gave a sense of security and a reason for strength. The long war years made everything one did seem urgent, even if it was only temporary and necessary to the moment. Soft words became important, for every man's heart was full of the secret knowledge that the fleeting hours were all that was left. Out of the deep sympathy one felt, one had to take these fleeting intervals and build an eternal kingdom in the spirit.

When one day my friend proposed that we marry, I was reluctant to face the idea of another ceremony. I felt guilty that I had not done more with my other attempts, and because I attributed the failure to myself, I felt spiritually beggared and defeated. Marriage in terms of settling down to what might become an affectionate boredom would not be enough; I still believed it should possess more mystical meaning and fulfillment than I had yet discovered.

Besides, at this time I was concerned with the social changes that would present themselves when the war ended. I had been for some time interested in the Fabian Society. It attracted me because the Fabians themselves rejected the idea of a political party but had always urged the trade unions to form a party of their own. (It will be remembered that eventually H. G. Wells hastened events by reorganizing the Fabian Society, a scheme that caused much controversy between him and Mr. Bernard Shaw). Since the Fabian Society always stressed the ambitious idea of reconstructing society in accordance with the highest moral possibilities, it especially appealed to me. I sought active contact with the workers and their leaders and had been seriously thinking about opening a labor hostel against the time when the war ended, in order to get a clearer understanding of the theories and fundamentals of organized labor and at the same time work with people who were themselves preoccupied with the problems. I had in the past seen a great number of fine, intelligent men and women devote their lives to the cause of the worker, and recalling the fire and enthusiasm of the Irish political leaders of my childhood, I was interested in instilling a spark of that fire into the new movements then taking shape, that those who returned might not lose themselves in a labyrinth of discomfort, poverty and despair.

In such a mood, I felt that perhaps a trip to Ireland would refresh me and help me make up my mind about my next step. There I could recall the old atmosphere, the independence and courage of some of the leaders of the caliber of Redmond, O'Brien and Dillon. I went, however, at a time when everyone was still doubtful, sullen and resentful; there were no great leaders to lift the people out of their despondency. As a sentimental Irishwoman I, too, could weep tears over the suffering of Ireland, but I could not find myself in actual sympathy with the too-nationalistic policy of the period. I did, however, feel that the true spirit of the country I remembered from my younger days had been kept alive, encouraged and stimulated by the vivid and living faith of the literary and intellectual groups, especially the beloved A. E., Yeats and that fine woman, Lady Gregory.

I returned to London knowing that I would never find satisfaction in politics alone, but that my heritage and background would always beckon me from the quiet roads to fight in my own measure for the cause of freedom. I was often disappointed at the overimportance a man placed on himself and the underimportance that he gave to the ideals of the particular movement of which he was a part. My estimation of these values was reversed. I never lost my realization of the fact that the ideal of any movement must continue to be held greater than the individuals who support and sustain it. At the heart of every man there exists a faith in some ideal, and though men commonly forget and fail to make sacrifices, there are those who do remember and who keep the faith.

I went to the hospital to talk over my experiences with my wounded friend. He was very understanding of the complexities that had sent me to Ireland in search of the answer to what I really wanted to do next. When he again brought up the subject of marriage, the far-off hills were green but hazy, and I was a little more inclined to listen.

I confess I drifted into my third marriage without any thought of its being permanent. The war was then in its fourth year and everyone was a little distraught and tired. The years had been very hard to endure, for no day had been free of tragedy; as one day succeeded another, so one by one the names of friends and relatives appeared on the casualty lists. There were so few friends left, so little to cling to, and most of the young people had no tomorrow to which to look forward. Friends greeted each other in the streets with sad hearts, and the usual parting words were, "I never thought he would be killed or that the end of our happiness could come so soon."

Within a month of my wedding, the Armistice was declared.

❖ NINE

NEW DEMANDS OF MY PSYCHIC SELF

The war years had made settling down to a comfortable marriage relationship very difficult. The transfer from the vital activities of four tragic but exciting years to a peace that promised more hardship and discomfort than one could readily have foreseen was not easy to accept. Victory had been gained, but — one often asked the question in these first years of peace — by whom? No one could depict the goal, since it had never been reached, and the pathetic fallacy of victory left everyone in England, as well as in Europe, drained of the spiritual qualities and resources that make for grim determination. On every hand, the deep desire for social changes and the stubborn resolve to bring them about were surprising.

The transitional period between war and peace was a bitter one for all concerned. It was surely also the moment to test my own character at a time when so many of my friends were up against it. In such a time it was difficult to think in terms of one's own happiness, but more difficult still to contemplate a wedded life of comparative ease, a state which had never really appealed to me. Besides, it was better to make the experiment in the high noon of a halcyon day than to persuade oneself when adversity arrived that one had been really strong. All this I explained to my husband, urging him to realize my needs. But he referred to my past illnesses and begged me at this particular time to cease to drive myself. Even while I listened I still secretly and happily contemplated going ahead with my new plans to open a labor hostel. The idea of new responsibility attracted me, and in a little while I was once again committed to work in which my ideals of life and conduct could manifest themselves and still give me leisure for my home.

About this time I was fortunate in meeting Edward Carpenter. He was then a man of more than seventy years. We first became friends on the basis of our interest in the changing social scene.

Before meeting him, I had been deeply stirred by his social and political writings. His deep spiritual love of his fellow man and his comprehensive understanding drew me to him.

In the early days of our acquaintance he told me of his love of the earth and all living things. He was himself the possessor of the password that took him at all times to that place where he was content to give all and ask nothing in return. He had the power to understand and merge with the life-force in nature, and it was easy to speak to him of what I sensed and saw. His was a spontaneous nature; there was something continually arising from below his ordinary consciousness which could neither be quenched nor stopped — something that was out-of-joint with accepted things and yet never inconsistent with the moment.

He took time to explain to me at great length that I had been born to what he called a state of "cosmic consciousness," a condition many sought in vain to achieve. He also spoke of the lives of those personally known to him who had succeeded in reaching this state of "miraculous living," as he called it. He took me back, step by step, through my early childhood experiences, asking me to relate them in the order in which they had happened. Then he would explain sympathetically that they were not the ordinary memories and experiences of childhood. The way in which I described them to him led him to comment that they were not subjective imaginings but external and objective impressions. He showed me the completely logical sequence in which my perceptions had opened, and he was regretful that I had not been brought up by someone who understood my "realizations" and would have encouraged me to follow instead of suppressing them.

He believed that my inability to hear music correctly was due to the repression and misuse of my own understanding of sound. He knew what I meant when I said the spectrum was not adequate to express the range of color that I saw, and he suggested that my knowledge of color might one day manifest itself in painting and design, for he felt that through some artistic outlet I would conceive ways of revealing both vision and inner perception.

He advised me to read certain books on the psychology and physiology of sex, but only afterwards did I realize how profound his purpose was. He had wanted me to know that the people who possess these special sensitivities blend in their natures both the masculine and the feminine qualities. In this way he led me to understand that the variations in sexual types were not to be despised; he interpreted them as steps toward a higher form of mankind. Possessed as he was of a deeply mystical and benevolent nature, he regarded art and beauty as supreme expressions of God.

Edward Carpenter introduced me to the religious and spiritual movements of the day and singled out those leaders who had revealed the Cosmic Law. I heard through him of many religious movements that were then unknown to me, and among them was the Theosophical Society. I went to meetings and read the literature of the Society. When I told him of my negative reaction to this and to other movements of which he had spoken, he laughed and said, "I have my own conception of the Divine, and you have yours. Your judgment will take care of you, and you'll find your own way. Now that you're in the mood to know more, I am able to introduce you to the true sources from which these movements draw their original inspiration. First, read Emerson and know him well. Then digest *Leaves of Grass* by Walt Whitman. Fraser's *Golden Bough* will give you something later on, and one day get to know Spinoza. When you know Spinoza, you can disregard the lesser prophets. When you have carefully digested these great ones, take time to read the Oriental Scriptures, especially the Upanishads and the Mahabharata. Then go back to your Bible and read it with fresh understanding. When you have reread and digested all these writings, you will begin to understand the folly of modern man's attempt to create new religions."

In the two years of my close friendship with Edward Carpenter I had what I can only describe as the most profound spiritual experience of my life, one which gave me a sense of release, of being set free, of being reborn. He helped to liberate me from the burdens of my past confusions. I no longer carried a secret despair about my childhood or my parents or the failure of my first marriage. Through him, I learned that my intense curiosity and urgent need to live in two selves were not the products of an unbalanced mind but positive powers beyond the range of contemporary understanding. For the first time in my life, I realized that my perceptions were truly not hallucinations but the result of capacities for inner comprehension, capacities for what Edward Carpenter called "cosmic consciousness."

Whatever I might say of Edward Carpenter would be inadequate to express my spiritual debt to one of the greatest beings of the modern world. He knew better than anyone I have ever known the Region of the Self. The diversities of people's temperaments, which ordinarily distinguish and divide people, never troubled him. Life was a testing ground on which all were equal who had achieved the first struggle to be born. He lived in a region of his own making, a region where defects or accomplishments appeared of no importance. He spoke freely to me of the influence of Whitman on his life. He said this influence was as natural as the rain and sun and the air which yielded their laughter and secrets of him. He lived in the open air, and there, in the vast world between him and the sky, was his land of splendor.

About this time, my daughter had a series of long illnesses that followed one another in quick succession. These were the first illnesses from which she seemed unable to recover. One day I overheard the doctor telling my husband and the nurse that he could do no more then for the child, that the crisis would probably occur at about two o'clock in the morning, but that at whatever time it developed he was to be called. He also warned them that my own health might suffer if the child did not pull through. I burned with resentment against him for "abandoning" her. I knew that the child must get well.

She was gasping for breath. There was nothing I could do, yet I could not bear to sit in idle agony and watch her fighting alone. In desperation I took her up out of her bed and held her close, wishing to give her some of my own strength. Then I heard a voice saying to me, "Be careful! Do not stifle her. She must breathe more easily. Open the windows and allow a current of air to enter the room."

I did not dare to question the source of the voice; I just opened the windows. I remember watching the curtains flutter and wondering if there was too much air. Then, turning back, I saw the outline of a figure leaning against the bed — a short, lithe, ageless individual — , his face turned from me. I was startled, and my limbs were trembling, yet at the time this phenomenon did not seem extraordinary. As I laid the child in her bed, the figure became more clearly defined. It was that of a man clad in gray garments, and he was smiling in a kindly, sympathetic way with a contagious sense of cheerfulness. I was reassured and knew that he had come to help me. I cannot tell how long he remained, nor did I see him go. The next thing I knew, there was a resounding noise in my ears; someone was knocking. I rose and unlocked the door to find my worried household standing there anxiously waiting for news. I returned to the child's bed. She was breathing quietly, and I knew with certainty that she would recover.

The next day I collapsed from the long strain of my daughter's illness, and I was ill myself for many weeks. Out of that developed asthma, which stayed with me for years afterwards. Meanwhile, my daughter grew well, but the identity of the mysterious stranger who saved her life was still unrevealed, though the memory of the visit remained with vivid clarity.

I had thus had three visions of incorporeal personalities. Forgotten until this moment, I now remembered my uncle coming to me after his death and his promise that within two years I should leave Ireland. This prophecy had come true. Then I recalled the appearance of my Aunt Leone holding her tiny baby and that I had known that she was "going away" and would take the baby with her. Now I had seen the unknown one who had come and saved my daughter's life. I could no longer doubt that these visions were real. They had all been followed by developments in the lives of people — undeniable, objective evidence.

Among the many people who stayed at my hostel, there was a man who threw further light on the nature of my experiences. One day he stopped me in passing and surprised me by saying that he recognized my "latent powers," and he proceeded to explain that he knew this because he was clairvoyant and perceived that I had capacities that covered the entire range of psychic phenomena, including healing, psychometry, clairvoyance and clairaudience.

I was intrigued by this statement and asked him to explain to me the meaning of some of these words which I had heard for the first time. In response he gave me a brief and simple explanation of what certain groups believe about the capacity of the alleged dead to communicate with the living. He said that he was able to speak with his "dead" daughter, and afterwards I heard him address her as though she were in the room. I looked intently but could not see her, so I regarded him with sympathy and pity, suspecting that the poor man was unbalanced and imagining that his daughter was there. In that first reaction, I was wholly unaware of the fact that I was treating him in precisely the same way that others had treated me in the past when I spoke of my own experiences.

I might have dismissed the whole matter as unimportant if this man had not later handed me his watch, saying, "Tell me what you sense about this." I took the watch in my hand and gave him my impressions as they came to mind. He stated that the incidents I related of his son's life, among other things, were true. I was startled but interested and questioned him about the nature and use of this psychometric power.

He often spoke of his daughter as though all the thoughts, aims and tastes which had motivated her living were still the foundation of her new existence. I was disturbed to hear death interpreted as a change of place but not of consciousness. From the little that I had been able to observe personally, I was sure that at death a definite transformation took place which led to a state of new consciousness. Having watched the intense and dynamic movement of separation that took place at the time of death, I knew that the motives and activities that occurred beyond could not possibly be the same as those that operate on the plane of human living.

However, this man's explanation of his daughter's changed condition puzzled and interested me. When he suggested that I accompany him to the headquarters of one of the Spiritualist societies, I was not unwilling to go and make further investigation.

We attended a meeting in which a clairvoyant was giving the audience messages from the alleged dead. I went in a serious mood, prepared for revelation. The room was very still, the audience waiting; then the clairvoyant began.

"For the lady at the back of the room with the big black hat, I see an old man with a gray beard and blue eyes. Could he be your father?"

"Yes," said a voice in the rear.

"I see a large 'J.' Could his name be John? Or it might be James."

"That is right: James," the lady in the rear responded helpfully.

"He says you are worried about conditions that are changing for the better at the end of the month. Would you recognize that?"

The lady answered, "Yes, it fits exactly."

During this conversation I looked for the apparition of the father, but could not see him. For an hour one heard communications from the realm of the dead that consisted entirely of advice about the banal routines of the present. At the end, tea was served to the audience. There was a buzz of conversation. I overheard one woman tell another that she was not coming again, for she never received anything, and her friend replied, "Oh, but my message was good. I knew Eric was there, because he described the initials on the fob that his father gave him before he went to the war." Another woman complimented the clairvoyant on the wonderful message which she had received. I waited for no more. Outside, I told my friend how puzzled I was by this performance. Was it possible that the profoundly important change that death involved could be reduced to the level of banality?

As far as I knew, the visions of the dead which I had experienced had come by chance. Now I wanted to know how the clairvoyant functioned and whether she saw her visions of the dead objectively. I was also interested to know more about the "mechanism" of the phenomenon which was so readily accepted by the group. I took out a membership in a society and attended meetings which included lectures and demonstrations in psychometry and clairvoyance, but I remained baffled, finding no clues to the way in which these experiences occurred.

Within the society, everyone was sympathetic. They related their own psychic experiences and encouraged me to read the literature. They suggested that, if I needed further enlightenment, I should join a group who gathered once a week at the society's headquarters. When the proceedings commenced, I was requested to place the tips of my fingers on the surface of a table as the others did, and the table would tap out messages "from the dead." The ladies claimed that whenever I joined the circle, much more happened. For instance, the table moved more definitely and spelled out the messages more swiftly.

Much interested in these experiments, I tried them out at home with my husband and friends, who were skeptical and very amused. Once, when a cousin was sitting with us, he asked the communicating intelligence to inform him of the address of the place where he had been born. At that time he did not know the address himself, but verified at a later date the truth of what was told him. This type of verification impressed me sufficiently to continue my experiments.

One day during an experiment in the rooms of the society, with table tapping, something extraordinary happened. I became drowsy and dropped off to sleep. I was awakened by being vigorously shaken by one of the members, all of whom seemed frightened and upset. I was nauseated and giddy, with lights dancing before my eyes. They told me that, in my sleep, their dead relatives had communicated through me. Astonished at their reactions, I hurried home to tell my husband.

"This is awful!" he said. "You must not go to that society any more."

For a moment I had a tremendous sense of relief that his decision should thus put an end to these experiments, for I had no desire to lend myself to experiences beyond my control. However, the secretary of the society, who had been worried about the extraordinary manifestation, later wrote and advised me to consult a Swiss friend of hers, Mr. Huhnli, who had considerable knowledge of psychic matters and could help me. Still curious, and anxious to learn more about these powers, I went to see Mr. Huhnli and was relieved to find him a gentle and simple person. He had heard a little about me from the secretary of the society but asked me to give him the whole story. I told him of my experiences while he listened sympathetically; then he suggested that I sit quietly in my chair and relax. I did so, and again began to feel sleepy. Then, I lost consciousness.

When I recovered, he said, "You are potentially a trance medium." I was naturally surprised, but he explained that it was a condition dependent on an extreme passivity of mind, and that it could be either of a light or deep nature. Deeply entranced, the individual lost control of his own consciousness in what appeared to be a sleep-like condition, and at such times some entity would control a part of the sleeper's will. "This is what happened in your case," he said. "I spoke with an entity while you slept. He is one of unusual intelligence who declares himself to be an Oriental and wishes to do serious work to prove the validity of the theory of the survival of the alleged dead. He gives the name of 'Uvani.'"

Mr. Huhnli's words were both unexpected and disturbing. I left quickly and returned home to tell my husband the story. He was much displeased that I should have again undertaken such experiments, and he told me that, if these things had actually happened, I was not only on the brink of insanity, but I must already have lost my mind. I half believed he was right, and a new fear overcame me—a fear of not being wholly my own self.

For weeks I never slept without a light burning in my room, was constantly and anxiously wondering if this "Uvani" saw and heard everything I did in my daily life — if, in fact, he was responsible for some of the strange patterns that unfolded themselves before me from time to time. Or could it be that this Oriental was a creation of my own subconscious mind? I could not believe that I had subconsciously imagined him. The most terrifying aspect of the situation lay in the fact that it seemed possible for him to express himself through me only when I was incapable of knowing what he might say or do.

I endured this state of new confusion as long as I could; in desperation, I went again to see Mr. Huhnli and explained my misgivings to him. If this "control personality" really existed in such close relation to me, could he not know my most intimate and private behavior and relations? Mr. Huhnli assured me that the "control personality" would not be interested in my daily life — that his whole purpose was based on a profound wish to be of service to humanity. "Moreover," Mr. Huhnli said, "your 'control' may not approach you unless you make it possible for him." I replied, "Since I have the power to avoid the trance state altogether, I can dispense with him." But he doubted if this would be possible and feared that, if I did so, I might have further mental confusion to cope with. According to Mr. Huhnli, the "control personality" had already established his contact through me and had made his purpose clear, having stated beyond all question that it was destined that he should prove the truth of human survival after death.

I doubted the reality of the entire situation relating to the "control," yet Mr. Huhnli's integrity led me to trust what he disclosed about the hitherto unsuspected areas of the subconscious mind. In order that I might better understand the "control personality," he suggested that he would help me deal with myself if I would permit him to speak with "Uvani." My avid curiosity caused me to accept his suggestion, and, as time went on and the statements of "Uvani" accumulated, I began to speculate as to what would happen if my capacities could be developed so that in time I could become a competent sensitive.

In order to continue these experiments with Mr. Huhnli I felt that the less my husband knew about them the better. Any mention of the trance condition convinced him that I should be examined by a psychiatrist. Remembering former like suggestions, I refused, even though he and his friends were terribly disturbed by what they suspected to be a new and very dangerous preoccupation. He became so upset at times that he threatened to place me under observation, but I was not to be frightened. My stubborn insistence brought about other differences of opinion which did not add to our happiness. However, I wished neither to deliberately wreck my marriage or to give up interest in my experiments. My hostel made continual demands upon my time which could not be ignored, but I found it not only stimulating and educational but, more importantly, the preserver of my financial independence.

My husband had never welcomed the many preoccupations which left me little time for the more social life which he wanted me to share with him. I knew that he was disappointed in me and that I worried him, and I even seriously considered giving up the hostel in order to devote more time to him, but to do so would have seemed like a betrayal of those with whom I worked, as well as a negation of the very aims which, I had begun to realize, must be continually treasured. It would have been easy to echo the cynicism of the hour and hold oneself aloof from the despair of the moment by accepting the fallacy that one cannot change the mood of the world alone. However, I knew that hard work — with honest and impartial aim — went a long way toward producing positive results.

Most of my friends tried hard to settle down to a normal state of existence but were disillusioned by the trade depression which followed so soon after the rosy dreams of postwar reconstruction. The trade unions themselves had shed the overly optimistic who had entered the ranks through the abnormal influence created by the war and early postwar period. Unemployment and falling wages were heralding the onset of the grave depression which followed the temporary boom and led eventually to greater distress. Too many of my friends were losing hope. However, the recent illness of my daughter, the new psychic developments and changing situation within the country did not encourage any settled pattern in our married life.

The National Strike of 1926 solved my problem. I took advantage of this unhappy turn of events to dispose of the hostel. The decision to do so was helped by the fact that the time had come to send my daughter to boarding school away from London on account of her health. It was not without regret that I resolved to make so drastic a change, but on the other hand the changing scene justified taking time out to explore further the mental and psychical processes that were taking place in me in an almost mechanistic way — processes that were not absolutely dependent on my will.

To find a physical explanation was neither easy nor comprehensible in terms of everyday consideration, and the occurrences of trance were "inconvenient facts" which troubled my friends, who were beginning to doubt my sanity, if not my respectability. Within myself, I knew that I would have to find a physical explanation and more seriously understand my own mental processes if I were to continue to live a balanced life. I found it necessary to look into books dealing with philosophy and psychology in order to understand the interrelation of body and mind, and to make this possible I formed the habit of being alone a good deal of the time. As though destiny itself had taken a hand, circumstances made it imperative for my husband to go abroad at this point. He was very reluctant to leave me, but I did not want to stand in the way of anything that would be to his advantage. Besides, I had an almost prophetic sense that this marriage would not last.

I experienced a secret joy at being alone, for now I had ample time to consider all that had occurred since I had first gone to the Spiritualist society. I could hardly believe that all these strange things had happened to me and that events could crowd so strangely and quickly into the life of any human being. Sometimes I was appalled to think that I had allowed myself to be drawn into such extravagant activities without knowing more about them. I saw that the validity of the "control personality" depended on the word of a single individual, Mr. Huhnli, and I realized that he might have been mistaken. With a kind of natural aversion I turned from the idea that any intelligence but my own should have access to my mind. For several months, then, I avoided all philosophical groups and maintained an objective attitude while I absorbed what I could from reading.

I had never really grown very strong since my daughter's illness, and further lung trouble again overtook me. During the period of enforced rest, I examined myself and my past and made certain discoveries about the manner in which my life had fallen into shape. I saw that the trance state might be a part of the pattern of my own development. I began to comprehend how the pain and suffering of my early days had made me withdraw from the world of people. Indeed, I had been able to withdraw so completely that, although I had seen my aunt's lips moving as she scolded me, not a word of what she said penetrated my bearing. I remembered how, when the pain or punishment became almost unbearable, I could retire within myself and become numb, negating the painful effects. I also recalled the repetition of "blotting out" or amnesia which had occurred during early years of my first marriage and during the tragic episodes of my sons' deaths. These, too, were forms of escape. Throughout my life I had unconsciously developed the technique of escape in order to avoid suffering. I could now perceive how this practice had perhaps prepared the way for the development of the trance state.

I recalled the gypsy woman who first taught me to read the cards, to see omens in the dark glass and to gather meanings from the patterns in the sand — all of which stimulated levels of my consciousness —, symbols under which deeper values were now discernible. In my attempts to understand these perceptions, imagination operated my sensory being, and, briefly, between my seeing and the surface on which my gaze was fixed, areas were visualized where different patterns dawned, moved and disappeared: fragmentary events, some strange and unfamiliar. Soon consciousness would pass beyond imagination, and that state of inner alertness to which I have referred would supervene. Immense, colorful figures moved swiftly before my inner vision as upon a stage; words and phrases came out of the air; form after form would appear and disappear, swiftly and unaccountably, yet the kaleidoscopic pageant always held a sequence and a meaning.

Thus I reviewed the panorama of the inner mind, full of significances and banalities. I knew that thoughts were things, formed of the purpose and power of the one who creates them, and they are capable of transforming the lives of people, of communities, or of the world itself — as, for instance, the idea of Columbus, that by sailing westward he could reach the fabulous East. Every created object carries the mark and quality of the life of him who made it, like the unmistakable brushwork of a master's painting or the patina of a great ceramist's matchless glaze. Even in the marketplace, differences in *quality* are recognized, and at deeper levels of perception more subtle values in the natures of things become discernable.

It was at this point that I began to feel a growing sense of impending change, a growing restlessness. I was suffering from an overdose of philosophies and concluded that a unified self might be more easily realized in a new country. The very idea was in itself stimulating. Obedience to the inner will meant continual sacrifice of the exciting, external events of life.

This, then, was the answer. I should be truly virtuous and remove all the existing patterns of conflict by starting a life in a new country where reorientation would in itself be an intrinsic education for the emotions. To think was to act. When my husband returned I would get as far away from England as possible and find release from all of the past in a fresh environment and a new country.

❖ TEN

SERIOUS STUDY

One day, having arranged everything for my departure, I set out to buy tickets to Australia. My way led through Southampton Row, only a few steps from the Spiritualist society. I felt a strong impulse to call upon the secretary of the society, who had been very sympathetic. A stronger destiny than my own decision was at work, for this call changed the course of my life.

The secretary was pleased to see me and expressed her regret that I had given up my interest in psychic matters. She stressed very strongly the importance of continuing with my training, and she told me that recently, while sitting with the well-known trance medium, Mrs. Osborne Leonard, she had been told by the control personality, "Feda," that she would meet me again and be instrumental in helping me to continue my own studies. At first I resisted the idea, but her genuine sincerity led me to promise at least to see another friend of hers, who knew a great deal about the subject, before I made any final decision.

It was in this way that I came to meet Mrs. Kelway Bamber, who told me that she also had been informed by the control of Mrs. Osborne Leonard that she would meet me and aid in my further psychic development. Mrs. Kelway Bamber was a very capable woman with a strong personality. She had lived for many years in India, was herself a sensitive and had received a series of letters, automatically written, from her dead son, Claude, which had already been published. I was impressed by Mrs. Kelway Bamber. She struck me as being a woman of fine, keen intelligence, not given to wild imagining or sensational statements. She was most anxious to help, and when she heard that the control personality was alleged to be Oriental, she felt that she could aid "him," for she had a deep understanding and sympathy with the East and its philosophy. I was intrigued with this new diversion and postponed my journey for a while. Mrs. Kelway Bamber arranged that I should meet esoteric groups in London and have the trance examined by them, in groups or individually.

I fell easily into an autohypnotic state, and apparently the control "Uvani" came through and spoke. From all reports, these early experiments contained evidence that "Uvani" might in time give proof concerning survival after death. This, I found, was the only subject that interested the majority of the groups. Among the prominent people I met at this time was Mrs. Hewat McKenzie, who, with her husband, had founded and organized the British College of Psychic Science. I was impressed by her honesty and intelligence and also by her cautious approach to Spiritualism, although she accepted its doctrines. She suggested that I meet her husband, who was reputed to be an authority on psychic phenomena.

Hewat McKenzie had a remarkable personality. His humorous outlook and generous welcome made me feel at ease, and, as I came to know him better, I realized that he had a greater knowledge of psychic matters than anyone else I had met. When he suggested an experiment in order that he might judge the nature and quality of my control personality, "Uvani," I was relieved and pleased to have another objective opinion. Mr. McKenzie eventually told me that I possessed potentialities for becoming a trance medium, provided these capacities were properly trained. He further remarked that I had undoubted psychic power which would manifest itself anyway, but he stressed the fact that, in trance mediumship, the most important thing was the adequate training and development of the control. In the entire period of my development, he was the first and only person who seemed to realize that the spiritual quality and level of communications expressed through the trance were dependent on the degree of mental and spiritual development of the control personality, as well as on the degree of responsibility one took for it oneself.

Hewat McKenzie was the only one who refused to take a pronouncement of a control personality as inevitably the word of some "higher power." He explained that, in his estimation, the possibilities of trance mediumship had been wasted and allowed to deteriorate through the centuries, so that trance mediums had come to function mainly on emotional and sentimental levels. This was due to the fact that when a control first made an appearance, no one regarded it as a personality who itself needed help and training in order to understand the highest use of its own functioning. He explained that a control personality is only an interpreter of what reaches him from other states of consciousness, and, therefore, each control has to be taught to make the purest use of its powers and transmit only the highest levels of truth available to it.

This attitude of Hewat McKenzie threw a different light on the possibilities of mediumship, and I felt that with his assistance I might find a clearer understanding of my psychic capacities. I came to value and trust the friendship and sympathy of Hewat McKenzie and his wife, and I decided to enroll for training under their joint direction at the British College of Psychic Science.

Hewat McKenzie considered that the most profound philosophies of the early teachers and the inspiration of all great scriptures through the ages had been received and channelled through the passive mind. He emphasized the responsibility which the possession of this power placed upon me and stressed how necessary it was for me to exercise care and and control over my daily habits of living. What I had to do was lead a simple and controlled existence, a quiet and harmonious life, free from excesses or indulgences of any kind, and he assured me that under tuition the control personality could be trained to take good care of the other aspects of my mind.

He showed a profound understanding of the nature of the conscious. He considered it as containing the entire memory of man, its form being that of a vacuum which drew everything to it. The conscious mind he regarded as a surface and continuous expression, on one level, of what was being "patterned" in the deep subconscious. To Hewat McKenzie, the nature of man and his subconscious were one. Believing that the subconscious absorbed impressions of everything in its environment, he made rules for the protection of my subconscious self while he trained my mediumship. He explained the danger of blurring or interfering with my own clear functioning, and he prohibited any attempt at this time to open up other aspects of my perceptions. He insisted that I avoid all reading on philosophic and occult subjects. He paid special attention to the methods by which the control must give his evidence, emphasizing that he bring through types of information as far removed as possible from the conscious knowledge of the investigator.

Believing that both suggestion and hypnosis could aid in producing a deeper separation between the conscious and subconscious minds, thus creating a condition in which the subconscious would be freed from the influences of external conditions, he regarded both of these techniques as valuable. With the subconscious thus freed from outer effects, the control would have a clear channel through which to work.

Thus for some years I worked under the care and direction of Mr. and Mrs. McKenzie. Once a week during this period I sat with Mr. McKenzie for the development of the subconscious and for its direction into phases that were not related to the type of communications that proved "survival." My work at the College was limited to one or two appointments a day, and, following Mr. McKenzie's advice, I shut out all other aspects of psychic activity. In those years I built up a reputation as a trance medium, and, from records made, it would seem that my trance utterances dealt with survival, with precognition and even with clairvoyant perceptions in the trance state.

During those years in which Mr. McKenzie trained the control personality, I never fully accepted for myself the reality of the control's existence. In mental conflict, I often voiced my doubts about "Uvani's" individuality and my suspicion that he might not be a separate personality but only a split-off of my own subconscious mind. Both Mr. and Mrs. McKenzie were indignant at this suggestion, and they told me frankly that I was in no position to judge the reality of the control's existence, which was true. In this doubting mood, I often referred to the "Uvani" personality jokingly, which shocked Mr. McKenzie, who took the matter of mediumship most seriously.

As I continued at the British College, I became familiar with the reactions of the people who sought me there, and I began to question how these people made use of the information they received. In time I began to differentiate their types. There were a few who came because they were drawn by an earnest desire to communicate with someone dear to them who had died. But I discovered that many of the people who consult mediums use the sittings as an opiate and not as an aid to more responsible living. There were those who came with a purely personal and selfish desire to receive messages of consolation and encouragement. Such messages were not always forthcoming, and, when this occurred, upon awakening from my trance I was indignantly asked whether I was ever able to give any satisfactory results.

This troubled me, for I could never guarantee results, and I began to feel the futility of continuing work at this level. Such responses had none of the fine feeling and deep significance with which Hewat McKenzie approached the entire undertaking. In view of this, together with my own lack of conviction in the reality of "Uvani" and my uncertainty that the communications transmitted by the control were necessarily from the alleged dead, my deep interest began to flag. Nevertheless, I continued with my work as a trance medium at the College until Hewat McKenzie died in 1929. His death removed the one person whose lofty attitude toward psychic matters had made possible a serious interest in developing trance mediumship. His quality had sustained me up to that time, and it continued to sustain me in the years that followed. What integrity and success I have been able to achieve in the use of supernormal sensitivities I owe to the untiring patience and high faith of this tireless and courageous man.

After the death of Hewat McKenzie, it seemed impossible to continue my work at the College. Yet I found myself so deeply committed as a trance medium that I could not easily withdraw from that activity. I decided therefore to continue with several other well-known philosophic groups. By this means I hoped to gain more varied contacts in the psychic field and to obtain a clearer understanding of the types of people who are attracted to these other philosophies. I discovered that their interests and motivations were no more profound than the interests of those who attended the College. Those who sought evidence over a period of time seemed to be well satisfied with the communications they received, but I concluded from my own observation that, instead of gaining strength and independence as a consequence, they became more emotional and seemed less able to think out and determine matters for themselves. I was perturbed by this, for it seemed to me to indicate a gradual weakening of their mental and moral fiber.

Gradually I had developed a serious sense of responsibility for the effects of the trance communications. I saw that I was responsible, in some measure, for the consequences of the material for which I was the channel of transmission. I could not escape the impression that deterioration rather than improvement showed in many of the people who sought evidence, and I began to have a feeling of revulsion at my part in the production of such results. I wondered if I should not give up mediumship forever. My daughter was happy away at school, and I began to consider a new phase of living for myself.

Then, as so often before, I became ill again, and two serious operations suspended all my activities for many months. The doctors remarked that I deliberately retarded my recovery by "busying" my mind with too many things. However, during this long illness, I again lived close to my own being, glad to immerse myself once more in the realm of the two minds and forget the problems which the trance work kept constantly before me. During my convalescence, I had time to explore further my world of light, sound and movement, and I found that color had power to heal. For example, by wearing certain colors, I could produce exhilarating effects, and I began to contemplate the use and value of color in establishing the momentum and equilibrium of some phases of my life. In fact, during this period I did much to revitalize myself by means of this new comprehension, and, when my friends saw me again after long months of illness, they were amazed at the vivid impression of new vigor that I exhibited at times, even though my physical recovery was not yet established.

I also had time to examine my attitude toward my marriage, which had continued in a civilized and friendly way. It was as though we had established a covenant of friendship between us and were content to be understanding and undisturbed about each other. There were roads without number ahead, and there was often a voice that cut through to my heart like an unseen flash of lightning — a voice that reminded me that I was meeting only a part of myself face to face and had not yet taken hold of the helm of the ship that I alone must guide. Despair often came to choke back the life currents that surged within me and demanded action. But I still kept my senses bound and, in consequence, was made more guilty by the deeper knowledge that I had not given enough of myself to marriage at any time. I had been content to follow a certain routine of action as the shadow follows the moving lamp. However, I was very certain that self-mortification held no answer, and when I eventually recovered, it was with the decision that I would truly be a comrade and a wife rather than a woman who nourished disappointment because marriage contained no great fulfillment.

However, it was not to be. My husband had different ideas and was not at all interested to hear that I was prepared to devote "the labor of a lifetime" to make love all, for this response in my heart had come too late and could not make for the airy lightness with which I had dismissed marriage in the bygone years. Very gently he told me that he had found the more perfect woman but had hesitated to speak of it because he did not wish to hurt me. I despised myself a little that my own unconscious drive toward freedom had blinded me to his deepest needs. Thus it was no longer necessary to surrender to a vow. My husband, in freeing himself, released me from it.

I now felt free to make a final test of my attitude toward my activity as a trance medium, and I returned to this work. Up to this time "Uvani" had been the only control who relayed messages in my trance state, but now I was told that a new personality had spoken through me. His name was "Abdul Latif," and he claimed to be a Persian physician and astronomer who had lived in the 12th century and had been associated with the Court of Saladin. From then on, he had remained to extend his work to many people interested in health and healing. "Abdul Latif" was already known to Sir Arthur Conan Doyle and to others. He had worked through a number of sensitives in different parts of the world before he revealed himself through me, and he continues to do so up to the present time. When I first heard of his appearance, I was afraid that this new manifestation might indicate a fresh split in my own personality, and although I watched my own physical condition, as far as I was able, to discover if there were any disturbing consequences from this new association, I found none. I gathered from the reports of others that the level of the trance communications had changed with the introduction of "Abdul Latif." He was concerned with healing and philosophy and discussed both spiritual and philosophical problems, but, unlike "Uvani," he gave little time to the proof of survival.

I had always needed to find my own answers to my problems, and in this case I finally came to the conclusion that the level of communication had changed because the needs and wishes of the people who now inquired were different. I began to understand that the subconscious mind could reach out to many levels and, if this were true, then I saw two possible conclusions to the problem of the change which had occurred. Either the control personalities were parts of my subconscious, or the subconscious might be far more vast and profound than anyone had yet imagined. It was impossible for me to determine this subtle and extensive problem. I was giving satisfactory results, yet I could not frankly and fully accept the significance which most people attributed to them. It occurred to me to gather further evidence for myself from the works of others. I could do this justifiably, for my own mediumship was firmly established. I attended a number of seances for both mental and physical phenomena, and, while I saw many remarkable manifestations, I did not find what I sought for my own clarification.

There were those who suggested that the separation in my personality due to my use of trance might well be the cause of my many illnesses. This implication, together with inner uncertainties, finally determined me to give up my work as a sensitive. Friends protested and could not believe that, having carried on my mediumistic experiments successfully for many years, I would give it up now. Some, very much concerned, undertook to discuss the matter with the control personalities, who made light of my intention, declaring, "This is only a step in her further development. She will go through with this, but she will not, as she thinks, give up her experimental work." Nevertheless, I went ahead with my own plans.

Then one day again I heard a voice, toneless and cold, saying to me, "Make the most of your happiness; it cannot last." I shuddered, remembering the warning that had predicted the death of my son. This present warning applied, I thought, not only to my feeling of freedom in giving up mediumship but to my determination to find some personal happiness and to marry again.

Life was wonderful and everything progressed smoothly in this direction until the day when the banns of the marriage were announced. On that day both my fiancé and I fell suddenly ill. He, having a chill, developed septic pneumonia, and I was taken to the hospital with an active mastoid and ruptured appendix. I was operated upon for appendicitis and a few days later had regained sufficient strength. I was told that my fiancé was dead. The shock caused a serious relapse and aggravated the ear and throat condition, and I had to undergo another operation, this time on the throat.

I was told by my own physician, long after I had recovered, that the doctors and nurses in the operating room at that time had clearly heard the tones of a voice which spoke just after I had become unconscious from the anesthetic. No one seemed to know exactly what the voice had said, but my physician, who had been in India in his youth, told me that he had recognized certain words in Hindustani, spoken in a commanding voice. I had no knowledge of any Oriental language, and, in any case, at the moment when the voice had spoken, the operation had already commenced, so that it would have been impossible for me to utter a word. My doctor was so impressed by the event that he prepared a letter of verification for those interested, recording the exact circumstances of the occurrence. G. R. S. Mead, the well-known scholar who often communicated with "Abdul Latif" through my mediumship as well as through others, reported that he had been informed by "Abdul Latif" that he had been present in the operating room during my operation.

One evening, very defeated and weak, lying in my hospital room, I became aware of the ebbing away of my vitality until I was at the point of losing consciousness. I wondered, could this be death? Then I perceived that the wardrobe standing against the wall opposite my bed was tottering, while crackling and explosive sounds were coming from its direction. Terrified, I rang for the nurse. The moment she entered, the manifestations ceased. I explained to her what had happened and begged her to stay with me. She stayed a while — to humor me, I suspect —, but scarcely had she left the room when the wardrobe began to shake and a violent interior explosion threw its doors wide open. Only just able to touch my bell, I did so and fainted. It took me fully twenty-four hours to find my voice or recover from the effects of this experience. The nurse told my doctor that, in the hallway outside, she had heard the explosive noise that had occurred in my room and that, hurrying in, she had found me unconscious. Whatever the actual nature of the event may have been — and to this day I have no sure explanation — the experience did heighten my sensitivities.

During my convalescence I had plenty of time to consider my future. I had now disposed of my marriages and had to ask myself why, once having gained my freedom, I should want to remarry. The answer became very clear when I sought it. The zeal that I first exercised to make marriage a mystical and sacramental bond had, in the end, defeated me. Had I been more mature, I would have accepted marriage on a less romantic level and would have fared better. Relentless effort, however, drove me to make the material formality a significant, unique and almost sacred experience. What the marriage ceremony lacked in emotion, I was determined should be fulfilled by unceasing effort. The mystical formula most probably stemmed from my Bible; the heat and splendor of imagination did the rest!

Then, too, I remembered that I always wanted to give. The "savings" of my school days were devoted to the needs of others, and my later marriages were arrived at because they happened along at times when the men I married had need of me. The moment the need was taken care of, I began to lose interest. In my early dreams of growing up, my adult world was peopled with many children. When I lost my sons, I turned automatically toward social service, and I rather suspect that husbands became identified with my own deep need to give and to serve. That I should rely on their superior strength, regard them as breadwinners or beings to whom I was morally responsible, never occurred to me. My intuitive self demanded that I should always find happiness in work and that the road ahead, whatever it held, must be forged by my own efforts.

Whatever means I used in my relations to the external world, I was related to it only by intuition. This had been the indispensable groundwork at all times, until it would appear that I was given over to myself through intuition and became dual in my motivations, the subject as well as the object. I could not, at this point anymore than I can now, see any fixity or permanence in a relationship that did not depend on need and spiritual understanding. Thus it often happened that the intuitive "I" saw the beginning and the end of a situation as one, while the more personalized "me" decided to act out the play in the world of external circumstances.

When I finally realized that the marriage ceremony must always remain symbolic for me, I knew that I would not contemplate marriage again.

Months passed before I had recovered sufficiently from this protracted illness to consider my future seriously. There seemed to be no escape from my psychic destiny. My friends urged me to return to my experiments, but I decided that, if I did, it must be in a new and very different manner. I determined that I would use trance communication for the purpose of serious objective research, for the appearance — if such it was — of "Abdul Latif" in the operating theatre and the violent explosion in the hospital room had led me to believe that there were principles underlying phenomena which I had yet to discover. No sooner had I resolved to do this than the way to proceed presented itself in an almost miraculous manner. I received an invitation to visit New York and work under the auspices of the American Society for Psychical Research.

❖ ELEVEN

TRANSATLANTIC JOURNEY

I sailed for the United States in the autumn of 1931 and spent a few months in New York, demonstrating trance mediumship. I had hoped that the American Society would be much more scientific in its approach, especially since I knew of the fine contributions to psychic research that had been made by Professor Hyslop and Dr. Walter Franklin Prince. However, at this time there was little attempt to keep objective records of investigations.

I also visited the West Coast and found that here, too, objective research was almost nonexistent, although I did have the pleasure of doing some experiments with a number of groups, including those of Hamlin Garland and Stewart Edward White. At this time an opportunity presented itself to work at Johns Hopkins, where I spent some time working in analysis. However, the results of these studies were not published until thirteen years later.

Many of these trials were described as being telepathic, but I suspected that I had not as yet been able to separate these subtle perceptions, and although I was often asked to explain how I worked, I liked to examine the method and significance of the phenomena for my own better understanding. In precognitive mood, I conceive of standing outside of time, as I did in my childhood when I waited breathlessly to examine the spiral movements of color and light.

Then, as now, the long in-drawn breaths, together with a tightening of the muscles, prepared me for a state which I have unconsciously evolved in order to calm the conscious and so allow all the senses, keenly working in unison, to reach the desired goal. In such an *alert* state, I conceive of yesterday, today and tomorrow as a single curve, and on the in-drawn breath time loses reality and the past and future are present in one instant.

While imagination plays a part in the beginning of the experiments, the sensation may be likened to that of a pigeon circling to find its bearings or the alert intentness of an animal stalking its prey. The intensification of desire quickens and exhilarates the senses until one can actually imagine the sting of the sea on one's skin, smell the perfume of the blossoms, see the birds on the wing, and hear the beat of the waves against the shore — and yet simultaneously be in winter in one locality and register summer in the region of one's inner perceptions. The phenomenon appears as the gradual forming of an image out of a deep blue or nebulous background. Sometimes it is not even an image. It can be a sound, a deep intuition or a certainty about something of which one had no conception a moment before. This process is not indefinite but is almost electric in its reception. One *knows.*

While the written language requires an eye to observe and identify, the unwritten language translates itself from an inner light which needs an outward feeling of passivity but an inner and very active perception, causing the most delicate cognitions to be translated into ideas. In such sensing the minutest detail becomes important. Initials stand out as large as a window, while a miniature may assume the dimensions of a large portrait. The fluid and flexible state in which one finds oneself registers in incredibly quick time and often in almost surrealistic form, blending objects together or suggesting them by taste or smell. I cannot always say through which organ these delicate impressions first begin to manifest, though I am sure that further acute observation of these sensations will lead to "lawfulness."

In order to illustrate what I mean, let me explain the conditions of a test which had been arranged for me by a well-known analyst in New York with a medical man in Newfoundland. Two notetakers were present, as well as the participants and observers in the home of the New York analyst. (I might also mention that I had not previously been in this house, nor in that of the Newfoundland doctor, whom I had not even met). When I entered the telepathic state I found myself outside a house, where I was able to see both garden and ocean — sense the damp atmosphere and see tiny flowers growing in the ridgeway between the rocks that lined a path to the door, and beyond the door I knew there was a staircase. Then I could actually see a man slowly descending. Speaking aloud as though he sensed my presence, I heard him say, "I think this will be a successful experiment." The words sounded like a toneless voice a short distance away. Caught in his movements I watched him as a hypnotized person might, as he approached a table. There he paused for a moment as though to focus my attention. The objects on the table, as well as the man, were now visible.

After I had described them they faded and I knew that the doctor was again speaking to me. "Make my apologies to the group. I have had an accident and cannot work as I hoped to." Impelled to examine his face more closely, I saw that he lifted a hand and pointed to a bandage around his head. He walked slowly toward a bookcase but before he reached it the title of a book by Einstein flashed into my mind. He looked at a volume. I did not know if he was reading aloud but, like an unseen flash, the impression of what he was reading revealed itself. He then directed my attention to several objects, including two photographs, on the other table. "But these," he said, "are in the house of the New York experimenter which has been recently redecorated and the photographs are not where he saw them last."

Here the experiment ended, and the observers stated that it had lasted fifteen minutes. This was described in the report issued as a study in telepathy, but had I relied upon telepathy alone, it would not have been comprehensive. For while I might have gotten the thoughts in the experimenter's mind as well as the sense of the words he addressed to me, without clairvoyance and clairaudience I would not have been able to hear the doctor's voice or see the objects.

The record was checked and sent to Newfoundland, but in the meantime a telegram was received describing the doctor's accident, which had occurred shortly before our experiment commenced. A few days later a letter arrived listing the steps of the experiment executed by the Newfoundland doctor, proving that I had been able to justify his hopes for a successful result. I had seen the series of objects laid out on the table and had successfully noted the book, its title and subject matter, and in addition had recognized that he had projected himself into the home of the New York analyst, since he had mentioned changes that had been made a few weeks previously in another part of the house.

During this time I also engaged in other experiments with Hereward Carrington, the well-known psychic researcher, in an attempt to test the validity of the control personalities as separate from my own. For this purpose, two types of testing were used — measurement by psychogalvanic reactions and the well-known association word tests. Should the reactions of the trance personalities and myself be different, then presumably these personalities would not be drawing from the same subconscious source as myself and, therefore, the minds of the two controls might be regarded as psychologically apart from my own.

The experiments, as far as they went, showed certain striking differences in response, but a more intensive study would have to be made in order to draw final conclusions as to the connection of the trance personalities with my subconscious mind. The following spring, I returned to England to repeat these same experiments with several groups in London and to recheck some of the work that had been started with Hereward Carrington and others in America.

❖ TWELVE

NOTES ON THE VALIDITY OF CONTROLS

Following this period of experimentation, I found no one very much interested in encouraging me in a deeper investigation of my mental mediumship, so I returned to work with the English societies. Then an extraordinary thing happened. Having given successful results for a number of years, I now found myself unable to produce results. I wondered then if my trance mediumship was coming to an end. Many people who had not been sympathetic to my need for scientific investigation honestly felt that my period of experimentation had probably interfered with the trance activities. From one of those I gathered that "Uvani" expressed reluctance about giving advice about purely personal matters. Over many years, he pointed out, he had given proof of survival after death, and the time had come to deal with the more serious aspects of living. I was interested in this statement, since it again brought up the identity and true meaning of the controls and my relation to them.

This relationship had never brought me complete peace of mind. I had never fully accepted the controls as realities, yet I was certain that some unexplained power worked through me in the production of supernormal manifestations. I had been able to thrust "Uvani" into the dim shadows as "something" that aided my experiments, but now I was not readily able to produce the results upon which the studies depended. "Uvani's" expressed wish not to cooperate further seemed to be in line with my own thoughts, and I asked myself in all seriousness what the nature of the control could be? Did he have any reality apart, and if so, how could I penetrate into my own subconscious and find the answer?

For a number of years I had acted as a channel through which alleged communication had taken place between the living and the dead, but I was now at the place where the whole process was either a tremendous self-deception or a method of revelation which should never have been allowed to be casually handled.

There are many who express the wish that I might come to some final conclusion about the control personalities. I long ago ceased to regard them with doubt but have failed to arrive at a complete understanding of their functioning. Since they continue to be consistent in their appearance, I have not the effrontery to suggest that a part of my personality which has afforded the blessing of understanding to many in the past should be coldly looked upon or arbitrarily decided upon by me. However, what these changes in personality may be are questions that continue to interest me, though my own attitude toward them must always remain fresh, spontaneous and wholly objective.

The trance, as I saw it then, operated for the purpose of alleged communication, because it was in this environment that my mediumship had received its initial impulse. Had I been born into another culture — Indian, Chinese or in the Congo — I should then have become the channel for an entirely different type of communication. This realization led me to a reexamination of the process by which communication is received. Assuming that the control exists and functions as the individual intelligence that it claims to be, then three personalities are involved in the communication process: the control, the medium and the investigator. Each is necessarily conditioned by his own experience and has his own consequent point of view.

This is what takes place in a typical experiment. The investigator arrives, the medium goes into trance and the control speaks. He first introduces to the enquirer whatever "dead" personality is present. Let us suppose that this enquirer has come to speak with a dead sister, sincerely convinced that this is possible. The control correctly describes the dead sister as she looked in life and mentions her name: "Prudence." The statements are acknowledged as correct. Then the brother may be advised to dispose of family effects in the near future. This is an important and evidential matter to him, but before he accepts the advice, he asks for more evidence of the sister's identity. She refers to the ring on his finger which belonged to their mother; she speaks of the accident which occurred to him when he was nearly drowned at the age of eighteen and she describes the death of their older brother after an operation. "Prudence" is asked for more evidence and, finally, where and what her present activities are. She speaks of her happiness but does not go into concrete details about her environment.

This may be taken as part of the report of a successful sitting. "Uvani" has been questioned as to the process he uses in communication, and he has stated that he receives messages by means of visual and mental impressions whose meaning he interprets through my mind.

I have always been troubled about the sad lack of detail that reaches the enquirer as to the environment of those who have gone beyond. But since I have used my own clairvoyant faculties, I can understand some of the difficulties. The mind works with pictures and symbols that are dependent upon the individual for interpretation. The state beyond would seem to be an extension of this life, or, better, this life would seem to be a mirrored reflection of the greater grandeur that surrounds us. In reflecting upon this "other world," I find myself devoid of words. The whole is a form of ecstasy, a breathless exhilaration in which every part of the being is caught and held suspended. It is a state in which every sense experiences the emotion of beauty in light and color and fast-moving rhythm. While one is within the experience, the senses work together and not independently of each other. That is why, in my estimation, it is so difficult to put words together that will do adequate justice to the experience.

It is true that I do clairvoyantly see the alleged dead and clairaudiently receive impressions of the messages they wish to transmit. These I receive in a process of "light" in which images and symbols change so rapidly that the transmission of the experience can only be sketchy, and also these symbols and experiences have to depend upon my limited interpretation. I can only compare the experience to visiting for a brief moment a country of great beauty where the habits and language are entirely foreign. One would be able to communicate only a hazy and confused impression of the experience.

Examining my own clairvoyant process further, I suspect that I may draw the energy and knowledge to build the images from the subconscious content of the sitters. If so, it is possible that the control does likewise. If this were true, I reasoned, it may not be necessary to use the control personality in order to obtain supernormal knowledge. In this mood I decided to devote a greater length of time to understanding the clairvoyant state. In so doing, I realized that even if it is possible to reach another dimension or level of life, I am still confined to the use of my own imagery and symbols, and therefore I wondered if, when I contacted another intelligence, could I ever fully understand what he desired to transmit? If these later impressions of mine were correct, then I could understand that the trance state and the controls were very necessary to obtain what may be termed "supernormal knowledge."

These realizations amounted at once to a release and illumination for me. I perceived one of the basic principles underlying communication. Consciousness is capable of indefinite expansion and of making contacts in all realms of mind that it may choose to seek. The conception of this capacity to reach into areas of existence that lie beyond the borderland of conscious knowledge is an exhilarating one. I hesitated to be too positive on this point, because I realized that the majority of trained and experienced people interested in communication might not agree with me.

Examining trance objectively, it would appear to be allied to sleep, yet differing, since it is used by an apparently objective state of consciousness that is aware of its own identity. The levels from which these communications arrive have never been adequately defined. The entranced person withdraws as in sleep, and yet some measure of awareness must continue to operate, for questions presumably reach the aural capacities, as in hypnosis. There is another slight difference between sleep and the trance. In sleep one brings back more or less fragmentary dream phrases and events which contain material relating to one's own experience, and the common feeling is, therefore, that it is out of the subconscious that the dream material is brought forth; but from the trance state one returns with only a relaxed feeling and an innate freedom from restriction or limitation, as though one had gone within oneself in search of refreshment, or as though one had surrendered to a complete relaxation of will yet one knows, from the evidences of trance activity, that levels of the mind have been alert, busily transforming symbols into active thought. Trance activity, then, like all artistic activity, begins where practical activity culminates.

At another level of consciousness, the inner eye perceives and translates from a larger level of knowledge. The objective mind, as it were, has cast off the practical everyday vision, to transport the senses beyond the strains and stresses until the inner vision becomes the serene spectator, freed for an interval from objective experience. In fact, the experience of trance might not have happened to the individual (so easy is the transition) if it were not that the notes and the words of the enquirer account for the time lapse.

❖ THIRTEEN

ESP EXPERIMENTS

I had exchanged the atmosphere of Ireland for the more prosaic one of London and the more exciting one of America. I had proved to my satisfaction my capabilities as a business woman, and I had realized that marriage was something that required more time and thoughtfulness than I had been ready to give to it. I had developed and deepened my psychic faculties, but I still lacked complete understanding of them. Chance had taken me to America, and I had traveled extensively through the United States, returning each year, like a homing pigeon, to Europe. I was always searching for something — something that would convince me of the timeless values of psychic powers. Wherever I went, the drive behind the journey was my preoccupation with further development and further investigation.

I therefore returned to the United States. Still intent on further scientific investigation of psychic phenomena, I got in touch with Professor William McDougall, who was then at Duke University, to inquire if any objective work was being carried out in America. He told me that studies in the field of parapsychology were then taking place at Duke University and invited me to participate in these experiments with Professor J. B. Rhine.

I was eager to cooperate, and on meeting Dr. Rhine I was impressed with his directness, simplicity and enthusiasm. He showed me the specially-designed cards which he used in his experiments — the Extra Sensory Perception (ESP) cards which have since become well known. He employed the term "Extra Sensory" to describe any type of perception which would not be attributed to the normal operation of the five human senses. I entered into the work with enthusiasm, never doubting that it would be a simple matter for me to produce significant results by means of this technique. However, after a few of these card tests for clairvoyance, I was astonished to find that my scores were unusually low. I was naturally disappointed, but as I had done successful subjective work in telepathy and clairvoyance for many years, I re-examined these psychic activities with new penetration in an effort to determine why I should produce poor results with Dr. Rhine's ESP cards.

It then occurred to me that radiation lay at the very core of the supernormal activities. I concluded that clairvoyance and telepathy depended upon an active emanation registering between two people or between an individual and an object, and since the ESP cards lacked "personality," they did not stimulate my perceptions. Clairvoyance (as I knew it then) cannot be directed peremptorily to any particular object. I may or may not be able to secure knowledge clairvoyantly concerning a specific person or thing. I can do so only if I receive the response of an adequate energy stimulus from the individual or object in question. When this energy stimulus exists, I sense and see simultaneously by means of a series of images, animated but simple, like a child's drawings. After I have received impressions and visions in this way, I then interpret them to the listener. What I receive may be much or little. This depends upon the degree of the energy stimulus that I receive and also upon my own condition of psychic sensitivity at the time. I had believed up to this time that both people and objects must give out an energy stimulus to enable me to work psychically.

I felt that Dr. Rhine's ESP cards lacked the energy stimulus which would enable me to see their symbols clairvoyantly. In fact, it would seem that the handling of the cards and their inanimate symbols inhibited, for the time being, whatever supernormal powers I possess. On the other hand, in working on clairvoyance tests with Dr. Rhine, I discovered that by being passed through the mind of another, the symbols came alive. My scores rose perceptibly. In the telepathy experiments, I was freed from direct concentration on the cards themselves and was able to receive the symbols from the mind of the transmitter, where they acquired vitality and provided the energy stimulus necessary for my perception. Up to this moment I had worked mostly with personalities who, consciously or otherwise, supplied me with the emotional keys which I felt were necessary to unlock the door of my sensitivities. I now know that this was simply an acquired habit which was not really connected in any way with the perceptions. What I have, since childhood, seen as a nebulous *surround* enveloping each living organism has a definite use and purpose as receiver and transmitter of life substance throughout the universe, and in recent years I have for myself defined this aura or surround as a protective and magnetic field.

Dr. Rhine made many thousands of tests with the ESP cards, but I remain convinced that my tests in clairvoyance with the cards were no better than guesses in their quality, and that the only successful work I did at Duke in that year and the next was in telepathy. I still feel that Dr. Rhine contributed greatly to the success of these early telepathic experiments through his interest and enthusiasm, which provided the energy stimulus to permit me to perceive the card symbols and produce good results. This held true throughout our work together, although as time passed I overcame my "resistance" to the cards and welcomed working with him and various others interested in the field of parapsychology, because I believe this method necessary in the interests of scientific acceptance. As the years went by, I spent many pleasant intervals at Duke University, participating in the various studies, theories, experiments and investigations with the same enthusiasm as when I first began.

On my return to England in 1934, an opportunity for further research presented itself. Dr. William Brown, the well-known English psychiatrist who founded the experimental laboratory of psychology at Oxford University, was ready to undertake research into the nature and mechanism of trance. Previously, he had conducted some trance experiments with me in which he communicated with the "Uvani" personality. Following this, he made one attempt to hypnotize me and succeeded in reaching "Uvani" under suggestion. This led Dr. Brown to propose a study of multiple personality and analysis under hypnosis. I had reached a point where I welcomed the prospect of further light on the nature of my mediumship and the reality of the control personalities. I was fully prepared to risk the disposal of the trance condition and the possible disappearance of the controls should they prove to be no more than evidence of a "dissociation in my own personality," as the psychiatrists asserted. I also wondered privately at this time if those physicians were correct who had suggested that these splits in personality might be contributing factors in my almost constantly ill health.

While I underwent analysis, Dr. Brown's assistant recorded my galvanic reflexes. In the first session he asked me to recall, while in the waking state, whatever memories I could recover from my childhood. The rest of the work took place while I was under hypnosis; however, it is interesting to note that Dr. Brown did not reach the controls by this method. At the final meeting he asked me to go into trance under my own suggestion, which I did. Upon waking, he told me that he had spoken with "Uvani."

After this there were no further experiments, and although I had not gained greater understanding of my mediumship, I did achieve a new mastery of my supernormal self, and in the course of the following months I was able to penetrate new levels of consciousness. As a result of observance of the method by which Dr. Brown had been able to make me recall on awakening what I had said in hypnotic sleep, I applied to myself the principle of autosuggestion, for if I had been able to speak under hypnotic control, I could also write in that state. I therefore experimented daily, using the process of automatic writing to reach as yet unrevealed phases of the subconscious mind. It is necessary to explain for those unfamiliar with the mechanisms of mediumship that, up to the time of this analysis with Dr. Brown, all my trance utterances had been transmitted through one or other of the two controls. Yet never at any time had I been really able to accept the trance personalities who claimed to communicate through me as separate entities, although I had admitted as genuine the information drawn from those other levels of consciousness through which these controls purported to work. This had, therefore, left me in the somewhat paradoxical position of doubting the reality of the controls while recognizing the validity of the source from which they drew their supernormal knowledge.

I was well aware that automatic writing might be no more than an expression of the unconscious contentions and desires of the one who produces these writings, but even though many scripts are the result of subconscious conflict and self-delusion, there are those which reveal paranormal results. While I regarded my own experiments at this time as of no importance to anyone but myself, I refer to them here because they played an important part in beginning to free me from dependence on the control personalities in further development.

My automatic writings dealt not only with the subject of my immediate life but also with what seemed to relate to possible previous states of consciousness. Some of this material was undoubtedly drawn from my subconscious, but a great part of it, I am convinced now, came from areas of the superconscious.

How then did I, during this experience, come to distinguish between levels of the subconscious and superconscious mind? The subconscious I had long recognized in both picture and symbol as representing the nature of mental operations not present in consciousness, as well as the conflicts and confusions of daily life and memory. But beyond this level I discovered still other areas which needed to be explored, and gradually I saw that I was drawing from a less personal and more extended region that reached beyond the limits of the experience of the subconscious, within which there were vivid pictures of distant and unknown places and people, fragments of strange music, rare colors and unfamiliar languages that reached me like silver streams of light. These experiences were happy ones and seemed unrelated to those subconscious fantasies of the conflicts and problems of daily living. In these more profound and delicate sensations I realized that I was related to areas beyond those, either in my waking or subconscious states. I could only explain my deep sense of connection with such remote but nevertheless soul-stirring experiences as due either to their association with possible other lives I had lived, with race memories or with the vast reaches of universal mind. Further contemplation of these supernormal areas made me aware of a universal consciousness greater than anything I had ever before conceived, in which events not known to me consciously were taking place and being revealed. A supreme awareness pervaded me. It was a state in which I was permitted to participate and to receive knowledge from some ultimate source beyond the limit of personal being.

Since the controls had not been dissipated — nor any new interpretation of their meaning been revealed during my work with Dr. Brown — I wondered whether the whole structure of mediumship might not depend on information drawn from the subconscious mind of the seeker as well as from the great storehouse of the universe.

❖ FOURTEEN

CLAIRVOYANCE AND PSYCHOMETRY

Back in America again, I sought the advice of one of the greatest scientists, Dr. Alexis Carrel, about the impasse of my investigations of trance mediumship. He possessed a very comprehensive understanding and knowledge of supernormal phenomena and the laws governing them. He suggested that if I wanted to penetrate more deeply into the problem of my own mediumship, a study should be made of the physiological states, in and out of trance, so that science might reveal what a psychic state really is.

I found a doctor willing to undertake such an examination. He made a series of experiments, first in the waking state and then on the alleged controls while I was entranced. Unfortunately, these physiological tests, how ever revealing and interesting, were interrupted by ill health. However, the outcome of these efforts suggested that there were extraneous thought processes operating within the physiological trance state — influences that differed greatly from my own conscious realization of self. This pattern tended to give substance to the statement made by the controls that they were discarnate entities. The differences were sufficient to convince me that there is a great deal yet to be discovered within the self-created substance of personality.

The capacities of a sensitive are an integral part of that person's life history. I know that my "sensitivity" was rooted in my early childhood. My first seeing and sensing of movement, light, color and sound were the operation, at instinctive levels, of what were later to become my conscious and selective supersensory capacities. From earliest childhood I have been aware of the nebulous surrounds or auras of all plants, animals and men, and have observed how they expand and contract, as though the bodies within breathed by means of this outer lung.

From these sources came the first discoveries about my own breathing. I can now consciously shift my breathing when I choose, and by doing so I can constantly change my activity from one phase to another. Control of the breathing plays a most important part in all of my supernormal work. It develops a sense of excitement and eagerness, such as one feels on entering some unknown or forbidden territory. Without this "acceleration," I can make no claim to working supernormally. Even in ordinary, everyday exchanges between people a stimulation of the senses occurs, but in "visioning" and "sensing" all physical and emotional faculties are speeded up. This process occurs in a fraction of the time it takes me to describe it, and no such conscious analysis accompanies the experience. Simultaneously, in a state of easy contemplation, one sees through, around and about an object and becomes associated with its nature and quality. Sometimes the clairvoyant forms or symbols are preceded by a heavy, inchoate darkness which is charged with vibrant movement, finally bursting in curving lines of light and color. These lines in turn split off from the parent rays to move out and form themselves into other lines which develop an animated fourfold movement. They take on swaying, rhythmic movement as they interlace and move in spirals in what would appear to be measureless space. From these rather simple forms others are continuously born. It is within these shapes that I sense energy transforming itself into substance.

These warm and pleasant sensations lead to a clearing and an expansion at the back of the brain — a sensation which continues to grow until the area of oneself would appear to be suffused with soft light, and one enters into a condition or dimension which might be described as one of color. Peace is the quality of this stage, bringing with it a freedom from any connection with time, space and external events. Thus does clairvoyance function. The action which then takes place may be related to an actual event relating to today or to an episode that was enacted a century ago. In the moving panorama of color one sees a series of swiftly moving forms. The actors in the scene may be those who are now alive or may be those who have lived in the distant past. During this time my only conscious physical act consists of deep breathing in order to expand the diaphragm and alert the solar plexus, that important nerve center which would seem to experience instinctive sensation first, for it is from this area that I am aware of energies flowing through the body. It is from this center that the faculties appear to awake to sensitivity and to alertness, and this alertness is the *sine qua non* of sensory perception, an eagerness to contact, apprehend and translate the "story" revealed in the search.

Clairvoyance is dependent upon those subtle inner capacities of sight that motivate vision. I believe I first learned to be clairvoyant in the early days of the garden in Ireland. Then, in order to control and hold my breath, the practice was natural enough. It was an accompaniment to my childish awe and wonder before the whirling world of life and movement that repeatedly caused sudden "breathless" suspense, in which I sought to see more deeply into things and farther distances — not distances of space only but distances of being. Each type of life had then, and still holds for me, its own particular kind of radiation. Every stone, metal, flower or animal, substance or organism was contained within its own field of light and color, radiating both toward and away from its inner form of active, potent rays. I enter "within" the very life of this world of light, sound and color, using them as one might use a telescope to see what lies within and beyond. Thus I am able to sense the *history* of the organism or object whose nature is revealed by the quality of its radiation which I am able to contact and enter.

From time to time I have referred to movement, light and radiation as being a present and necessary stimulus to clairvoyance. As a child I watched the surrounds of living organisms, and it seemed as though these enveloping substances acted as an outer lung through which all forms of life not only sustained themselves but at the same time joined with the life principle of the universe. Color and odor, as well as the stuff of life itself, operate through and in this surrounding mesh. That is why I find the theory of radiation reasonable; I am convinced that every living organism has its own type of external being by which it contacts other energies. This nebulous outer substance not only protects and feeds from the forces of life, but it shields the form within from intense and impacting forces. (Everyone is aware of the way in which one can accustom oneself to sleeping in spite of noise and disturbance, and very soon the body learns to shut out the things that would register intense pain and discomfort.) From studying this enveloping substance, I conceive of its role as being that of a condenser of experience, sifting through its mesh, as it were, all atmospheric radiations of light, color and movement and, in consequence, becoming the receptor of all external sensations. This "magnetic" mesh, then, is a map through which illness of the body and mind can be reached and studied by those who understand its principles and its functions. There are such individuals, though they may not understand the laws by which they work.

Since I conceive of this "magnetic field" as possessing an outer reality, might it not also be possible that it contains the localization and structure of the greater mind that helps shape the more limited consciousness of man?

Since the magnetic field interpenetrates the physical body and also reaches out to relate itself to other energies in the universe, man becomes closely linked to all the cosmic forces that play upon our planet through his magnetic field. There are patterns which indicate what diseases or illnesses we may have had in the past. Analyses of such "scars" have been verified on many occasions. To those able to perceive this pattern, the surround becomes a map which can disclose the condition of mind, body and spirit.

The psychochemical interchanges between us and the things around us are in constant operation, and the perception of them depends upon a natural human faculty that is readily subject to development. For instance, a coin is concealed in an envelope and held in the hand. As I hold the coin lightly, the actual presence of the person who has given it to me fades out, and the object takes on increasing importance. A tingling sensation announces that inner expectancy has begun, and the coin begins to reveal its story. I may have a glimpse of a stately columned building standing on a height. People are passing in and out of it and moving about in its vicinity, Greeks of an ancient time. This is a temple of Aesculapius; I see his statue here. He wears a long robe, his breast is bare, and he holds the symbolic staff with its twining serpent. The picture changes, and I am in a dark cave from which I look out on a wide blue sea, empty and beautiful under a pale sky. I feel that there are coins scattered on the floor of the cave, but it is too dark to see them. Then I see a glass case in which various coins are exhibited. All of these things — the temple and its statue, the cave, the glass case — are seen clairvoyantly; they require interpretation. So, summing up my experience, I consider the sequence in reverse order, as to time, and I say that the coin is a museum piece, an ancient Greek minting (I cannot cipher its date), that it was found in a cave in Greece and that one of its owners — probably the last one — was a wealthy Greek, possibly a physician but, in any case, a devotee of the god Aesculapius. When the envelope is opened and the coin revealed, it will turn out to be one of Greek or Roman origin.

We are apt to be skeptical about the "personal" nature of nonsentient objects, yet Alpine lichens do not grow in the tropics, nor are orchids discoverable in the Arctic. The "nativity" of any substance marks both its nature and its natural destiny, and in the case of manufactured things their making and the purpose for which they are made amount to rebirth into a new life. Their fate is thus recast, their relations destined to be radically different from those that were possible to them in their original natural state. Iron becomes steel, sand goes into glass, trees become paper and new categories are born into the realms of Nature. Thus every object has its individual quality and its individual history. Psychometry would appear to supply the key to the perception of these qualities and these histories.

Psychometrists are artists in temperament, for these impressionistic flashes in the mind have to be formulated promptly by the person who perceives them, and a large part of successful psychometry consists of the ready expression of these subtly felt impressions.

Personally, I do not like the word "psychometry" as a designation for the process which it commonly represents. The word means "to measure by means of psychic capacity." But to me, the process is not a measuring. I prefer to think of it as experimentation in psychochemistry, and I believe that this word more clearly represents what occurs. We know, or think we know, that everything in the world is reducible to the ninety-odd basic chemical elements. Behind the countless combinations of these basic substances lies the immense field of differentiable energy, and it is in this diverse field that Life moves, both manifest and unmanifest to human perception. Psychochemistry consists in a relationship that comes into existence at energy levels that lie beyond the sensory field.

We all psychometrize more or less. Having had a really interesting experience at sensory levels, we do our best to understand it — to discover its quality and meaning — at levels that lie beyond the reach of the senses. But here we commonly make the mistake of limiting the freedom of our perception by permitting thought, memory, imagination or emotionalism to play upon our theme. Thus the field of our apprehensions becomes crowded with images that either preclude or smother the more tenuous but more illuminating appearances that actually emerge and move at still deeper levels.

Instinctive awareness, which I find to be at the base of all supernormal sensing, is not confined to man. It also directs the behavior of all other living organisms. There is a perceptiveness which is the activating principle in the lives of both man and animal, preserving them against the hostile forces of their environment. This alertness in all living creatures is created by the synthesis of their five physical senses with the one Life, and this instinctive vigilance is the foundation of all self-protection which involves the manifestation of Life itself. Supernormal sensing, therefore, is but the refinement of that dynamic power of being which propels all life forward through the growth and development of its own evolution. And to this, man is committed by his relation to the universal nature of things.

❖ FIFTEEN

CLAIRVOYANCE AND TELEPATHY

There are various types of clairvoyant experiences. Not all of them are dependent on the flow of imagery but may occur in the unaccountable appearance of a strange picture, in which one sees through and beyond barriers that would completely balk our ordinary sensory vision. A road may wind among hills for any distance. One sees the hills, and as the road reaches away, perspective operates and its farther dimensions diminish, as they would diminish to our sight or in any picture. Nevertheless, at the same time one sees the entire road completely, regardless of the intervening hills, and its farther reaches are as meticulously discernible as the areas that lie close to the spot from which one is seeing. Each rut and stone is individually seen and can be described with precision. The leaves of trees and the blades of grass are countable throughout the landscape.

Such a picture may be of the "visionary" type, occurring mysteriously and sometimes without a known significance. It may be, and often is, a picture of no known place — a purely "imaginative" creation, vivid and seemingly real, though it is not the imagination that creates it.

A woman comes to see me. Her life is being torn to shreds by a long-sustained tension between her hopes, her fears, her growing despair. "My son George was reported missing months ago," she tells me. "I have had no further word of him. He was my only son. Can you tell me whether he is alive or dead?" In the present case, in which I am seeking a particular man named "George," I know in my mind that such a person exists somewhere in the universe dead or alive, for a woman who claims to be his mother has declared his reality. In my clairvoyant picture, a man stands out prominently as though my attention were volitionally centered on him. This is George, the man I am seeking. I see every detail of his person from his bare feet to his unshaven face and his unkempt head. I am able to assure her who sits beside me that her son is alive. If she asks me how I know, I say that I have "seen" him. And if she is too distraught to understand that I have truly seen her son, I describe him, with emphasis on some personal peculiarity which she, his mother, can recognize.

There is nothing extraordinary about such a picture — we are all familiar with it — , but my picture is not an impressionistic reproduction of anything that I have ever seen before; there is no element of memory or imagination in it. I note raggedness, his beard, the look of despair. I discern the countless details of his environment, the surrounding bare countryside and a lonely bit of shore. It is more clear to me than it would be were I present on the spot, for I see it all at once, all together in a breath of time, and I do not have to shift the focus of my vision from one part of the picture in order to see it whole, entire, complete. Here are two different experiences in relationship: my contact with George and my contact with his mother. My perception of George and his environment was instantaneous and complete. It occurred in a stream of being which is not conditioned by our conceptions of time and space. Upon the mother's entrance into my office, I caught an equally vivid impression of her disturbed state, long before the usual greetings could be exchanged at conventional and rational levels. There is another difference here. While I may forget the mother with whom I had contact, I will never forget the clairvoyant circumstances surrounding the son. The full perfection of its original clarity will always be preserved.

Very often in the clairvoyant flow of images I see one in whom a limb or some facial feature suddenly becomes emphasized and grows out of all proportion to the rest of the figure. When this occurs, I know that there is meaning in the distortion. For instance, on one occasion, the hand of a man whom I was seeking clairvoyantly grew to a great size; I could not avoid observing that it lacked a thumb, and this disfigurement was of evidential significance to the inquirer. At this point I may find myself projected into the garden of the house where this man had lived. I may find myself standing under an apple tree. It is winter; I see the tree stripped and bare, but before my eyes the same tree changes and appears in several phases of season and change and growth. What aspects I see it in are factors over which I have no control, but its aspects may be vitally evidential. I may see it as a young tree not yet bearing fruit, or in spring bloom when I can smell the odor of its blossom, and in a breath it may be laden with apples. On the other hand, I may have but a single glimpse of the tree in some particular aspect of its history as it relates to the late owner's life. In these examples of clairvoyant experience which I have chosen at random, sight, smell and taste contribute to the unity of the whole impression.

At this climax of clairvoyance, a precognition, clairaudience, projection and vision-at-a-distance occur simultaneously. It is a state of inspiration in which one is identified with all that vision holds. Had I not learned to control these powers of perception, to protect myself from the impact of these experiences, such intensive sensing and receptivity might utterly exhaust me. But actually, as my body becomes increasingly exhilarated, my mind steadily becomes more tranquil and clear.

When I have an appointment with someone who is in deep need, I have been told that before my visitor's entrance into the room I have a habit of busying myself. I will move the objects on my desk or accelerate my body by attending to several things in a great hurry. Only afterward do I realize this, at times when it is jokingly brought to my attention. I am not objectively conscious of working toward this nervous release. It is probably a means of clearing the mind of all objective material. I remember that it was required of me in the early days of my experimental work that I should spend some quiet time in concentration and meditation. This I was never able to do. Contrary to all that I had been told, it was necessary for me to be in a state of nonchalance — in fact, an attitude of high carelessness.

In clairvoyant vision I do not look *out* at objects in my fields of observation as in ordinary seeing, but I seem to draw the perceived object toward me, so that the essence of its life and the essence of mine become, for the moment, one and the same thing. Thus, to my sense, clairvoyance occurs in states of consciousness whose relations exist as a fact in nature, on levels of being that transcend the present perceptive capacities of our sensory faculties.

I have referred to an inner condition of "alertness" which is the essential factor in many of these activities. It is a realization of superior vital living. I enter into a world of intensely vibrant radiation; I am extra competent; I participate fully and intimately in events that move at an increased rate of movement. Though the events that I observe are objective to me, I do more than observe them; I *live* them.

The principle difference between clairvoyant and telepathic experiences lies in the relatively clear and simple nature of what one perceives telepathically. These pictures appear as things in themselves and are generally understandable as they appear. But in the clairvoyant experience, one follows a process. Light moves in weaving ribbons and strands, and, in and out of these, fragmentary curving lines emerge and fade, moving in various directions. The perception consists of a swiftly moving array of these broken, shifting lines, and in the beginning one gathers meaning out of the flow as the lines create patterns of significance which the acutely attentive clairvoyant perception senses. The lines and the pictures that they form do not always appear as clear representations of people, places and things, as in telepathy; rather, they are symbols whose meanings are not instantly clear to the sensitive as things in themselves. Nothing appears whole and finished; everything that is "caught" is built up out of fragments and related to something else. It is necessary that the clairvoyant sensitive shall translate or interpret these if they are to have any value for the person on whose behalf they have been sought, and this he does by means of that clear inner *knowing* which is also an element in the clairvoyant experience. His interpreted message may have little or no meaning for *him,* since it may have no relation to anything else in his experience, but it usually happens that the names of persons and places and references to objects and things are readily understandable by the person who seeks the information.

I say this is usually so. Yet sometimes the message may have no meaning for the person who receives it, for on clairvoyant levels there exists simultaneity of time, and the clairvoyant message may concern future events and future relationships which today seem impossible, incredible or meaningless to the person to whom they are revealed. Such "failures" have occurred a number of times in my own experience, but in each case the incomprehensible meaning of the message has been made clear through the passage of time and the occurrence of subsequent events.

When telepathy and clairvoyance operate together, the case is usually simpler for the sensitive. He is then less dependent on his correct interpretation of fleeting symbolic formations; pictures come clear and whole, and his knowledge of their meaning is a high adventure in supersensory realizations. He knows the meaning, though the meanings may mean nothing to him. The process might be thought of as resembling the sensory reading of a figure: 76982. One knows the number but not what it means. It will assume its true significance, so to say, only when it is transmitted to the person to whom it belongs.

Clairaudience may also enter into the same given experience, and one's knowledge is then amplified by "hearing" as well as "seeing." In my clairvoyant picture of a village, I see the bell ringing in the belfry of the little church, and I know that it is ringing; if clairaudience enters into the experience, I hear its tone as well.

Clairvoyance, clairaudience and telepathy are different processes. A person whose sensitivities are developed over a wide range is at home in all these operations, and in living at such sensitive levels one does not ordinarily differentiate among them any more than one stops to consider whether he is seeing, hearing or touching a thing.

It is impossible for me, except theoretically, to separate clairaudience from clairvoyance, for I have the clear impression of clairvoyance creating its own sound chamber; it is always accompanied by its own musical rhythm. My aural sensitivity undergoes refinement; I become receptive to tones that my sensory ears never hear. As I have repeatedly intimated, I do not think of the psychic capacities as alienated from the five senses. Though I have used the terms "extrasensory," "supersensory" and "nonsensory" to carry the general meanings which the terms commonly convey, I feel that no one of these words accurately expresses the true nature of experience.

Thus the clairvoyant experience is frequently multiple in terms of the five senses — the five senses amplified and extended, superactive and extraordinarily sensitized and with the clairvoyant *alertness* always dominant. Clairvoyance is an intensely acute sensing of some aspects of life in operation, and since at clairvoyant levels time is undivided and whole, one often perceives the object or event in its past, present and/or future phases in abruptly swift successions.

In the manner which I have described, then, telepathy only enters into the clairvoyant experience, and many which are called "clairvoyant" are telepathic as well. Strictly speaking, clairvoyance is clear seeing, and telepathy is a knowing of distant realities, and both are achieved by sensory means.

Telepathy would seem to be supersensory knowing. It transcends time and space, and when it operates one becomes aware of real things that lie beyond all the possible reaches of our five senses as we commonly think of them. Telepathy and clairvoyance are not the same thing, but they frequently rate together, and when this occurs the supersensory experience differs from the experience of clairvoyance alone or of telepathy alone. In clairvoyance I may see a picture or an image clearly without understanding its significance, and in telepathy I may know of some fact or event occurring at a distance which has no known relation to anything else in my consciousness. I am constantly receiving such pictures and such knowledge. They constitute a flow of perception that resembles the flow of unconscious thought that moves in everybody's mind all the time, and I pay no more attention to them than people usually pay to their secondary flow of thoughts.

In order that the revelations of either clairvoyance or telepathy shall be significant for me, they must have some relation to something else that I know. Otherwise, the experience is like scanning the pages of a book printed in a language which I do not understand.

Someone has said that all we can ever know of the Divine Mind is its subconscious aspect, and I sometimes think of this supermental imagery as the flow of subsidiary thoughts in the subconscious of Divinity, resembling that flow of secondary thought that moves in the minds of human beings.

❖ SIXTEEN

TELEPATHY AND PRECOGNITION

Telepathy, in its simplest definition and as I have experienced it, is direct knowledge of distant facts achieved by extra-sensory means. It may be thought of as a sublimated and perfect kind of intuition. It is an experience that does not always have to be sought. Often one's first intimation of its occurrence is a sense of restlessness that arrests one's attention, so that awareness has to be released from whatever it is concerned with and set free in the supersensory field. It depends upon the vibratory nature of all things and upon the existence of a measure of affinity between the two poles of the telepathic experience.

The secret of telepathic sensitivity is very difficult to define. Even after years of observation of the processes involved, one cannot be certain that one has discovered all the means. Telepathy produces full and clear impressions in a way in which clairvoyance does not. It is an acuteness of very being. One sees, hears, feels emotionally, suffers physical pain, hunger, and cold — is at one in sentiency with the people, things and conditions that enter into the perception. Telepathy is a process of knowing through being, and it is a swift process. Entire scenes flash before the vision. The experience may be likened to watching and reporting on a motion picture that is run at high speed, though it is not always continuous and coherent. I not only see the people who appear, but I know them — who and what they are, what they feel and think. At the same time I seem to know that they are not necessarily aware of my presence.

Telepathy is perhaps the most mysterious of the conscious psychic activities. The perceiver's sense of unity with what he perceives, and at the same time the complete objectivity and lack of response of all that he shares in so intimately — together, these two factors, which are somehow contradictory, constitute a puzzling problem for thought after the experience. Except for one fact, however, telepathic perception may be likened to walking up Broadway in New York City, observing the theaters, the display signs, the vehicles and the crowds of people. Here and there a bright color display attracts one's attention, a lovely face wakes admiration, some other faces may move one to pity or revulsion, some beggar or cripple may stir one's sympathy. In the telepathic experience all such things and more may appear and be felt and understood, and the principal difference between the two experiences — sensory and telepathic — lies in the acceleration with which the telepathist perceives and in the depth and clarity of his knowing and understanding.

For many years I have noted telepathy in dreams. It consists of taking into a part of my mind, as I go to sleep, the problem which someone has brought me during the day. In order to do this, I recover a clear impression of the person, of our interview and of the problem. This is not simply a recalling of our meeting out of my memory but a definite recovery of all the elements — sensory and extrasensory — which I had at the time of our interview, including the depth and intensity of my visitor's emotional state. Then I deliberately give my consciousness the task of finding the answer to the problem while I sleep, and in the morning I find, at the threshold of awakening, the information I have sought. In both my waking and my dream telepathy I participate in a process that occurs outside myself; somewhere in the regions of universal Life where these people live and act, these perceived events occur. And believing as I do that consciousness is universal and coexistent with Life, I suppose it also to be true that through purposeful direction of my consciousness I am permitted to find what I seek. Accepting the universal Consciousness as a fact and realizing my unity with it, I gain admittance to its all-inclusive areas and records.

Discoveries, refinements and progressive achievements in the field of mechanisms all arise out of the field of consciousness. I am very sure that in conceiving the expansion of man's consciousness toward wider areas of the Universal, and in conceiving of the development of man's perceptive capacities into vastly deeper areas of the same limitless field, I am not without good support in present-day practical fact and action.

Precognition is a supersensory experience which raises the problem of the unity of time and also the problem of the relation of consciousness of time. Because I have experienced some events before they come to pass, others as they are taking place at a distance and still others that occurred both far away and long ago, I cannot help knowing within my own sum of knowledge that time, space, and consciousness exist and operate together, that each of them is an indivisible continuum, that they are mutually interpenetrable and that their nature contains that element of simultaneity which is but vaguely apprehended.

From our general training in self-centered thinking we believe that we project consciousness outward into space-time — into past, present or future, at whatever spatial distances. But instead of this, I believe what we actually do is release the mind from the confines of our present interests and so discover and come to know in our minds that consciousness is ubiquitous with time and space.

The idea of the unity of time is gradually taking form in human understanding, and many people have frequent, dim perceptions of the reality behind the phrase "the eternal now." It is only through such mental enlargement, however, that the concept of the eternal now could ever have been achieved by the human mind. It is much more difficult to grasp a sense of the unity of space than of the unity of time, because our eyes are so wonderfully useful to us within the limits of their capacity that, in order to achieve any conception of limitless space, one has to escape from an ingrained sense of distances, and this is a most difficult thing to do. To encompass the whole of infinity in the finite consciousness is not possible, of course; one takes it piece by piece, by whatever means and in whatever strange forms of symbolic imagery.

To reach any kind of a practical conception of the space-time continuum, one lets one's consciousness follow its own unrestricted way in space-time. I am convinced by my own experience that man's consciousness constantly operates in regions where the mind cannot follow — that it remains forever in its own right and in its own nature, and that at base it is not conditioned by experience as the mind is. Things are constantly happening to our consciousness of which we have no mental awareness.

Some, but not all, of the effects of both sensory and supersensory experience come to the mind for judgment — for criticism, acceptance or rejection — , and the mind deals with them according to the particular quality which it has developed: with disbelief, disregard, wonder, awe or understanding, and, according to the nature of its relation to each particular experience, the quality of the mind is itself affected.

It may even place further inhibitions on the freedom of consciousness (we warn ourselves against so many things!). But just as the reality of the giraffe in the zoo was not affected by the farmer's doubt that the animal existed, so the free and fundamental quality of consciousness remains unaffected by the mind's judgments on its experience.

Precognition is perhaps the soundest evidence, the best proof, of the reality of the whole of supersensory experience, because so many events perceived in this way are later verified beyond all doubt, at the sensory levels of life.

Clairvoyance, clairaudience and telepathy may all cooperate in the precognitive experience. One not only hears, sees and knows clearly all of the elements involved in what one witnesses, but one may also feel emotionally the essence of the scene or the event.

To be able to account for this element of feeling, I am again led to mention emotional energy, which I have referred to as the motivating force in all supersensory experience. My own precognitions are nearly always related to people or things that are close to my personal interest, yet in *experimenting* in precognition, I have come to know that, during the whole of the experimental period, some phase of my consciousness has been focused at precognitive levels, and under all the activities of my sensory field — meeting people and carrying on conversations, eating, reading and writing letters, enjoying landscapes, situations and events and listening to the repartee in a group of people — the precognitive phase of my consciousness was constantly awake and alert.

In order to clarify the process used in prevision, let me describe the experiments as set up in 1947 and repeated many times since then. The trials were carried out by means of pictures that at the time of the experiment were not known to anyone. (The pictures were somewhere in the building, but what they might portray when discovered was not known to anyone.) My job was to draw telepathically and describe clairvoyantly the subject matter contained in the pictures that would be chosen by an agent after the drawing experiment had been concluded.

The impulse that generates the foreknowledge is in no case derived from the known self or by any known or learned procedure. One sits at a desk and from the empty canvas of the mind a "key" emerges which may be only a suggestion of a perfume, a sweet smelling flower or a country scene; or one may hear a bar of music or a haunting melody, see an airplane in flight or a boat upon the ocean. One accepts the clue, and presently the outside world is shut out, and one is possessed by the idea. Like intuition, one idea flows from the other, actively presenting themselves out of space. Sometimes one instinctively feels that one is going to draw or describe one particular thing, but a line will arrive and change the whole contour of the scene. In the realm of this unsubstantial thought process "near" and "far" would seem to lose their meaning; presenting outlines of the picture can be likened to the free drawings of a child. It is almost as though the brain had a series of rays that speeded to a secret storehouse, as the bee does, and there discovering certain elements, flashed them back in inspirational fashion. This impulse is so arresting that during the descriptive process one feels that the subliminal self predominates to translate the crude lines into beautiful patterns. The known will or desire capitulates in front of the experiment. The governing impulse selects the material that is most agreeable to the mind of the sensitive. For instance, I have noted that there is a "reluctance" to accept or describe scenes that are disagreeable to the conscious self; on several occasions I have "rejected" scenes of battle or, if total rejection did not take place, I drew a rough outline of the picture as though I might hurry away from the scene before content or real meaning revealed its itself.

An example will make this statement clearer. On one particular occasion I had "described" four pictures in the order in which the agent would eventually find them at a later hour. I numbered each drawing as I imagined the agent would later choose it. Picture 3 was noted but vaguely and hurriedly outlined. When the actual picture 3 was selected by the agent it was found to be the picture of a soldier with a wound in the head through which the blood flowed. On the other hand a pastoral scene or a seaside picture will reveal much detail and I find it easy to linger over the execution of such a picture. At no time, however, is the conscious self concerned with the reception of this material, and while one is alert and very happy with the game of previsioning, one is unaware of any direct process of brain control.

One is led to conclude that the human personality can be a great storehouse of unsuspected eyes, ears and subtle signals that can be attuned to the Universal mind, a great potential that has yet to be explored.

There is an element of surprise and adventure about the experience of precognition which would appear to free itself from all conscious direction — even personality itself — , for when any action becomes automatic and effortless, it ceases to evoke consciousness. One enters into a place of participation which has no connection in time and space with conscious direction or conscious telepathic communication. The experience remains as "real" as any other and suggests that there must be a timeless and spaceless communion between our intuitive selves and the great eternal laws of nature.

In his book, *Something of Myself*, Rudyard Kipling wrote, "I am in no way 'psychic.'" Yet he records a dream which was purely precognitive:

> I dreamt that I stood, in my best clothes, which I do not wear as a rule, one in a line of similarly habited men, in some vast hall, floored with roughjointed stone slabs. Opposite me, the width of the hall, was another line of persons and the impression of a crowd behind them. On my left some ceremony was taking place that I wanted to see but could not unless I stepped out of my line because the fat stomach of my neighbor on my left barred my vision. At the ceremony's close, both lines of spectators broke up and moved forward and met, and the great space filled with people. Then a man came up behind me, slipped his hand beneath my arm, and said: 'I want a word with you.' I forgot the rest: but it had been a perfectly

> clear dream, and it stuck in my memory. Six weeks or more later, I attended in my capacity of a member of the War Graves Commission a ceremony at Westminster Abbey, where the Prince of Wales dedicated a plaque to 'The Million Dead' of the Great War. We commissioners lined up facing, across the width of Abbey Nave, more members of the Ministry and a big body of the public behind them, all in black clothes. I could see nothing of the ceremony because the stomach of the man on my left barred my vision. Then, my eye was caught by the cracks of the stone flooring, and I said to myself: 'But here is where I have been!' We broke up, both lines flowed forward and met, and the Nave filled with a crowd, through which a man came up and slipped his hand upon my arm, saying 'I want a word with you, please.' It was about some utterly trivial matter that I have forgotten. But how, and why, had I been shown an unreleased roll of my life-film?

It may, perhaps, be objected that the Kipling experience that I have quoted occurred in a dream. But there is no point in such an objection. The precognition of a dream differs in no appreciable way from a precognition experience in the waking state; the human consciousness is active in the same way, and both are true precognitions — the true experiencing in the consciousness, in advance, of an immaterial event which later occurs in the physical and sensory fields. I have no doubt that in sleep one learns many things through the supersensory activities of consciousness. That one does not remember more about such experiences is undoubtedly due to the fact that, in sleep, awareness is somehow disassociated from the perceptive levels of the mind; yet we know that consciousness is capable of outriding the reaches of the mind. It is generally accepted that the remembered dreams are those that occur at the mysterious edges of being in which awareness is returning to the restricted areas of sensory perception in the "real" world. But it is an old conviction of the human race that we solve our problems by sleeping on them; certainly, a new clarity of mind, a fresh point of view, often comes with the morning. Many dreams contain clairvoyance, clairaudience and telepathy, and some are precognitive, such as the one I have cited.

I have my "telepathic dream" state, in which many problems are solved. I have put a good deal of emphasis on the emotional values involved in supersensory activities, and I have a clear impression that in the telepathic dream the emotional tension which caused the problem, its acceptance and its transposition into my intention to seek and find the answer to it are the elements that determine the associations of my consciousness in the dream state and insure the success of the endeavor.

My telepathic experiences, whether dreaming or awake, are frequently precognitive, as the Kipling dream was. For instance, though physically tired, I find myself restless and unable to sleep at night. I take up a book and begin to read. But under the attention that my mind gives to what I am reading, the restlessness develops at the secondary level of my mental activity. I presently become aware that this secondary awareness is concerned with a dim picture of my bathroom, and I know immediately that there is a spider there. This is no ordinary spider, but a large, black, demonic-looking thing measuring three inches across and capable of rapid movement. He is native to the place where I am staying at the time, and though people assure me that he is quite harmless, I have a very definite temperamental aversion to him and his kind. So I get out of bed, determined to face and rout him, and I turn on the bathroom lights.

My impression of his presence has shown him in a precise position — say, at a particular point of the patterned tiling. Now, if I find him poised in that position I know that I have had a true experience, however unimportant. But if I do not find him there? Many people would suppose that I had imagined the whole thing. But there is a difference between "seeing," "knowing" and imagining, and in the present case I know that I have not imagined the spider's presence. Nevertheless, a search does not disclose him, and I finally give it up and go back to bed. And when, three days later, I find the spider in my bathroom, poised at the foreseen particular point of the patterned tiling and apparently observing me with malice (as well may be, for I do not mean to be kind to him), I know that my experience was of a precognitive type.

In one form or another, the "restlessness" to which I have just referred seems to be a preparatory phase of my psychic experiences, whether these occur at random, so to say, or are consciously undertaken. I am busy in the office and my secretary tells me that Mrs. A. has arrived. The lady has an appointment with me at eleven o'clock, and I say, "Ask her to come in." I know that Mrs. A. has problems that she wishes to discuss with me, and I have been told that during the two minutes that elapse before Mrs. A. appears I perform a ritual of preparation, to which I have referred elsewhere. Quite unconsciously, I move the papers, books, flowers and other objects on my desk, for no particular purpose that I am aware of. But because this is all so spontaneous and unconsidered, I have no doubt that it has its importance as a preparatory phase in the adjustment of my consciousness to psychic levels.

Whether or not this preparation is a really essential aspect of the work, I do not know. I sometimes think that it points back to the early days in which Hewat McKenzie so definitely differentiated my psychic work from the rest of my life.

I was in the south of France in the most desperate early days of the war in Europe, after Munich, and during the evacuation of Dunkirk. Britain had stretched her very life across the Channel and made her offer of national unity with France. The southern country was already crowded with refugees of all types, and a few who had been living there and still stayed on had opened a *foyer de soldat* and soup kitchen. Throughout the whole of France resentment against England moved like a plague: she was secretly collaborating with Hitler; she had sold France out; she would fight to the last drop of French blood. I knew that this wild hatred of England had been hatched in Germany and that it was being propagated by German agents who moved through the French countryside and the French cities, dropping hints, making vague suggestions, asking endless questions barbed with poisonous innuendo. I watched France swallow this bait, submit to this deception, and I saw the national morale going to pieces day by day. I thought in my heart, could this be possible in France, where the life of the people and the life of the sea and the soil were one life? If this were possible, was this then the beginning of the end of the world, of the reversion of mankind to savagery, of the extinction of the human race? Humanity seemed to be moving toward madness — a madness destined to end in self-destruction. All about one, people were fleeing from an annihilating force, as those other people, long ago, had fled before the rising water till there was no longer any land to flee to, and the deluge destroyed them utterly.

I kept myself as busy as possible, but in the privacy of my own room and my own spirit I brought the situation to an issue, demanding some sign that would enable me to verify my faith in England and justify my hopes for a world of honorable peace. I saw a large room with high windows, like a turret, and a man sitting in a chair in a mustard-colored uniform from which shoulder straps, buttons and all insignia had been cut away. The man was unmistakably Hitler. He was fatter than most pictures had made him appear, and tears were running down his soiled and bloated face. As the picture cleared to my perception, another man went out of the room through a doorway. I saw only the back of this second man — a "von Stroheim" back, with cropped hair and the thick crease of flesh above the collar. This man was no dignitary; he was dressed in a rusty black suit, and I had an impression of him as some kind of artisan, maybe a concièrge. He did not look back as he went out, but his hand cast back into the room a knife with a short wooden handle and a curved blade. My sight followed the knife as it slid across the floor, and I had the impression of thinking, "That's the Russian sickle." But a voice said, "No, not Russian. That's an Afghan knife."

I looked again at "Hitler"; he sat immobile in his chair, his shorn uniform awry, while tears ran slowly down his cheeks. Then and there I was filled with a transcendent pity too deep and poignant for any words — pity for that life spent in senseless and futile war against its own kind and against the time to which it belonged. Shorn of his flimsy honors, power had gone out from him completely, leaving him — a foolish, lonely, human creature — to the slow, perhaps eternal realization of the crimes he had committed against humanity, against the life and peace of the world.

For me, that vision was the key to the assurance that I needed. Through it, I knew within myself, deeper than all desire or hope or reasoning, that Germany would never win the war. Through all the ups and downs of success and disaster that filled the years that followed, I suffered with my kind for the base and heartless cruelties of the war, but never for a moment did I fail to know that in the end, and whatever the cost, the United Nations would be victorious. At times, my family and friends lost patience with me when I tried to ease their anger and their agony over Coventry or Lidice by reminding them of the end. I would mourn over the disasters and loss of life, but within myself I knew with a constant and steady assurance that Germany was destined for defeat.

There is one phase in this experience which I have never been able to translate into understandable terms for my own satisfaction. I do not yet know the meaning of the statement, "No, not Russian. That's an Afghan knife." As the war ended in Europe with Russia's occupation of Berlin, one could easily find a connection between my impression of "the Russian sickle" and the final downfall of Hitler's Nazi dictatorship; but one will be wise not to make one's own acceptances and rejections among the symbols of such an experience, and it may be that the fate of Germany is bound up with the fate of Asia in some future too far ahead for our minds to penetrate.

❖ SEVENTEEN

DISCARNATE ENTITIES

During the years of my work in London, I had several opportunities to study poltergeist phenomena. Various calls for help to deal with these vigorous, sometimes boisterous ghosts reached the British College of Psychic Science. I had often seen cases of such outbreaks reported in the press — outbreaks which usually consisted of china and crockery, as well as other small objects, moving mysteriously from place to place.

When such an outbreak took place, a boy or girl of adolescent years was usually alleged to be associated with the disturbance. If this were all, one could be indifferent to the calls for help, but these calls came from intelligent people not given to unseemly and bizarre conduct. This latter fact aroused my interest, and I was frequently called upon to help investigate some of these phenomenal happenings. Through a series of these investigations I became keenly interested in understanding the mystery of the poltergeist and various other types of physical phenomena that were related to these entities.

The poltergeist phenomena differ from the ordinary hauntings that one reads of and can be regarded as violent outbreaks of long or short duration. My own observation led me to believe that such outbreaks, occurring as they did at set intervals, were centered around an unusual, unhappy or tragic event within the house and were not always necessarily connected with the people who might be thus afflicted. Whatever the cause of the outbreaks may be, the fact remains that the phenomena happen, and cases are reported from all over the world. The interesting fact about these phenomena is that all reported cases have a sameness to them — bells ring spontaneously, crockery and household objects move mysteriously — , though sometimes these happenings are accompanied by explosions, and from nowhere there may appear showers of small stones or small pebbles (even fishhooks have been known to arrive in quantities). Such occurrences can be not only disturbing but very frightening. On the other hand, these happenings would seem to establish the existence of an unusual energy or rudimentary unseen intelligence. Although many people may remain unconvinced of the reality of such phenomena, there are so many authenticated records of these mischievous entities that one must accept them and draw one's own conclusions as to their cause.

Since my mind was never quite made up as to the reality of spirit phenomena, I was glad of the opportunity to assist at the investigation of poltergeist phenomena which promised to help us to a greater understanding of what might be at the root of the "infestation." Thus it was that whenever an "outbreak" occurred I was always more than willing to be of use. I shall now give some examples of these unhappy occurrences.

A retired Admiral in the British Navy, who was living outside of London, called upon the officers of the College of Psychic Science for help. He was a man of action and something of a bon vivant, accustomed to command. He was master of the external conditions of his life and that of his family, who, one assumed, were well disciplined by him and free from all "nonsense." He had a pleasant wife and two sons. When his younger son, who was still an adolescent, began to be disturbed at night by the idea that there was someone in the room where the youths slept together, Father was unsympathetic. This was "nonsense" — a neurotic breach of discipline, order and good form.

The boy had the support of his older brother, whom he had waked on several occasions to witness a mysterious visitation. Neither of the boys saw anything, but both heard unaccountable sounds from the wardrobes, especially one in which they kept their shoes, and in the morning they would find that these had been moved. These annoyances continued for some time. The effect of them — his father's disapprobation and the consequent nervous tension which developed throughout the household — made the younger boy moody and nervous to a point where his health was being affected. His parents decided to send him away, and on his departure the mysterious disarrangement of the shoes ceased.

Then the mother became nervous. She testified to hearing footsteps at a time when the house should have been quiet. Being unafraid of ghosts, she encouraged the visitation, but no enlightenment came from her response. At first she did not tell her husband of the footsteps, and as the disarrangement of the shoes had ceased, and to all appearances everything restored to normality, the father decided that his absent son had better return and that the family would forget the whole episode.

Before the boy reached home, however, the Admiral was sitting alone one day with his scotch and soda on the table beside him when the glass began to move away from him without visible means to account for its movement. The man was astounded and somewhat awed, and without lifting a hand he watched his glass of scotch and soda move across the table and crash to the floor. Naturally, he went and got himself another drink and attempted to dismiss the occurrence from his mind, but when a day or two later a jug that he was using executed a movement across the table and crashed to the ground, he realized that something very wrong was happening. Shamefaced and embarrassed, he called upon a friend for advice.

The friend advised him to seek help from the officers of the College, and so the case was referred to them. "Uvani" cooperated in the investigation, and the sad story was reported through trance communication. The story, as revealed, was that the mother of the boys had a brother of whom she had been very fond who had died two years previously. During the last months of this brother's life, he had been mentally ill, and in this period — as so often happens in such cases — his affections had changed toward his wife and his lawyer, two people whom he had been most fond of and most devoted to. During this time, he had made several wills. The only one produced at his death bore a date corresponding to the time when his mental aberrations had commenced. This was accepted by the Court and allowed as his last will and testament. It deeded his property to a distant cousin, and the wife, whom he had sincerely loved through the years, would receive no more than her legal widow's share. In death it would appear that he had been able to realize the situation in which he had placed his wife, and, disturbed by it and unable to rest, he had desperately tried to attract attention in order to adjust this grave mistake. His memory was bent upon finding another will, an earlier one which bequeathed his property as he really intended and wished, and in which his distant cousin was remembered but the bulk of his property was left to his wife. He could not tell where the missing will was to be found, but some part of his memory recalled that he had a habit of writing and hiding things in his shoes when anyone approached. During the seance his sister, overcome by emotion, left the room. She had had a previous "conviction" that it was her brother who was trying to reach the family.

He had been especially fond of the younger of his two nephews, and he felt that the boy's sensitive nature could furnish the line of least resistance by which he could make his presence known. Failing at that point, and not wanting to lose the possibility of contact, he continued to make his approach through other members of the family, including the Admiral. Since the occurrence with the shoes in the cupboard had been an outstanding aspect of the whole episode, the "dead" man, when questioned about this, explained that his mind had been filled with secret things which he wished to set down in writing, and that often, while he was noting down these important ideas, he would be interrupted by some member of the family; when this happened he would put the secret papers away by placing them in his shoes. While he could not quite remember where he had hidden the document, the place of hiding was repeatedly associated in his mind with an idea of shoes.

Through this clue, the lost will was found in a cupboard. The distant cousin neither needed nor wanted the property that had been left to him. Disturbed and overcome by the manner in which the existence of the first will was discovered, he decided to honor it and to distribute the dead man's estate according to his first will and intention. Apparently, having made these necessary adjustments the dead man proceeded on his way, since no further disturbance in the house was reported.

Later, my daughter and I were the participants in a very unhappy but spontaneous haunting experience of another variety. Motoring in Germany, we had planned to reach Cologne by twilight, but on reaching Kleve we decided to pass the night at a comfortable little inn where our host wanted to renew a pleasant acquaintance with the landlord. The place was clean and comfortable, but from the moment I entered the inn some vital note, some necessary élan, was missing. I charged this to the absence of the friendly landlord who, we were told, was away. I made a brief toilet and went down to the sitting room to await my friends.

Relaxed in a comfortable chair with my back to an inner wall of the room, I watched the waiter setting the table in a corner of the room. Sleepily, I felt the familiar pricking of my nerves and a gooseflesh sensation in my back, which is usually a signal that I am not alone in the room. My daughter entered at that moment, and I remarked to her, "Is there anybody behind me?" She looked at me and answered, "No." But just over my shoulder I "saw" a man hanging by his neck from a large beam and knew that it was in a room behind me. As I looked, I could see from the final spasmodic twitching of his body that he was at the point of death. I also "knew" that he was the owner of the inn.

I have no idea why I should have seen him at this particular moment of his self-destruction, unless it was due to the fact that that was the moment to which his consciousness, instead of being fully released by death, was anchored by strong emotional ties. Normal death is not an instantaneous event but a process that in some cases involves a long time before life is finally and completely released. I have known of cases in which there has been evidence of a partial "consciousness" remaining in ghostly form for years after the death of the body, as though some part of the mind were reluctant to release itself. So far as my own experience goes, the lingering here is due to some injustice, injury or moral wrong which the consciousness has not been able to forgive or forget and which, under the mysterious law of compensation, arrests its progress and holds it in the place of its deepest life relationship.

In the case of the landlord of the inn at Kleve, I knew none of the facts or circumstances of his life, yet there he was, sometime after his physical demise, impinging on my consciousness, demanding attention and holding me to the picture of his suffering. I could see that he had been a strong old man, single and sincere in his desires and devotions, and in that hour my unvolitional clairvoyance was so acute that I saw with perfect clearness every button of every garment that he wore — not in a flash or briefly, as is so often the case, but the perception continued to hold. Seeing thus clearly that no wound or illness of body existed as a cause of what he had done to himself, I also knew that his self-destruction had been the culmination of a series of events and circumstances which, for him, had been tragic in their nature.

My friends came downstairs, and presently supper was served. Though I made an attempt to eat, I had no appetite. As soon as I could, I excused myself and went for a walk, taking my daughter with me, to whom I told the story. I have learned from long experience to accept such happenings, examine them objectively and accept them in the spirit of adventure. Such an attitude in no way lessens my sympathy and desire to help. In the present case, I found that my daughter was a little disturbed.

"Oh, mother," she said, in a tone that might be interpreted as 'here we go again,' "if he is downstairs, that needn't keep you from sleeping. We might as well undress and get a good night's sleep."

That was not to be, however, for there was a level of my consciousness that would keep contact with the suicide throughout the night. I was out of my bed early in the morning, and, not knowing what else to do, I waited until the verger of the little local church arrived, and there I lit a candle for the peace of the dead man's spirit and asked that he might be released.

We started for Cologne in the early morning, but I could not rid myself of the feeling that I had not done all that was necessary for the dead man. I knew instinctively that he had been a Catholic, and when we approached the Cathedral I went in and asked that he might find rest. By nightfall I was completely released from his presence. He had withdrawn as unaccountably as he had come.

When I recounted the experience to my friends, my host made further inquiries. It was then revealed that the old landlord of the inn, whom he had known, had indeed hanged himself from a beam in the cellar stairway, driven to desperation by a nephew who, uninvited, had come to live and work with him and, gradually, by guile and by force, to rob the old man of his inn, his peace of mind and eventually his life.

Many such instances have occurred through the years, and it is interesting to conjecture about the source of the stuff of energy that such discarnate beings use to manifest themselves and their natures. Science makes no declaration in this field, but the voluminous records of the psychical research societies no longer leave any room for doubting that some potent factor of the life-force of a human being can, and often does, survive the death of the physical body, continues to be conscious at its own level and is capable of affecting the destinies of people.

My own conviction is that, in the life of each such discarnate entity, there has been developed a nucleus of emotional intensity so potent that not even the dissolutions of death can completely dissociate the consciousness from the field of its most poignant life-affinities. This lingering of the individual consciousness in the areas of its deepest associations may occur in the case of every human being who dies; we do not know.

In the ancient East, where the processes of death are perhaps better understood than with us, the period between the end of breathing and the time of interment (of whatever type this may be) is normally filled with instructions, suggestions and exhortations to the passing consciousness relative to its change of condition and the future into which it is advancing. The Chinese *Book of the Dead* and the Tibetan *Book of the Dead* are compilations of these rituals. And though we in the West leave each passing entity more free to find its own way into its own future, practically every normal death is marked by some blessing of love and devotion from the world and often by the symbolic or magical ministrations of religion as well. It would seem to be that, out of the millions that are dying all the time, relatively few are caught and held in midspace.

And this is well. For as I have intimated above, what seems to hold them is the effect of some moral injury or wrong that has been done to them — an aggression which they can neither forget nor forgive. It is well that such lives are not more numerous — at levels that are perceptible to us, at least.

There was, for illustration, a peculiar case that occurred in England. A widowed woman, a stranger to the region, had come to a small town and opened a rather meager little shop where she settled and waited for trade. She had a child, a young daughter who was anemic and never well. The two of them had not been there very long before the people of the village became aware that strange rappings and other disturbances frequently occurred on the premises. Meanwhile, the little girl steadily failed in health. All of this continued for some time, and the gossip grew, but nobody interfered until finally someone wrote the circumstances to the late Sir Arthur Conan Doyle. He referred the letter to Hewat McKenzie, who was then at the head of the British College of Psychic Science. The case seemed to contain some of the elements of poltergeist phenomena, and as I was particularly interested in poltergeists I accompanied Hewat McKenzie to the scene. The woman was aggressive and uncooperative when she learned the purpose of our visit, but she was afraid, too — as she had reason to be — , but she finally permitted us to enter her home and to see the child, who appeared to be quite ill. Almost as soon as we came on the premises an unaccountable series of rappings began. Presently I went into trance, leaving McKenzie to take down a report of whatever might come through.

What did come through was a message from the woman's dead husband. He had died some two years before, leaving some money to enable his widow to care for the little girl, his only child, of whom he was very fond. But the lawyer who handled the small estate had "got 'round" the woman, who was not vicious but weak, and the two of them had been gay and frivolous together until the money was nearly all gone. By that time, either tiring of her or having some other interest, the lawyer abandoned the woman to her conscience, letting her know at the same time that she had put herself completely into his hands, legally as well as physically and morally.

The rappings and disturbances were expressions of the dead man's protest against all this. He simply could not abandon his precious child to such outrageous conditions. And there were two extraordinary intimations in what he then declared: one was that the strength or energy that he used for his manifestations was strength that he somehow absorbed away from the child, and the other was that in order to "save" the little girl (and as soon as he could accomplish it), he would take her away from her mother and care for her himself in the place where he was.

Whether or not the "dead" can use the life-forces of the living for the manifestation of their own purposes, I do not know. If such a thing is at all possible, it would seem as though it could occur only in some special case and relationship. We are all familiar, however, with the fact that in this life there are people who stimulate us and others who depress us or exhaust us mentally and nervously; and though we do not know very clearly how such effects occur, it will be easy (for those who do know of their own experience) to imagine how disruptive of one's normal peace and vitality such pressures might be if they were persistently and intimately applied over a long period of time.

That certain discarnate entities have the power to affect us in our bodies and our consciousnesses I know of my own knowledge, for they frequently demand my attention, as did the poor man who hanged himself at Kleve. Most of the discarnate beings that I have any knowledge of through my own experience have seemed to operate not by draining off the life-force of living beings, but by the innate power of their own existence — the power of that part of them which remains alert in the sphere of our conscious living — the power of that unforgettable, unforgivable emotionalism that still ties them to particular places and people, demanding the justice that is their due.

What they seem to need is a chance to *express*, to get rid of what is troubling them; and it is a question whether, in becoming aware of them, the sensitive gives them some measure of energy which they are able to use in some subtle way, or whether all that they need is a channel through which to project an energy that is all their own.

In the valley of the Severn there lived a family of fishermen: a man, his wife and several grown sons. There was another son, younger, who had been born during the time of his mother's change of life. This youngest boy was delicate and very dear to his mother, but he was also a favorite with his father and his brothers. As he approached the age of puberty, with his parents beginning to be old, he suffered a time of terror, for he discovered a "ghost" about the home-place — a dark, rough, swarthy, threatening man. When the boy spoke to the others of this apparition, they all knew what he meant; they had all heard of "him" on occasion, but, said they, he was harmless, and they paid no attention to him.

It was not so with the youngest, however, for the strange visitor seemed to be attracted to him in some way. Sometimes the boy, crying or screaming with shock, would rush into his mother's room in the middle of the night, and when she tried to soothe him he would tell her how he had been awakened suddenly by the ghostly one snatching the clothes off his bed. When she would go into his bed with him to reassure him, the bedclothes would sometimes be snatched away again. Yet the dim visitor never troubled the other members of the family.

When the report of the case came to the attention of the officers of the College, several members of the society accompanied me to the Severn valley and met the family of rough but simple men. When we arrived they were polite and cordial to us and very curious, in their shy way, to see what "magic" thing we intended to work.

Hewat McKenzie was not alive at this time, and Stanley Barber, a member of the Society, explained to our hosts that they need have no anxiety; presently I would go to sleep, and then we should see what developed, if anything.

"Uvani" cooperated, as usual, and a communication came through from a personality who bore a distant relationship to this family of young men — he was an uncle in some remote degree. He had lived in this same house several generations before, and he still had a fondness for the place, coming back to it at those seasons when the fishing should be at its best.

He was not a pleasant person, and he told a gruesome, tragic story with a gusto that revealed how definitely he was still living in, and enjoying, the passionate past. He and a brother had smuggled as well as fished together, and at one point in his talk he offered to conduct the group to the local church where they had hidden the laces, wines and other contraband goods that they were able to smuggle over from the Continent — and also to reveal the path that they had used coming up from the sea, through the lich gate and leading to the church's great strong box where the plate and other treasures were kept — a beautiful, old, carved chest, six feet long and a treasure in itself.

He recounted that, eventually, he and his brother quarreled and that he had shot and killed his brother — an act for which he evidently had neither regret nor penitence; he continued that he had had to keep the dead body in the house for several days before he could dispose of it without endangering his own safety. He spoke frankly of treasure that had been hidden in the garden, and he said that digging would supply evidence of the truth of his story. He reported how the family had at one time owned immense areas of land and considerable wealth and how everything had been gambled away — money, land, horses, women — ; anything and everything had been risked on the fall of the cards or the dice — risked and lost. Later, when some digging was done in the garden, a number of old coins and some human bones were unearthed. Whether or not these were the bones of the murdered brother was of course uncertain.

But in the meantime a strange thing happened. The father of the present family brought out of hiding a small strong box of his own. It had been given to him by his father, and it contained a number of ancient coins and papers so old as to be scarcely decipherable, yet sufficient to give a touch of authenticity to our communicator's story of the family's former wealth. The father of the present family had also received from his father a belief in the legend of the family's former greatness, but this little box of ancient remnants was the only surviving evidence of it that he knew. He had never revealed either the box or the story to his sons, because he was ashamed to have so little to give to *his* family out of what had once been so much.

When the alien "one" was asked why he came here, he said truculently that this was his place, and he liked it. He did not know who these present occupants of the house were, and he resented their presence in no uncertain terms. When he was asked why he had been troubling the youngest son of the family, he declared that he hadn't meant to frighten him, but that he liked the lad and wanted to attract his notice.

The unquiet spirit of the man who had been dead for several generations was finally convinced that his place was no longer here but elsewhere, and I was later informed that he had finally given up his visitations and was seen no more.

I am repeatedly surprised at the comparative ease with which these "visitors" accept dismissal from the scenes which have held them so long. One would suppose that a tie strong enough to defy the dissolutions of death and hold a consciousness to the scenes of its life on earth for a century or more could be broken only by some extraordinarily definite consummation. But on the whole the findings of the psychical research societies do not indicate this to be so. The keys to such survivals seem to be emotion and egotism. In the case I have just cited, the man's naive admission of crimes committed, his cooperative offer to take those interested to the church and his friendly indication of where the digging should be done in the garden — all were given in a spirit of braggadocio and boasting. That's the kind of man he was in life, and that's the kind of "ghost" he was. He loved himself and he loved his life, and he clung to it decade after decade of our time, though time as we understand it would not seem to exist outside of bodily sensation. Those who return in such fashion would appear to be in a half-world of confusion, a world caught between waking and sleeping where the dream experience becomes a reality and, too often, a nightmare. Indeed, the whole process of haunting seems to be related to a nightmare experience, for the ghostly visitor can be released from the world of substance not by force but by patient suggestion coupled with loving reasoning.

The appearance of such entities appears to be directed and dominated by some emotional fixation of the past. When they are released by the argument that they do not belong to this world any longer and that it would be well for them to forget the past and find the place that is now their rightful one, the effect is to release them from bonds that would appear to be a nightmare state in which they act as though they were still alive and responsible.

Dissociation has been considered an abnormality and a destructive condition in the lives and personalities of many sensitive individuals. But it would be well to remember that every "normal" person has his moments of dissociation in fantasy and daydream. Is it possible that such dissociation can continue after death, and if this is so, would it not help to clear up some of the mystery attached to the phantom and to hauntings?

The returning entity acts like a fever-ridden patient or one whose mind is "released" under the effects of an anesthetic. It exhibits memory in connection with certain places and happenings in its past and refers again and again (as does the fevered one) to these unhappy emotional relationships. It is as "out of time" as is a person under the effect of any of the time-deranging drugs.

It would appear, then, that death is but an exchange of one experience for another, for during all human history there has been a belief, not confined to any particular country, creed, level or culture, that through perceptions beyond the five senses men have been able to get in touch with phases of existence unfamiliar to everyday experience.

❖ EIGHTEEN

PSYCHOKINETIC MANIFESTATIONS

Many learned men have testified to the genuineness of raps, the movement of objects without visible means and to ectoplasmic substances, all of which come under the heading of physical phenomena. Notwithstanding, there are many who do not believe such things occur. I, however, am convinced partly by the large amount of evidence which has been made available from many sources, and partly because I have been exposed to them myself.

I have also participated in a great number of experiments conducted by Harry Price with Rudi Schneider, the Austrian sensitive of international renown, and I also was one of the group in his series of experiments held in London in 1921 with Stella C. under conditions that had been electrically arranged with all the niceties that scientific ingenuity could conceive. I have seen a bunch of lilacs thrown onto a central table with never a murmur of telltale bells or a flicker of the sensitive electric light that would have flashed if Stella or any one of us had moved in our chairs.

I have seen an "ectoplasmic" hand that resembled a human one form itself in space, and I can assert with conviction that it was not a mere "appearance," for on invitation it grasped a handkerchief that was held toward it, and in so doing gave evidence of its strength.

I have seen a one-hundred-and-twelve-pound table lifted to the ceiling of a room, there to hang suspended while the best efforts of the group could not bring it down. When at last it fell, it was ripped apart in the falling.

These were not random exhibitions but controlled experiments that took place at South Kensington, London. They were arranged by Harry Price, one-time honorary secretary, University of London Council for Psychical Investigation. A report of these experiments was published by Mr. Price in 1926. I attended many of these meetings at which Mr. Price took care to have a nurse and doctor present during Stella's manifestations. "Women are no good for this job," he would comment. "They become sympathetic and emotional and more easily deceived — and have less knowledge of deceptive methods." He believed that if a medium were genuine, he or she would not object to medical examination and such controls as he considered necessary. Those who would know more about his methods will find many of them discussed in his book, *Confessions of a Ghost Hunter.*

The experiments I have referred to were conducted in the presence of officers of the accredited societies, doctors, newspaper reporters and a panel of scientists, military men and engineers, among whom one would see Lord Raleigh, Sir Robert Gregory, Sir Vincent Caillard and Professor C. E. M. Joad (whose interest in magic and related subjects were well known), Sir Ernest Bennett, and Professor F. C. S. Schiller, to mention only a few. These men were interested and open-minded. They found the facts strange and wonderful and pleaded at all times for an official and unbiased examination of the evidence for paranormal phenomena. They lent a sympathetic ear to Harry Price's plea that psychic research be rescued from the unhealthy emotion which promised to submerge it and keep it away from the serene eye of science.

It is undoubtedly an excellent thing that the human mind should be skeptical of these types of phenomena. Such demonstrations appear to touch the fringe of little understood energies and leave us completely mystified by the techniques which they manifest. We know how radically the discovery of electricity altered the entire life of the civilized world, and we have seen the destructive uses to which man can turn the powers of nature that have so lately come into his hands. So it is little wonder that we find such phenomena disturbing.

The danger of Sinbad's genie escaping from his servitude, the fate of the final owner of Stevenson's bottle imp and the story of Faust are all symbolic indicators of the dire fate of the man who associates himself with amoral forces. One may readily imagine that the energies evoking these physical phenomena rise out of secret areas of the creative process in which the life-force of the universe seeds all forms of physical being, particularizing, specializing and developing them for existence in the world as the human embryo is prepared and developed in the womb.

I have *seen* such a world where forms and half-made shapes moved and struggled, vital and conscious but strangely unaware — as a tree is, and yet not as a tree, since they did not seem to be impregnated with the fire and movement of life that we know on this planet. Such experiences in the early days of my training held a warning for me of a danger that reached far deeper than my physical being, not active but suspended, a dim potential animus to the very core of sentiency within. I frequently wondered if I were the victim of hallucinations, and I found no voice to tell me clearly that I was not. Nevertheless, I continued to experience, observe and reflect.

Before this I had already had some experience with physical phenomena. Hewat McKenzie would have none of it and in my early days had warned me against such experiments, but a group of friends who were interested in physical manifestations urged me to join them in a series of experiments in spite of McKenzie's veto. I sat with a group to see what might occur, and eventually some measure of success was achieved. Then I had an eruption of conscience and told Hewat McKenzie what I had been doing. He reprimanded us all, and since he had such a reputation for disinterested probity, the experiments in physical phenomena were discontinued for the time being.

There are other types of psychokinetic work that are performed with conscious purpose and in full waking awareness, and which produce very definite physical forms and effects without the aid of a medium. (For interest and emphasis on this point, one can read the report of an experiment of this kind that was made by Madame David-Neel in her book, *Magic and Mystery in Tibet.*)

Such experiments as this are not recommended, for, as is indicated in the report, one cannot escape from the responsibilities and consequences of such creations — or any others for that matter — except by paying the full compensatory price. In fact, it is impossible to escape. There is no such thing as escape. One pays and receives payment for all of the commitments and activities of one's life.

The following is from Madame David-Neel's report:

Besides having had few opportunities of seeing thought-forms, my habitual incredulity led me to make experiments for myself, and my efforts were attended with some success. In order to avoid being influenced by the forms of the Lamaist deities which I saw daily around me in paintings and images, I chose for my experiment a most insignificant character: a monk, short and fat, of an innocent and jolly type.

I shut myself in *tsams* (seclusion) and proceeded to perform the prescribed concentration of thought and other rites. After a few months the phantom monk was formed. His form grew gradually *fixed* and life-like looking. He became a kind of guest living in my apartment. I then broke my seclusion and started for a tour with my servants and tents. The monk included himself in the party. Though I lived in the open, riding on horseback for miles each day, the illusion persisted. I saw the fat *trapa,* now and then it was not necessary for me to think of him to make him appear. The phantom performed various actions of the kind that are natural to travelers and that I had not commanded. For instance, he walked, stopped, looked around him. The illusion was mostly visual, but sometimes I felt as if a robe was lightly rubbing against me, and once a hand seemed to touch my shoulder.

The features which I had imagined, when building my phantom, gradually underwent a change. The fat, chubby-cheeked fellow grew leaner, his face assumed a vaguely mocking, sly, malignant look. He became more troublesome and bold. In brief, he escaped my control.

One, a herdsman who brought me a present of butter, saw the *tulpa* (magic, illusory creature) in my tent and took it for a live lama.

> I ought to have let the phenomenon follow its course, but the presence of that unwanted companion began to prove trying to my nerves; it turned into a 'day-nightmare.' Moreover, I was beginning to plan my journey to Lhassa and needed a quiet brain devoid of other preoccupations, so I decided to dissolve the phantom. I succeeded, but only after six months of hard struggle. My mind-creature was tenacious of life.
>
> There is nothing strange in the fact that I may have created my own hallucination. The interesting point is that in these cases of materialization, others see the thought-forms that have been created.
>
> Tibetans disagree in their explanation of such phenomena: some think a material form is really brought into being; others consider the apparition as a mere case of suggestion, the creator's thought impressing others and causing them to see what he himself sees.

Madame David-Neel has given no further opinion of her own concerning the realities of the experiment thus reported in her book, which leaves everyone free to draw his own conclusions. From my own experience in observing the products of physical mediumship, I cannot help supposing that Madame David-Neel's monk was a reality of some kind — some kind of a real existence in himself. In such conception one does not have to go to the length of believing that the creature was a fully developed, organically functioning entity; but he was, without doubt, a real "creation," the offspring of particular purpose, creative intention and concentrated energies. He symbolizes one aspect of the whole vast field of psychology and natural mystery in which the immaterial energies of the universe are transposed into material form through man's creative intention. And it is worth remembering that our present civilized scheme of life is the product of man's intentions.

Since my own early training days I have experienced spontaneous phenomena which have led me seriously to consider developing telekinesis to a point where it may be controlled and studied by laboratory techniques; it is toward this latter phase of experimentation that I shall devote some time in the future. I still believe there is an unexplained source of energy within mankind which is automatically drawn upon in moments of deep need and emotional stress. The significance of these energies cannot be overlooked, and while I shall expect many setbacks in such a study I feel that, in this age of intellectual unrest, any road that promises to throw more light on the question of man's heritage and survival is worth long years of sustained research effort.

❖ NINETEEN

THE BREATH AND THE BLOOD

In the human constitution there is a point of focus that is the physical seat of the psychic faculties. It is the solar plexus, that great ganglion of nerves that lies behind the stomach. It is situated far from the brain, and it thinks differently from the brain, for it is a brain itself. When in a situation of silent danger a twig snaps, it is in the solar plexus that one first *feels* the effect. That the ear hears and the brain registers the sound are incidental facts, remote from the center at which life is then concentrated. In such a situation, the blood pounds and the breath comes fast and shallow in the lungs, because a part of it is held deep in the region of the diaphragm.

How rarely are we thus animated in the daily round of our routines! We lose the tension of a vital alertness that is native to us and spend our energies casually along the lines of least resistance.

It is in the vicinity of the solar plexus that one first feels fear. But fear is the prelude to courage, to the focusing of energies, to the facing of issues, to going on. Courage and important sacrifice are accepted in the mind — if at all — *after* they have been determined here. And it is as a result of having *satisfied* these deep compulsions that thought and feeling fuse in a sense of completeness.

It is at the level of the solar plexus that human nature makes its deepest concessions to Nature. It is here that those who die in battle first make their acceptance of destiny. Having done so, they pass beyond fear and face the universal life. And if, having accepted destiny in this way, they do not die but live, they are never again completely released from the depths, however unaware they may be of the nature of their inner strangeness. This is the key to the courage of youth and to the silence of those who have suffered much from the world. It is also the quality above all others that makes for success and is inherent *in* the world of perception. Plato long ago reminded us that God forever geometrizes. There is always a language at hand — the language of nature and the soul — for the engineer, the poet and the mathematician.

The majesty of the unknowable has always recognized the breath and the blood. He breathed into the nostrils of the creature He had made, and the creature became a living soul. He put Jacob to trial by demanding the blood sacrifice of his son. The ignorant may scoff, but the truly wise — whether religious or not — will know that, today, victory over the dark forces of death, destruction and enslavement has been won only through the shedding of the bright, brave blood, the giving up of the breath of life by the young of the nations.

One looks on with awe and pity as the sacrificial price increases war by war. One wonders if, in the end, humanity itself must die defending the spirit that is in it. There is no great prospect of anything less in civilization, for unfortunately civilization is not based in the integrity of natural man but in the balancing of symbolic powers. One might suppose that the eighty-odd cents' worth of chemical substances which, with water, constitute the human body stood as the actual value of a man. But it is not the value of a man. No monetary figure is the value of a man — neither how much he owns nor how much he earns. The value of man lies deeper than civilization's knowledge can penetrate and is discoverable only in the categories of nature's species. This is the realm of darkness for us; we know only the values of the market place.

This is not to say that I advise that one resign one's job, abandon responsibilities and go out with a begging bowl, trusting to nature. No, for we have neither earned the right nor learned the way. But I am suggesting that we take some notice of the natural sources of our existence, to think of the breath and blood, of their sources in the universe and of the universal energies which, through them, animate the being.

Direct knowledge of the Infinite through perception is the common goal of both the Eastern and Western mystic. There are many roads toward the inner experience, all of them leading toward the achievement of perfection. Perhaps the personality which we are today exists because we are not yet ready for fuller participation. We are, however, beginning to turn away from external authority and to rely upon inward experience.

The medieval scientists, who believed in the transmutation of the baser metals to gold and in the universal cure of illness and prolongation of life, would not find themselves in strange company among the atomic chemists of the modern age who have succeeded in the practical transformation of matter into energy on a large scale. These pioneers of atomic transmutation may well lead mankind to slow energy down to that place where he will gain ascendancy over time and space and understand these continual levels of energy through his own expanded consciousness.

The logic intuition, instead of being suspect, may well be more fully understood. Man's experience of the universe depends entirely upon his desire for knowledge and observation of the phenomena that he lives with. Existence becomes reality for him according to his horizons, and unless he has the curiosity to persist and persevere in his search for knowledge, he leaves the world's scene with much of the huge territory and its subtle atmosphere unexplored.

His picture of his "new country" will differ vastly from that of the man who has pushed his boundaries into a world of speculation, into a world of adventure.

The river of human experience has flowed across the plains of this planet for a long time, but always there have been those in every age who have wanted to survey the rapids; today, with the accelerated force of science, there are more. Each one has used his territory with different feelings, and when the traveller returns to speak of what he has found, it is claimed that the results are often incoherent and insignificant.

When man dies, he will not have changed much, and the reports of what the next dimension may hold will be equally as limited as were his reflections on this side,where the limitations of human thinking impose almost insurmountable difficulties. When one seeks to understand the fundamental nature of oneself, logic ceases to serve, and one's "illumined" statements can only be accepted as speculative. For, since each one accepts the formula of life differently, each one will still continue to relate his "after-life" experiences from his own deductions. However, when one desires to explore with the developed capacities of experience which are uppermost in our nature, there is an immediate quickening of one's better impulses. Conceptual thought enables one to escape beyond the primitive range of being and to analyze the crucial features of the mind's activity when it is fully coherent. The projection of oneself for travel into the levels of this experience is a highly stimulating one, not only to the mind but to the body.

From such exploration as I have made, it would appear that the growth of man in his next state is infinitely more resolved by his own conscious purpose. No matter how long the soul may dwell in a state of speculative dreaminess, finally it awakens to the necessity that the next step in development lies within its own desire for growth and expansion.

❖ TWENTY

A NEW VENTURE

The years between the first and second World Wars were waiting years. Most of my generation had, consciously or unconsciously, a sense of guilt for the unresolved political and social problems left or created by the Treaty of Versailles. We were uneasy during the years of the Armistice for we knew that powerful influences for evil were at work in the world. By 1938 there was, behind the nervous search for pleasure, the grim feeling that the worst could happen again. After the letdown of Munich, I felt impelled to visit Germany again in order to assure myself that the feelings of apprehension that I had were warranted; there one saw very clearly that what was happening to the Jewish people in Germany would undoubtedly break into a flame which, if uncontrolled, would one day sear the whole earth. There appeared nothing left to do but to decide in what way one's own efforts would be most effective. There was no doubt that, when the war came, I would work in France.

So I, like thousands of others, waited and listened to the fine words of unity being spoken — until hope died before our very eyes, and invading forces swept over Europe to be miraculously stopped at the English Channel. Much has already been written about these early days, days now almost forgotten, so quickly does history unfold and time erase the starkness of the drama. I remained in France until the end of 1940, working among children and refugees, but it was the suffering of the children that was hardest to bear.

After the fall of France, an Axis Armistice Commission composed of German and Italian officials policed the Cote d'Azur and made itself familiar with the movements of all foreigners. This was not to be wondered at, for everyone was doing his share to evacuate the soldiers, both French and British, who were left over from Dunkirk and hiding in France. My presence was not welcomed and soon it was obvious that I would be asked to leave. This did not trouble me much. The degree of my welcome was not important to me. What was important was my feeling of rightness in being there. As long as that feeling persisted, I stayed.

Then one day, in a flash, the "active movement" came; it was clear to me that my work in France was over. It was as if I had received a sudden order from the hands of my command. At that time I had no clear idea about returning to America, but I went to Lisbon, and, once there, it was inevitable. Ships leaving for England were few and far between, and planes, since the Dutch Airlines were grounded at that time, could not hope to carry the thousands waiting to leave for America. Journalists, economists, bankers, industrialists — all manner of important people spent weeks in Lisbon awaiting transportation. But on my arrival there, I found a refugee boat leaving for New York which miraculously offered me passage.

During the crossing, the plight of the children of Europe troubled me greatly; with them in mind, early one morning I walked the deck wondering when the horrors of warfare would end for them. It was then that the idea of starting a magazine came to me. It came in an instantaneous flash as something to be accomplished, and no logic came to proclaim the next step — that step that had, in the past, always seemingly revealed itself without judgment.

To define the moment when inspiration impels one is not easy. The urgency of the inner voice acts as an ordered and active movement. It cannot be mistaken for imagination or creative expression, which is the successful and well-rounded definition of any given experience. The inspiration that moves me from one step to the next is always instantaneous.

As I walked the deck I could hear the children's voices demanding of their mothers, "When do we eat, *maman*?" And the reply was always the same: "Tomorrow, we hope." There, in that often-heard question and desperate answer, was the name for my magazine: *Tomorrow*. Its reason for being would be to serve as a directive for youth and the problems of youth, for those young people who would one day, no matter how far off, drive out the alien violation that had destroyed not only the adult world but, more tragically, their own purer world as well. The nihilistic trend which had shown itself so vividly in the First World War was more noticeable now. The virus of revolution would become worldwide, and negation or inertia could not serve to avoid it. Within three months of my arrival in America, offices were established, and I had begun to gather the material for the first issues of the magazine. Creative Age Press, the book department, followed as a matter of course. It was then necessary to publish books in order to support the magazine venture. It was as simple as that.

It is true that I often dreamed, when young, of one day owning a magazine which would express my own ideals of creative living, but the years between had given little enforcement to the idea. But in 1941 *Tomorrow* was launched to become, not an expression of myself alone, but a significant monthly publication drawing nourishment from the still too small fraction of those who feel compelled to participate materially and spiritually in the shaping of the life ahead.

The scope of this book does not permit these pages to be a report of the business of publishing; the point that I want to make clear here is that this, and similar important phases in my life, have never come from within as growth that can be defined in general terms of experience. The compelling stimulus and the experience which allows for growth arrive without any inner search or known subjective belaboring. The nature, therefore, of such inspiration would appear to be wholly spontaneous and of external origin. It impels one beyond the field of experience, and it is so important in its consequences that one is led to search for the nature and meaning of a kind of stimulus that causes such a variety of reactions, not only in one's own life but in the lives of others.

I have often been asked — indeed, I sometimes ask myself — why I chose to go into publishing. If I want to find practical reasons for such a step, I can answer that the written and the spoken word had come to demand greater responsibility for their rightful use in a time when language had become a subtle weapon for propaganda. The pattern of making fine words the tools of base motives had become commonplace, and since language is basic to the business of civilized living, it is words, honestly used, that can turn an angry world in the direction of peace. In the face of the gathering storm on the horizon, publishing offers an exact and direct means of preparation.

My Irish heritage undoubtedly acts as a temptation to me; we Irish have a liking and respect for words. After the First World War, I was among those who helped gather together the posthumous writings of the young poets. Then, as now, I regarded writing and publishing as an honorable calling, rather than a business, and one that exacted responsibility for the written word. Had I been interested only in the escapes from living — which today make insipid so much of our daily living — I might have chosen a less exacting field of expression.

❖ TWENTY-ONE

IN SUMMATION

Man's spirit is sick of the confusion and futility in which we live, and for this reason I believe the sands of submission to orthodoxy and tradition are running out. A spiritual defense against apathy and unbelief is all-Important, and with this in mind I look forward with enthusiasm to the years ahead devoted to further research. The work in psychic research fields is the most fascinating imaginable, and in my estimation the most important work is yet to be done. Little by little the public is becoming aware of its importance.

Already there are not many in the scientific fields who are unaware of the experiments and studies carried out in universities in this country and Europe. Especially well-known is the work of Professor J. B. Rhine of Duke University and that of Professor Gardner Murphy of the College of the City of New York. The implications contained within their studies have deep significance for all religious leaders, regardless of their faith and belief, since they give promise of a revelation that can one day reconcile religion and science and give back to the former its spiritual potency.

Psychic research itself is not Spiritualism and it is not a religion. It is the scientific study of the human personality beyond the threshold of what man calls his conscious mind. Investigators are not superstitious people who decide to believe in something intangible, although the subject suffers from being erroneously identified with other occult and esoteric cults and beliefs. In order to clarify what it is, I believe a very short historical survey is indicated.

Modern psychic research is not of long standing, but the subject itself possesses a long history going back to primitive magic, for the phenomena with which it deals appear behind all the ancient religions, as well as in all primitive lore, so it cannot be regarded as a modern movement. Psychic research first originated in London in 1882. It is a branch of science which demands accurate observation and experiment. It has drawn scholars of renown from all other fields to contribute their knowledge to the study of man, his personality and his possible survival. One of its principal founders was F. W. H. Myers, author of *Human Personality and Its Survival of Bodily Death.* Since then this London society has never ceased to draw the support of intellectuals from all corners of the world; among them one finds the names of the Earls of Balfour, Sir Oliver Lodge, Professor H. H. Price, Dr. R. H. Thouless, Henri Bergson, Camille Flammarion, Dr. Alfred Russell Wallace, Sir William Crookes, Lord Raleigh, Professors Charles Richet, Geley, Carrell and Osty of France, to mention only a few. Through the years many other societies with the same scientific aims have come into existence. Prominent among these are the American Society for Psychical Research and the *Institut Métapsychique International* in Paris, while like groups have been formed in Holland, Italy, Poland, Denmark, Norway, Greece and Egypt. Since the end of World War II, these groups have all become active again. Harvard University has established a Hodgson Fellowship in psychic research, and the Perrott Studentship for the study of psychic research was founded as a memorial to F. W. H. Myers at Trinity College, Cambridge.

Before the war there was great attention paid to psychic research in Germany by the Department of Psychology at the University of Bonn, where the vital personality of William James, whose reputation and works are known to every student of the subject, was still remembered.

Here in America the work of Professor Hodgson, William James, Morton Prince and Walter Franklin Prince, as well as that of Dr. James Hervey Hyslop — one of the founders of the American Society for Psychical Research — has continued to expand these studies. The work started at Duke University by the late, beloved Professor William McDougall, and ably carried on by Professor J. B. Rhine, continues to add luster to the untiring work of others in the field who have been equally ready to sustain these studies.

But over and beyond what has already been accomplished, there are still many aspects of this research which demand continued attention. Such study may reveal the answers to many of the problems which cannot be solved until man's *reason* permits him to understand the truth that, through his intuitive self, he can reach beyond the conditioning of his environment. The doorway to the soul of man is through intuition, and it is through a knowledge of his soul that all his conceptual understanding must stem.

We have advanced so rapidly in knowledge of the mechanical and external things of life and have such command over the material forces of nature that we have little time for reflection, and spiritual truths of potentially far greater power are in danger of being stifled. Power and wealth are set up for worship; on all sides one hears the question, What do we get? rather than, What do we give? When man exists without knowledge of his individual and coherent function in life, belief dies, and the human foundation crumbles and decays.

If I seem to stress the need for more objective study and research, it is because I know that science and religion must eventually unite; the intrinsic and spontaneous word is needed to express this idea until faith becomes the directive of man's work and being. Since reason must submit, science alone can provide the answer to man's spiritual search. That is why the work of scientists in this field is of such supreme importance. Their work can give our "rationalists" exact evidence that man has a soul. It is, one may add, a sad commentary that these pioneers in scientific religion must continue to be hampered for lack of research funds when enormous sums are being spent by science to perfect ways and means to blot man's image from the scene.

From what I have recorded of my own life's experiences it will become clear that there are aspects of one's nature which are concerned, not only with the world of civilized forms of convention, but with states beyond. If I say that I know that the dead survive, that communication with those who have gone beyond is possible and does occur and that the human consciousness is capable of perception in other levels of experience, I know these things out of my own knowledge and experience.

It will also be clear that these certainties concerning the present and after-life affect and alter my attitudes as I pursue them daily. If I insist that the paranormal faculties are of general distribution throughout the human race, requiring only to be developed in order to become active and positive, I do so in consequence of the experiences that I have had.

There is nothing new or startling about these experiences. A moment's consideration will remind anyone that what I have experienced lies in the general direction of all that the seers and preachers of the race have testified to; but in the hurry of life we live in constant unawareness of the fact that we are natural creatures, and we have become so absorbed in the formulas of living that we look to these and not to nature for our very sustenance. It is well to remember that the breath and blood that are in us still remain the closed doors to the mystery of life. In them the vitality of the universe manifests through us, and we as natural creatures continue to exist.

One is often confronted with the statement that the next stage of existence contains many levels or planes, but that is also true of life here where there is a teeming growth in the earth, in the air we breathe and, indeed, all around us, of which we are totally unaware. The next adventure may seem subjective to us at this point, but once physical death has occurred, the ego will be as concrete and events will exist in sensation and memory, even as they do in our present days and years. The censor of daily conscience resists, transforms, or transposes the events and occurrences that represent our daily lives. The emotions of living in the moment are already vanishing into that abyss of alert and listening silence which is the epitome of man's short span on earth. However, this span cannot be lost, for life can be compared to the hammer and anvil, whose movements and results do not travel in one direction. While the heavy strokes may produce the desired shape and generate heat, the invisible vibrations travel out and beyond to produce sounds which in their way pass through walls and stir the imagination of the poet to weave a song, or affect the sad and cause discord in a life already offended with life's burdens.

I have learned that we live from life to the dream, and then to waking, for the dream state collects the rejected impulses and condemned desires and from them weaves the stuff of creative energy that will carry us with instinctive and driving aim toward the next day's satisfaction and beyond the dark areas of melancholy.

It is well to remember this in a world which is in flux, a world steadily growing better. Today it is possible to understand aspects of life which were foreign a few years ago, and it is now commonplace for people to understand most functions of body and mind completely and thoroughly. When I was a child, mental illness was considered witchcraft by the simple people around me, and my own visions were thought to be those of a changeling who had been left by the "little people." Today, mental patients are recognized as sick, and unusual human behavior may be evidence of maladjustment. There are many today who are not afraid to say that earthly achievement and attainment points to the spiritual in man, and that life does contain the promise of continuity.

Both in theory and human experience, I believe that personality survives bodily dissolution, to be contained in form again, though as yet one cannot comprehend the stuff of one's new being. But as long as the universe functions there will still be form through which to find expression. Whether one is conscious of this fact or not, one is always in communion with one's kind and with the eternal, with those who are no longer here, save in subconscious memory and through partial and immediate manifestations from within and from without our intuitive selves.

Form and dimension are the actual, qualified reality of man's struggle. The meaningfulness of this struggle is not clear to us. What is apparent, however, is that the common factor of *unintention* mostly directs the world from a center of the self which, in most cases, is unsuspected. By virtue of something external, there is a continuous flow at the level of free life and beyond the mechanics of existence.

The advance of man collectively would appear to take place not because of his increased effectiveness and awareness, but by external happenings, within which is the stuff of meaning, only to be comprehended as we advance toward a living fusion of understanding. This comprehension of the unique pattern of self reaches out to preserve all of us. It can be accomplished effectively by the understanding of mature love which is anchored deeply within the personal Cosmos.

As children, we accept life and are full of interest before the uncomprehensible. We are taught to discern between the symbolic and the factual, until we know the meaning of both forms and can evaluate their importance to life. Out of this understanding one achieves synthesis of being. The ideals of humanity, now brutal and false, can be taught to the young, and instead of instructing them that their sole duty is to the State and personal success, we can as easily reveal to them the truth and justice of the Sermon on the Mount. Thus, reason, by aid of mature experience, will itself reveal that we exist as one and each other at the same time, responsible for our own deeds and our brothers' spiritual and bodily well-being. Death, then, would become a natural event, and having once surrendered to eternal life and consciousness, one would abandon negation and fear. As clearly as one knows the time by looking at the clock, one knows that the regions of death are constantly at hand. These are not regions of emptiness and negation, however, but regions of reality, compact with consciousness and filled with substance. The value of such a thoughtful change can lead only to the amplification of consciousness, the opening of dormant areas of the mind to new ideas and impressions.

We have been through a great war in which millions of human beings have died in battle, in prison camps and as innocent victims of man's brutality to man; and there is passing through the world a great wave of desire — of need on the part of those who survive — for proof of spiritual being. It is for this reason that I continually stress the necessity for objective research in the supernormal. I have always been perplexed by the lack of common sense brought to the subject of this inquiry. Too much time has been taken up with the observable factor or event, and not nearly enough with the nature of the individual or the reasons that caused him to produce phenomena.

To my own satisfaction, I have discovered the electromagnetic field of my own being and external world. My object, then, must be to coordinate my own sensations and experiences into a logical pattern which I can examine, not only to gratify my own intellectual curiosity but to extend the value of my findings by means of objective experiments. I have gathered enough proof to assure me that there are areas of consciousness to be explored only through research.

It took half a lifetime to emerge through a world of external meaning in order to re-enter the fundamental nature of being within space and time, but it has been well worthwhile. I have found that the events of each day pass through my fingers like beads upon a string. Time becomes a new and exciting element flowing through me, its peculiar passage recording events within rather than without. I am now caught in its wholly intuitive meaning. I continue to make external arrangements so that outer events play their part in the shaping, but within is the continuum whose clock ticks never cease to be heard, even after all outward and visible sensations of body had been realized and laid aside.

I am often asked if such perception as I have written of here is painful. To this I answer no; but all of it contains a necessity for great precision. It is a knowledge revealed sometimes by pictures and sometimes by sound or feeling, for the flow of mobile symbols may be of every conceivable kind, some as hieroglyphics; but in some point there occurs a focus of significance and, quite suddenly, one has the meaning, which comes like a reflection of one's image in clear water. Perception, sensation and knowledge are not differentiated but united. It is this fusion of faculties, so definitely differentiated at ordinary levels of living, that makes explanation difficult.

I believe that in waking and sleeping one is exposed to a constant flow of images that move steadily, like the river, under the bridge of one's active interest. It only appears different because this flow takes place at unsuspected levels of consciousness and is related to the field of association and imagination in which all images —mental, emotional, and physical — are received.

It needs a poet's imagination to give complete expression to these states; and since this is a story of journeying in still uncharted territory, I leave the reader at the threshold of his own subjective experience — there to draw his own conclusions.

Eileen J. Garrett, President and Founder of the Parapsychology Foundation, died September 15, 1970 in Nice, France. She had been in declining health in her final years, but she had continued to be active in her writing and in her Foundation activities until a few days before her death hosting the Nineteenth Annual International Conference at Le Piol, St. Paul de Vence in the South of France. She was present at all morning and afternoon sessions of the conference and was hostess to the entire group at dinner and a reception. She had started to make tentative plans for the next annual conference, and at the urging of her publisher, she had also been making notes for a new book. She never lost her taste for adventure.

❖ EPILOGUE

EILEEN J. GARRETT'S CONTINUED "ADVENTURES"

Those of you who, like me, have found *Adventures in the Supernormal* fascinating reading, may be interested in knowing more about Eileen J. Garrett's life after this book was first published in 1949. Garrett's "adventures" certainly continued until her death in 1970. In fact, it may be argued that Garrett's most important contributions to parapsychology took place after the publication of *Adventures*.

In my opinion — and it is one I know other parapsychologists share — Garrett's major contribution was not in her psychic gifts (and the contribution they made to the field was by no means trivial), but in her work to support and organize parapsychology. Let me explain.

By the time *Adventures* was first published, parapsychology had moved from an emphasis on mediumship studies, apparition cases, and spontaneous ESP to an emphasis on laboratory experiments. Joseph Banks Rhine (1895-1980), considered by many to be the founder of modern experimental parapsychology, had established a laboratory at Duke University that was influential in changing research to such simple, easily-quantifiable tasks as card guessing. But regardless of the influence of the Rhinean approach, the field stood divided and fragmented. While Rhine's Parapsychology Laboratory became the dominant research site in the United States, and his influence was considerable in Europe and elsewhere, there were no overarching organizations to help to improve communication and understanding across language and cultural barriers. Neither Rhine's Parapsychology Laboratory, the American Society for Psychical Research, the Associazione Italiana Scientifica di Metapsichica (Italy), the Institut Métapsychique International (France), nor the Society for Psychical Research (England), were able to facilitate the overarching international connections that parapsychology needed to further develop the field during the middle part of the twentieth century. Complicating matters were funding problems: no agencies existed which devoted themselves entirely to the funding of the research of parapsychologists or psychical researchers. Organizations such as the Society for Psychical Research funded their own research when money was available, or, like the Perrott Studentship, funded students pursuing academic degrees. Although many conventional research agencies existed to underwrite research on more mundane topics, most of those were not interested in funding parapsychological research. Serious scientists in psychical research and parapsychology found themselves at a serious disadvantage. This is where Garrett came in.

In 1951 Garrett officially founded the Parapsychology Foundation in New York City. Different from previous groups which had focused on their own development and/or on national concerns, this organization, from the beginning, took as its primary purpose the supporting and nurturing of the field at large. In addition — again unlike previous groups — the Foundation had the money to achieve its goals because of the generosity of its donor and co-founder, Frances Payne Bolton (1885-1977), a twenty-year member of the United States Congress representing the state of Ohio, and a benefactor of a variety of important causes. But one must not lose perspective here: the real driving force of the Foundation was Eileen J. Garrett's energy and spirit. The same drive and determination that Garrett showed in her personal life and in such business ventures as Creative Age Press and the literary magazine *Tomorrow*, she also brought to the Foundation and its goals. The result was something unprecedented in the history of parapsychology.

The Foundation — known to many of us in parapsychology simply as "the PF" — was able to foster growth in parapsychology in a wide variety of ways. Garrett set up grants for researchers all around the world, funding many of those active in the main organizations of the field during the early 1950s. For example, Rhine was awarded many thousands of dollars for the work of his Parapsychology Laboratory at Duke University. Garrett's funding program knew no geographic boundaries; the international perspective was dear to Garrett's heart.

In addition to funding, Garrett organized a series of international conferences about which those who participated generally agreed were among the most intellectually stimulating meetings of parapsychology of the time. Perhaps the best known, and most important, was the First International Conference of Parapsychological Studies held at the University of Utrecht in 1953. The Utrecht Conference represented a return to the truly international psychical research congresses such as those that had been organized by Carl Vett and others between 1921 and 1935. To some extent, Garrett was able to create again a sense of an international community that had been lost due to the dominance of the Rhinean school, and to other geopolitical factors. But Garrett achieved something even more important at Utrecht. She provided a context in which researchers could discuss the state of the art of parapsychological research, and thus by taking stock of the most promising areas of research, set the agenda for the work to come.

The productive Utrecht conference was soon followed by many other meetings that have become legendary in parapsychology for a variety of reasons. While Garrett's conferences took place before my time, I have had the pleasure of hearing many interesting anecdotes both about their intellectual and scientific usefulness, and about the good times had by all invited. For many years these activities were held at a hotel owned by the Foundation at Le Piol, St. Paul de Vence, in the south of France. At these meetings, Garrett's biographer Allan Angoff recounted in his book *Eileen J. Garrett and the World Beyond the Senses* (1974), "Garrett was an imposing presence. Whenever she made her entrance conversations stopped and all eyes focused on her. Her personality was truly a magnetic personality, and she showed herself to be a clear and important leader as well, even among eminent professors and scientists."

For the rest of her life Garrett probably had more influence on the support and organization of the field than any single person before her had, or has had since. A good number of those who contributed significantly to parapsychology between 1951 and 1970 (the year of Garrett's death) benefited from PF grants, or from the opportunity to have a memorable time at Garrett's conferences, where much of the identity of the field and of individual researchers was developed, and, one may even say, constructed, through the unique interactions made possible by being in close proximity to one's colleagues in a comfortable and exciting environment. Garrett's contributions arose, of course, in the context of the work and the other activities of those who actually conducted the research and undertook theoretical work. But as modern trends in the history of science have shown, the kind of work that Garrett did is an important part of the social history of any field, as important in any understanding of the development of parapsychology as a scientific discipline as the actual research.

The Foundation continued after Garrett's death in 1970 and is still active today. From 1970 until now, Eileen Coly, Garrett's daughter, has served as President. Since 2001, Lisette Coly, Garrett's granddaughter and a long-time Vice President of the Foundation, has served as the Executive Director.

Apart from the Parapsychology Foundation itself, Eileen J. Garrett made other important contributions to parapsychology. She continued to publish her own books, such works as the one we have reprinted here, and as *The Sense and Nonsense of Prophecy* (1950), *Life is the Healer* (1957), and *Many Voices* (1968). Building on her previous publication experience at Creative Age Press, she created Garrett Publications, under which Helix Press was an imprint. This new house and its imprint provided a publication forum for serious parapsychological books that would not have been considered probable bestsellers — and thus not "good investments" by other publishing houses. Some examples of works published include Joost A. M. Meerloo's *Hidden Communion: Studies in the Communication Theory of Telepathy* (1964), A. R. G. Owen's *Can We Explain the Poltergeist?* (1964), and Suzy Smith's *The Enigma of Out-of-Body Travel* (1965).

In 1952 Garrett also created a new magazine entitled *Tomorrow*, which, like her previous literary magazine (which ran from 1941 to 1951), focused on psychic phenomena and related topics. (It was published until 1962.) Other projects more directly connected to the Foundation itself were: the *Newsletter* of the Foundation (1953-1970); and the *International Journal of Parapsychology* (1959-1968). The latter publication was a unique journal that focused on international and interdisciplinary aspects of the field. The *IJP* featured papers about research on psychic phenomena from a variety of countries as well as articles which connected parapsychology to physics, anthropology, literature, and other fields. The journal stopped being published during Garrett's lifetime (in 1968), but in 2000 it resumed publication under the leadership of Garrett's grandaughter, Lisette Coly.

Another publishing contribution the Parapsychology Foundation made under Garrett was the establishment of the series *Parapsychological Monographs*. Started in 1958, the *Monographs* consisted of studies too short to be books but too long to be scientific papers. Titles included those which reported research and those which undertook conceptual and theoretical work on parapsychological problems. The monograph series, I am pleased to say, continues to this day. The titles are widely appreciated by students, scholars, and researchers in the field. Among the most important of these have been: Karlis Osis's *Deathbed Observations by Physicians and Nurses* (1961), and Montague Ullman and Stanley Krippner's *Dream Studies and Telepathy* (1970).

Finally, Garrett continued to offer her personal psychic abilities to be studied by well-known researchers. For example, in 1964, Jungian psychologist Ira Progoff conducted a depth psychological study of Garrett's spirit controls which he published in the book, *The Image of an Oracle.* An unprecedented study of the dynamics of mediumship, Progoff's work remains valuable to this day. Other research conducted with Mrs. Garrett herself included Evans and Osborne's electroencephalographic studies of the mediumistic trance (published in 1952), Andrija Puharich's ESP experiments in electrical shielded surroundings (published in 1967), and Lawrence LeShan's psychometry studies (published in 1968). These, and other studies, are listed in the bibliography included later in this volume.

These are only highlights of Garrett's life after the publication of *Adventures.* The interested reader will find more information in the bibliography. In addition, I recommend reading the comments that follow. These reminiscences were written by people who knew Garrett well. Some were written specifically for this volume and others were excerpted from obituaries and letters of condolences received by the Foundation after her death. For those of us who never knew her personally, these remembrances bring Eileen J. Garrett to life, as we read about her personality, her interactions with researchers and others, and her continuing adventures in life.

Carlos S. Alvarado, Ph.D.
Chairman of Domestic and International Programs
Parapsychology Foundation, Inc.

❖ REMEMBRANCES

Eileen J. Garrett was certainly a very gifted person, most willful, devoted and generous. She paid the high price for using her gifts according to her equitable sense of duty. Her gifts were inextricably both psychic and moral — this is rare and when assumed leads to achievement. Such was the case with Eileen. I do keep and entertain of her a very vivid and pleasant, very friendly and respectful, very grateful memory.

Dr. Robert Amadou

Eileen Garrett was a powerful and yet gentle force that gave men and women and organizations and scientific experiments an intense humanity. She was sensitive to human needs and human suffering to such a degree that from early childhood she was looked on in awe as a supernatural being with supernatural powers. For more than sixty years she listened to these claims made for her with skepticism, humor, amusement, and curiosity even as she persisted in seeking out those who needed her and in helping those who sought her. As for the extraordinary sensitivity attested by childhood playmates and eminent scientists, let it be investigated and studied, she said, as it was, as it still is, all over the world. Eileen Garrett could not understand it and made no claims for it as she submitted to experiments that tested and weighed her powers, the psychic powers of others like herself, perhaps the latent psychic powers of all men.

She established a great organization to encourage research and study in this area. She infused it with the humanity and sensitivity of her own being. Then she went out into the world to stimulate and give hope and aid to the obscure and the famous everywhere.

I was privileged to travel far with Eileen Garrett on those astonishing journeys to distant places where men and women in libraries and laboratories were so often transformed by her powers and frequently went on to achieve with her urging some of the most important findings about human behavior. Her curiosity and overwhelming human sympathy increased. When ill health forced her to curtail her remarkable travels, she asked me to go, as her emissary to the people she knew needed her. "You must go to South Africa," she told me as she lay ill. "They are doing good work there. They have a small group, but it is an important group." And so, in Johannesburg and Pretoria, I brought them greetings and aid from this astonishing woman who had long reached out to them over two continents and worked with them and whom they had accepted so long as a leader and companion in the South African Society for Psychical Research.

Some months later, suffering greater pain and illness, she knew that the psychical workers in Israel needed her. Again I went for her and brought to the Israeli scientists the aid and encouragement to carry on the work Mrs. Garrett had helped them begin on her own memorable visit to Israel. When a great Israeli public figure and scholar who had studied the paranormal learned that Mrs. Garrett was ill, he said to me, "Let us pray for her." And that night he took me to the Western Wall, where patriarchal figures prayed under the stars. He, too, prayed there for the health of Mrs. Garrett, the girl from the mists of Ireland, from London, from New York, who understood so well the power of learning and the light it brings to all people. This Israeli scholar then turned to me to pray for Mrs. Garrett too, to write my thoughts on a scrap of paper and to insert the paper in a crevice of the Wall. "It is an ancient custom," he said, "and it will bring comfort to the great heart that sends you here."

Deep in India a leading scholar of the paranormal also prayed for Mrs. Garrett. When I explained only ill health prevented her from coming herself, he took me to the great Vishnuite temple at Simhachalam, and there beside peasants, who had traveled for days to reach this sacred place, he too prayed for Eileen Garrett.

These are some of the mystic ties and symbols, which revealed to Mrs. Garrett powers she valued more than her psychic powers. Let the scientists study the physical and non-physical aspects of those psychic powers, and may the Foundation she established continue to encourage psychical research all over the world. These were, these are very great contributions to man's knowledge. But far greater, Mrs. Garrett knew, was the manner in which her powers helped awaken a common humanity in people everywhere. This is what motivated Eileen Garrett, that common humanity that binds people. It infused all of her activities. Her great powers were devoted to that objective, in her family, in her office, in the strangers she befriended, in the scholars she helped.

I was given the opportunity to see her at work, to work closely with her for a quarter of a century. She did indeed have uncommon powers, and men and women everywhere who were touched by them know how unutterable is their loss to learning, to humanity.

Allan Angoff

I published my first parapsychological article in 1961. This was when I was still at the Queen's University, Belfast, shortly before I moved to the University of Edinburgh in 1963. The idea of using a random number generator came from Leonard Evans who was then a physics student at Queen's University and had heard a talk I gave to the student physics society on parapsychology. Although we did not get positive results, Helmut Schmidt has graciously acknowledged this effort as the first to use a random number generator to test for PK, which later he was to use to such good effect. Soon after this, both J. B. Rhine and Eileen Garrett took note of the fact that a British academic was active in parapsychology. In due course I visited Rhine's laboratory and, more to the point, I was invited to the conferences which Eileen Garrett then held at her summer residence in Le Piol in the South of France. I still treasure the proceedings of the conference which I attended there in June 1967 and to which I contributed a summary.

What can I say about Eileen as a person? She was, above all, very gracious. Although of humble origin — she was born and brought up in Ireland — she always struck me as a very regal figure, an effect enhanced by the presence of Allan Angoff who acted as her Prime Minister. After she gave up Le Piol, Parapsychology Foundation continued to hold summer conferences in Europe which I was sometimes privileged to attend; I recall one such in Copenhagen. I never knew Eileen Garrett well, there are many others who can say much more about her, but I am happy if I can pay this humble tribute to a remarkable woman on the occasion of Parapsychology Foundation's 50th Anniversary.

Professor John Beloff

I think she was the most extraordinary personality I ever met. Generous, sensible, fanciful, realistic, fragile, robust, devoted, autonomous and psi-gifted. I will never forget the charm of her personality and what she has done for parapsychology.

Prof. Hans Bender

A teenager, I first met Eileen Garrett socially as a guest of my parents in New York City in the mid thirties. I was immediately smitten. Although to me she projected a distinctive female presence, her force was non-gender with a remarkable warmth and ability to connect and communicate.

Our relationship over the years socially and in business — publishing — never faltered. Her awareness, participation, innovations, honesty and discoveries in the realm of psychic phenomena were and are a gift.

Allen Brenner

I did meet Eileen Garrett when she came down to Rhine's Parapsychology Lab in Durham when I was working there. What I remember most was J. B. Rhine's nervousness at her visit. I think each had a crush on the other, but J. B. was always concerned about propriety and his position. After much deliberation he decided the right thing was for him to come down the stairs (his office was on the second floor) to greet her since she was not in great health and it might have been difficult for her to come up to his office.

Later in the day, J. B. asked her to give a brief talk to the research staff about her experiences. Most of us were graduate students then, and we all gathered around the library table while "Aunt Eileen" told us ghost stories. It was quite different from the rather ponderous statistical approach we had all been taught at the Lab. Great fun!

Dr. Bob Brier

With the death of Eileen Garrett psychical research has lost its most striking and complex personality.

I knew her for almost half a century. We first met in 1923 at a séance in London. Even at that time I was no newcomer on the psychic scene since I had been attending seances for some fifteen years. We became very friendly and I had a feeling that, if a genuine medium existed, she might very well be one. At that time she was coming more and more under the influence of Mr. Hewat McKenzie who, sharing my feeling about her, did everything he could to divert her from the path of physical mediumship, which I wanted her to tread, to that of a trance medium for spirit messages. The battle was joined and Mr. McKenzie won. How often in later years we used to laugh over it.

Before she left for the United States I used to go to see her in her place near King's Cross. We had much to talk about. Eileen was an extremely well-informed person, full of curiosity about people and things and as interested as I was, and still am, in the odd quirks of human nature.

When she returned from the United States she was, in a sense, transformed. She had a mission to do something for psychical research. She wanted to raise the whole subject to a point where serious people would take notice of it and realize that there might be something there worth scientific inquiry. Gradually the idea of a foundation was conceived; a foundation that could give grants to students for special work that otherwise they could not afford to undertake. With the help of Mrs. Frances P. Bolton and others the Parapsychology Foundation was born and I have been closely associated with it almost since its birth. What Eileen hoped it could do it did and the great Utrecht Meeting was the first of the many international conferences that took place. These were of great value and their success was due largely to her own inexhaustible energy in planning and directing them.

Whenever she was in England we met on long consultations and on my numerous visits to New York many hours were spent discussing finance, future meetings and much else. It was at these meetings that I came to realize what a very remarkable person she was. We disagreed profoundly on much, but we never quarreled at these discussions. I hated to see her exploited by the many charlatans who are always holding out their begging bowls to generous souls who find it difficult to resist their flattering blandishments. It was but rarely that I succeeded in persuading her to refuse a grant to some patent swindler. After all, the Foundation was her brainchild and I loved her for caring for it. "You never know," she used to say, "there might be something and we mustn't miss it, must we?"

As the years went by we became closer for we understood one another very well. Although she was younger than I we both began to feel unable to do as much as we formerly did. Her courage and cheerfulness under the numerous bodily crosses she had to bear made me wonder more and more at the indomitable will power, which impelled her, always to further effort. My own disabilities seemed minor compared with hers, yet her determination to overcome her handicaps was ever present.

Her contribution to psychical research has been much greater than many believe. I doubt if we shall ever see another Eileen Garrett. May she rest in the peace that she has most surely earned.

Eric J. Dingwall

Eileen Garrett's life and work demands the skill of a particularly insightful fiction writer. Patrick Dennis, who had been on her publication staff, captured some elements of her ebullient, colorful personality when he wrote his enormously successful book, *Auntie Mame*. Aldous Huxley, who greatly enjoyed his frequent visits with her, embodied some of her characteristics in his final, futuristic novel, *Island.* Specifically, he caught her remarkable ability, when encountering a man or woman for the first time, to tune in on their individual abilities, needs and potential. It was virtually impossible for anyone to leave from such an initial encounter without the feeling that he or she had been deeply understood by such an obviously insightful and receptive woman. This particular gift, this talent of insight was, of course, a reflection of Eileen Garrett's mediumistic abilities.

During the twelve years that I enjoyed the privilege and challenge of serving as Administrative Secretary of the Parapsychology Foundation, I realized that the theme of Eileen Garrett's first autobiographical book, *My Life in Search for the Meaning of Mediumship* did, in fact, reflect her lifelong endeavors. Over and over, she questioned the reality of her so-called "control personalities" Uvani and Abdul Latif, wondering whether they were distinct entities or dramatized aspects of her own personality. I well remember that, when she planned her final work, *Many Voices*, I mentioned that her audience must be waiting for a definitive answer to the final questions concerning the survival of individual consciousness after bodily death. Still, she avoided any sort of dogmatic reply to this pressing, but ultimately ephemeral challenge. And yet, this was a forceful woman, outspoken, demanding, dramatic, attention-getting. She did not, to use an appropriate cliché, suffer fools gladly. At the same time, she was capable of deeply felt tenderness, generosity, and — above all — encouragement for the work of others, notably scientists and writers. She strongly identified with all those who were struggling with their personal unfoldment; she knew, from her own life, that our search for meaning must, in this life, remain without end.

Martin Ebon

At the University of Freiburg in 1968 I attended my first convention of the Parapsychological Association. There I got acquainted with Jarl Fahler, a Finnish psychologist and hypnotist who was on his way to meet Mrs. Garrett at Le Piol on the French

Riviera. This was during semester holidays and I decided to join him and drove both of us in my Volkswagen down to the Mediterranean. On the way down Jarl told me stories about this remarkable lady and gave me my first insider's view of the personalities in the field. Mrs. Garrett received us graciously and we stayed two or three days in her spacious villa. In those days research grants in the paranormal field were even harder to obtain than now, and Mrs. Garrett was like a beacon of hope for many researchers. Indeed, at one time or another, almost everyone in the field had obtained a grant from her. Besides, apart from her personal dedications, she had a charm and spontaneity with a bit of capriciousness that led to a fascination that made her a legend among researchers and a topic that was never exhausted.

When we met I felt an immediate liking for her, and I remember that the first thing she said was that if I ever needed something (for research obviously) I should let her know. A few years later when I did she had passed away.

In 1972 I started to work with Karlis Osis. He had worked with Mrs. Garrett at the Parapsychology Foundation for several years, had found her fascinating but was often frustrated by her. Psychic she was without doubt, he said, very generous at times but could be quite difficult to work with — a real primadonna. She was nothing that you could take for granted for long, there were always surprises, and never a dull moment if you were working with her. On the other side she showed a remarkable stability and her accomplishments were truly remarkable: the journal, the monographs and the books she published, the conferences organized, the library she established and, last but not least, the numerous projects she supported, and doing all of this without being born with a golden spoon in her mouth.

Professor Erlendur Haraldsson

When I first met Eileen Garrett I knew her as the publisher and guiding spirit of a progressive new magazine called *Tomorrow*. Some years later I realized that she was also the very unique medium who had set new standards in the field of parapsychology, and we eventually became good friends. I was privileged to work with her as a trance medium in a case brought to us by the late *Daily News* columnist Danton Walker, involving his colonial house in Rockland County and a resident ghost. Eventually, with the help of Congressman Frances P. Bolton of Ohio, she was able to establish a working Parapsychology Foundation, which flourishes to this day.

Eileen was always "right on" and did not mince words when it came to the quality of work she considered proper by working trance mediums, or, for that matter working researchers. Just as I was about to try my luck with a Broadway musical, she summoned me and told me I was to investigate haunted houses in the Eastern United States, and turn in a report about them. One simply *could* not say no to Eileen: so I did not, and went ahead and for two years investigated ghosts. When I wanted to return to my Broadway musical, she told me I was to write a book. Again, I could not refuse. The book, *Ghost Hunter,* went to eleven printings, and changed my life forever. Now, after 131 published books, I am finally getting back to my Broadway musical. I am sure Eileen will be in the front row, watching.

Professor Hans Holzer

Although I heard my father, J. B. Rhine, speak about his dear friend Eileen Garrett many times in my early years, my first clear memory of her was at our house on January 28, 1946. I remember the date distinctly because this was my 16th birthday. Eileen must have arrived with her entourage to visit J. B. at the Duke Parapsychology Lab and been invited home for the family dinner that marked the occasion. Now 55 years later I can still visualize the colorful exotic outfit and dramatic mannerisms of this elegant perfumed lady from New York City.

But the real reason that this evening was so engrained in my early memory was that Eileen Garrett in her magnanimity presented me, a shy teenager, with a remarkable gift — a heavy silver charm bracelet totally full of charms. This was a gift beyond belief for me at this time, as witness to the fact that I kept this bracelet with me my entire life, until only last Christmas finally passing it along to my daughter.

As a final touch to the evening Eileen Garrett read my fortune in the lines of my palm. She included such sage suggestions as "you'll always remember even at the last minute that you are a lady," along with at least one uncommon prediction that I remembered and realized in later years really had come true.

Dr. Sally Rhine Feather

My association with Eileen Garrett spanned 44 years from 1926 at which date she knew me as an infant and (to my mother's dismay) she would kiss the dog on its mouth and then me on mine! My link was fortuitous because James Hewat McKenzie, whose daughter was my godmother, had founded the British College of Psychic Science in 1920, had recognized the potential in Eileen's psychic gift, and for four years from 1925 until his death in 1929 he had, with my mother (Muriel Hankey) present, sat for at least four hours every Friday night developing Eileen's mediumship. I just happened to be there sometimes when she was training or working, and in a social context at other times.

Eileen could be called the personification of Generosity. I received munificent gifts and on three occasions was her guest in the South of France. She had known poverty and earned 2/6d (30p) per sitting in her early days, but when Dame Fortune smiled on her she shared her bounty magnanimously. By nature she was a giving person, although there were rare instances where generosity of spirit was startlingly absent. These seemed to occur when someone else was bestowing patronage (e.g. on one occasion when the Honorable Frances Payne Bolton lent me a fur wrap, and also when the same lady gave me a handbag.) It is not easy for two *grandes dames* to share the spotlight!

Although there are recordings extant, I am not aware that anyone has written of Eileen's voice. Obviously I had not known her young voice, but over decades it changed perceptively, and to some listeners it might have sounded affected, with its prolonged vowel sounds — almost a drawl. I think this may have been the result of overlaying sounds that had origins in Ireland, passed through youthful exuberance when she experimented with different persona, and settled into a voice of deep timbre. Her delivery was measured, which suggested maturity and gravity, but, at the same time, one could often detect wicked merriment. She was not afraid to say the most outrageous, almost libelous things, but somehow couched in language that was not deeply offensive, especially as her underlying sense of humor suggested that it was all great fun. And it was! Of someone prone to an over-active sex drive, she might dryly ask "... and how are his little goat feet these days?"

Even in older age Eileen always had tremendous Allure. Not beautiful in the classical sense, and with noticeable *embonpoint*, she fitted Alice in Wonderland's description "... as large as life and twice as natural." She had great presence. Her hands and feet were delicate. Her hazel eyes were almost hypnotic. To most men — but by no means all — of whatever age and background Eileen had enormous sex appeal. It was an education for me to watch distinguished men fall completely under her spell, some completely seduced. To everyone, of whatever sex, she gave 100 % attention when engaged in conversation, and I heard the late Miss Mercy Phillimore say that she attributed Eileen's extraordinary capacity to hold people's affection for a lifetime to this characteristic of making each person feel that he or she was all-important.

Although not tall, Eileen's appearance commanded attention. It has to be said that at one stage of her life her flamboyant dress sense was considered *outré* and she presented a gypsy-like figure, enhanced with large earrings (not then fashionable), but this resolved into a style more becoming to a woman with serious pretensions. In the second half of her life she was beautifully and expensively attired, though never dully. She still loved the unusual and exotic. She did not covet priceless gems, but had a few favorite pieces of costume jewelry of distinctive design and also for many years two wide gold wristbands. She would readily give away an admired jewel when it had "had its moment," and I have several of her brooches, necklaces, earrings, a girandole ring and an item of armillary from Haiti where she had been initiated into

Voodoo. Her homes in New York and in the South of France were beautifully and very comfortably furnished displaying good taste. She entertained lavishly, and when in London invariably stayed in a suite at Claridges. Fiercely independent, she nevertheless was nearly always attended by a devoted retinue, not least her long-term lover. She had an almost passionate love of, and need for, flowers in her homes and hotel rooms, and, whether they were bought en masse from the local French market, or were costly blooms showered by admirers, I never saw her without a surround of flowers and perfumes. She herself worked hard in the garden, starting at 6 o'clock in the morning when in France. She was methodical and disciplined in her daily routine of work, even when laid low by illness.

Despite the overt picture of grandeur, and at times of great opulence, Eileen's pleasures were essentially simple. From a humble start in life she retained a love of simple food: a supper of good home-made soup with a cracker, or a kipper, or merely some freshly-dug new potatoes with fresh runner beans, served in *La Ferme* at St. Paul de Vence. As an impoverished young woman I found it impossible to compete with the extravagant hospitality that Eileen extended and received, but she was equally appreciative of modest gifts, such as a novelty candle I found in a local craft shop — especially when it became her only source of light after an electrical storm.

Eileen was utterly Courageous. Physically she endured much (which did, regrettably, lead her to expect similar stoicism from others, and she was not always so compassionate of their ills as she might have been). On one occasion she left hospital almost immediately after major surgery in New York, against the doctors' instructions, in order to board the plane for London where she felt honor-bound to fulfill a speaking engagement. She looked radiant dressed in a long ice-blue satin gown as she delivered her lecture. Privately afterwards she showed us the long surgical scars, still sutured and bleeding slightly. Emotionally she endured much, undetected by all except those most intimately concerned. Her moral courage knew no bounds — in fact, she cared not a damn for people's contumely. She positively relished championing the social outcast, as when, in pre-War conventional London she failed to provide the name of her escort to a formal dinner (where it was customary for all guests' names to be printed in advance) and turned up on the arm of a miscreant who, to everyone's knowledge, had been "tarred and feathered" a few days prior to this public appearance.

Having sat with innumerable sensitives over my lifetime, it is a lasting regret that I never sat with Eileen in trance, although she spoke of her work, and I saw her dowsing, and of course heard from a number of people, notably Muriel, of her incredible séance room work. I have the original records of a little of this, and the reader will glean from the testimony of others something of the quality of her unsurpassed mediumship and, of course, of her literary output and, above all, the founding of the Parapsychology Foundation and all that entailed. Her great personality was many-faceted, but these memories encapsulate the Eileen Garrett whom I knew, admired and loved.

Denise Iredell

In 1967, I attended one of Eileen Garrett's celebrated conferences at St. Paul de Vence in Southern France. One of the invited participants administered LSD to Eileen and her friend, the English medium, Douglas Johnson. As the effects became evident, he gave both of them envelopes containing unexposed film, asking them to hold it to the part of their anatomy where it would "pick up the most energy." Eileen immediately hugged the film to her breasts, and Douglas clasped it to his crotch. Neither attempt produced images on the film. Eileen had greater success with a sealed envelope I had brought with me from the Maimonides Dream Laboratory in Brooklyn, New York. Inside the envelope was a smaller envelope that contained a photograph, unknown to me. One of her "spirit controls," speaking through Eileen, told the group that the photograph contained a picture of a man kneeling underneath an electric light fixture. The envelopes were opened revealing a photograph of the interior of a mosque in Washington, D.C.; a man was on his knees, praying below an electric chandelier. Eileen went on to say, "The picture does not interest me as much as the person who prepared the picture. He is a bright young man who is interested in science; before the end of the month he will be in the newspapers and before the end of the year, there will be an addition to his family." Upon arriving back in New York, I discovered that the newspapers had reported that he had won a city-wide "Name the Button" contest; his entry was "Ignore This Button." I told him of Eileen's prediction, and he told me that his sister and her husband were expecting a baby, but not until January. The baby was actually born on December 28th, fulfilling Eileen's prediction. But there was another statement that Eileen's "spirit control" made: "The person who owns this picture interests me most of all. He is very much like Dr. Stanley Krippner who is with us today." After her "spirit control" had departed, I told Eileen that I was the owner of the photograph, and she accepted it as a gift. These anecdotes not only reveal Eileen's extraordinary abilities, but her ribald sense of humor, her sense of surprise, and the personal interest she took in those around her. She is always with me, in my memories, and I will never forget the important part she played in my life, and in providing the funding that initiated our dream research at Maimonides.

Dr. Stanley Krippner

I have several very vivid, diverse memories of my interactions with Eileen Garrett. I will attempt to describe a few moments in time. We first met in 1946 at Brentano's famous bookstore, then located on 5th Avenue at 47th Street in New York City, where I worked. She was very charming and told me she would place my name on her advanced book mailing list of her Creative Age Press. Soon after we parted a messenger boy arrived with a big parcel of books. In expressing her gratitude for displaying her titles in our window display, she would often have me to a lunch or party and always at some smart or swanky place that I couldn't ever dream of affording on my pittance pay. At times I felt somewhat shy and obliged by all her goodness, so I thought it a good idea to entertain her at least once in my own small way. I would ask her to be my guest for cocktails at the Plaza Hotel! Knowing it was her birthday on March 17th, I phoned her personal secretary to arrange a 5:30 p.m. date for me. I left Brentano's earlier and bought a corsage of violets and tea roses. Neatly boxed corsage and I were already seated at a small table for two awaiting Madame minutes before 5:30, becoming increasingly alarmed as my watch crept past our appointed meeting time. I was nursing the martini I had ordered when at 5:40 p.m. suddenly Eileen Garrett arrived in all her Splendor. She was dressed in a dazzling, dashing green all-sequined long evening gown with several large, beautiful orchids pinned to her smashing gown. Smiling, she apologized as I embraced her for her lateness and again for the entourage that followed behind. She said that her employees had given her a surprise birthday party, so she had asked all to join her to meet me. Surprised as I was, I nevertheless kissed Madame on the cheek, and, wishing her a Happy Birthday, handed her my corsage of violets and roses. She held them awhile, then commented that I should not have spent my hard-earned money on her. Giving me another hug and thanking me heartily, she then removed all her orchids and handed them to her secretary standing by and placed my small corsage on her dress, saying that my violets were more precious to her at the moment. All in her group clapped their hands in agreement. Eileen quickly told the waiter to get a bigger table to seat all her guests, apologizing to me not to be offended, but that under the circumstances she would take the party over.

Being with Eileen Garrett there was never a dull moment. I remember once again walking with her through the Plaza into the Oak Room, my favorite bar, when Eileen spotted Marlene Dietrich and W. Somerset Maugham. She asked me if I had ever met them and if not if I would be interested in doing so. I was flabbergasted with the idea, as Dietrich was one of my favorite entertainers and, of course, Maugham was one of my favorite authors. We headed directly to their table and Eileen gracefully apologized for our intrusion, saying that she was with a friend who anxiously wished to meet two of his favorite artists. Dietrich extended her hand to mine with a great big smile; "delighted," she said. Maugham, on the contrary, never moved from his chair and only extended his hand in a sort of a forced way as if he was bored at such and never uttered a word, only nodding his head. We left with our thanks and Eileen wished them a pleasant evening. Commenting later on our reception, Eileen was as amazed as I at Maugham's strange and rather undignified actions, and she then stated that "he always acted like an old sourpuss." However, to me it all was a special treat regardless and I owed it all to my friend, Eileen Garrett.

Eileen was an unusual, different being entirely. There was sometimes almost an aura about her — not threatening, not visible, but one could feel it in her presence, rather a pleasant one — you sort of fell under her spell — one couldn't help but like her — listening to her soft voice — her charm radiated constantly. I was skeptical of her so-called psychic powers and I once challenged her and boldly asked her to tell me the real truth about her psychic gifts. I told her it would not make any difference in our relationship whatever if she admitted that it was all a hoax. She looked at me in the strangest way — sort of shocked like. Very seriously she said, "Dear Jan, please believe what I tell you, when I go through a deep trance I go through to another world — I lose my true identity. I am not my ordinary self. Believe me when I tell you that there is a phenomenon so strong all around that I become a part of it. There is something out there to be sure and sometimes it frightens even me. Please do not ever laugh or doubt all this — it is there all around us." She was so serious in this that it made me tense. She told me that it did not surprise her that I had doubts as many did. She said she would never try to sway me either way, as I had to find the truth within myself. The subject never came up again. Eileen, I am sure, did have some very unusual powers within her and she was indeed a rare human being.

Jan S. Mostowski

The happily anticipated day had arrived and Eileen, my husband Carroll and I were strolling the Philadelphia Campus of St. Joseph's University (then a College). A grant from Eileen was enabling us to do research in parapsychology and to establish a laboratory for research even through we were full-time Biology professors in a Jesuit institution.

As we meandered through the majestic halls of a cathedral-like building, bells tolled mournfully. Eileen exclaimed, "President Kennedy has been shot!" Simultaneously a young secretary screamed through an office door "The President is dead!" Eileen's sudden response confirmed the prediction of a medium acquaintance that a tragedy would occur during the President's visit to Dallas.

After being graciously chauffeured to our modest abode, I cannot recall what I served for lunch because in my home was the presence of a dynamic personality — a charming lady and a stimulating and witty conversationalist with a vibrant and positive outlook for the future of parapsychology.

I shed tears when I learned of her death for I knew that I as a person and the field of parapsychology had lost a true friend.

Dr. Catherine Nash

Eileen Garrett endeared herself to me the very second we met many years ago, when she was Editor of *Tomorrow* and I had gone to see her regarding some work for the magazine. I was a goner the instant I saw her and heard that wonderful voice. Then she said, "I didn't know you were a friend of Auriol Lee." Auriol, a director, actress etc. had just recently been killed in an automobile accident. "How did you know?" I said. "She loved you very much. She's standing there with you!" "Lord!" I said. "Don't be alarmed," Garrett replied. I never really knew why Eileen put up with me; my life went in such crazy directions. However, with that fabulous kindness and tenderheartedness, she did.

Michael O'Shaughnesy

What a remarkable woman — she well deserved the story she used to tell about her friend Aldous Huxley who said to her

"There are three creatures which really ought not to be: the giraffe, the duck-billed platypus and you, Eileen Garrett." She was very pleased to find herself classified among such marvels of evolution. I shall always remember my first meeting with her in the very tall building (was it 500 Fifth Avenue?) which had a superb view of New York Harbor with the Statue of Liberty standing out splendidly. That must have been in late 1954. It came about through Aldous Huxley, whom I had met in the previous years. From then on I got to know her increasingly well and came to admire her vision and her determination to ensure that the phenomena, which she herself had experienced, should be properly examined and enquired into. She sustained that determination over many years and through all kinds of disappointment.

She will be missed by all kinds of people for all sorts of different reasons. I suppose that one could make a substantial volume of those various views of Eileen Garrett seen from many different angles ...We shall miss her greatly for there is literally nobody like her, it is hard to believe that her vital presence is no more, but then perhaps, it is around and within us.

Dr. Humphry Osmond

One of the extraordinary aspects of speaking about Eileen Garrett is that the words go not only to this audience of her friends, but to Eileen. With her characteristic twinkle of skeptical belief and her equally charming appreciation of blarney, she would be the first to say, "But how can you be sure?"

That was perhaps the theme of her life — How can you be sure? She had a fierce integrity about this quest for certitude which she relentlessly pursued all her life. If she thought that an investigator had any common sense and some small idea for an experiment, she never turned down an offer to be personally investigated. She never really wanted to know the details of any experiment, and she never broke experimental conditions. Her confidence in her psychic ability made her fearless and she never showed the slightest doubt about the reality of her psychic world in action. But take her out of the arena of doing and place her in the arena of academic discussion, and she became the greatest doubting Thomas of them all — doubtful of her powers, in doubt of her controls and of all other pretenders to psychic powers. Which is not to say that she did not have friends among psychics — she certainly did. It was simply a case of self-doubt at a discussion level being extended to all other psychics.

In 1948 I took two years off from my work in medicine in order to find out if telepathy really existed. I was about to give up my quest when I met Eileen. She willingly offered herself as a subject for my Faraday Cage experiments, and proved to me that telepathy did indeed exist and on my own terms. I owe my subsequent efforts in psychic research in great part to this initial experience with Eileen, and her continuing friendship and encouragement.

She always had heroic qualities in all aspects of living. If she was your friend, it was a bountiful friendship. If you were an enemy you had better beware. Being a great judge of human nature she often became overconfident about the loyalty of her friends. She assumed that her big-heartedness and loyalty would always bring about reciprocation in kind. It was one of life's great cruelties to her to be wounded by a betrayal of trust.

I give these contradictory aspects of her character because in fact her character was made up of the dynamic tension of many such oppositions, and when summed up became her greatness. I do not for a moment doubt her place in psychic history. But if I know Eileen at all, I know that she did not stop her work when her heart stopped beating. Her indomitable will to aid and elevate humanity through knowledge of the physical and the spiritual has really just begun. I have never made a prediction before, but I will make one now: Eileen will speak, and her best works are yet to come. Truly, she always lived as if to die tomorrow, but she learned as if to live forever.

Dr. Andrija Puharich

I first met Eileen J. Garrett in May of 1962. We were friends until her death in Nice, France, September 15, 1970. She had a profound effect upon my life and in many ways sculptured my attitudes, interpretations and insights into psychical research and parapsychology. Like the character Auntie Mame, she "opened doors," created new friendships for me in the academic community, allowed me to travel to Europe to "ask questions" as a grantee of her foundation. She introduced me to numerous researchers and was always mindful of my association with the church. She was a deep, perceptive and controlling personality who gave the feeling of always looking within at those she liked and even disliked. She projected mystery and her personality was often stern and strong. Her psychic abilities were ever present. "I can do what I do in the middle of Times Square, Billy. I don't need a Cathedral. I look out over the hills of the South of France and this, this is my Cathedral." She was both telescopic and microscopic in relation to people and nature. Eileen was strong willed but anxious for others to describe her abilities using the scientific disciplines. I thought I knew her but she knew me better than I knew myself. Her circle of friends and researchers spanned the globe. Her sponsorship of research into the field of consciousness was of pioneer proportions. I credit Eileen J. Garrett as one of the truly great chapters of my life. She was other-dimensional in so many ways. I remember one of the last things she said to me, "Billy, when it is time for me to go, to blend with all that is, I will give you a call and as it is happening I will describe it to you." Her death in Nice did not allow for that moment but it was vintage Eileen. One evening, having dinner at her European headquarters at Le Piol, St. Paul de Vence, she looked at the full moon and also a bonfire on a hill in the distance. She commented, "That moon is not going to let that bonfire dim its light." Yes, Eileen was the psychic, the medium, the sponsor of research, the provider of many who labored in her conferences to explore topics of the mind and spirit, but she was also mystical in her view of here and beyond. Some almost felt uncomfortable or threatened in her presence. I did not. I saw a woman who was making things happen for the future. She was an explorer of "Awareness" and her many contributions changed lives. Her writings await a new generation who are learning that the study of consciousness on all its levels is surely, as she believed, the science of the future. I can hear her voice in my mind; "It is only by scientific patience, over long years, that real spiritual insight into reality can be achieved, and thus clear away the sentimental emotionalism that has long been the main enemy of true psychic research." She was truly magical in the best sense and her spell over my inner world remains with me. Thank you, Eileen J. Garrett.

The Rev. Canon William V. Rauscher

So much surges through my mind of what has happened since that morning when Eileen Garrett and her daughter first got off the train in Durham that it would fill books; she started many, many things, here as elsewhere, with her vigor, her initiative, her restless "creative age" mind, and yes, her generous readiness to help others.

How many there are who could say, as I do, "She helped me get my start!" She and I had what were for me great moments together. There will be eloquent words from others about her; we will all appreciate them too, but the personal sort of partnership Eileen Garrett and I had seemed to me somewhat unique, and it has meant a great deal to me and always will.

Dr. J. B. Rhine

Three individuals have played pivotal roles in my life as a parapsychologist: Prof. H. H. Price, my supervisor at Oxford, Dr. J. B. Rhine, who gave me my first job at the Duke Parapsychology Lab, and Eileen Garrett, who supported me for three years at Oxford, 1954-1956. This enabled me to work with Price and then led me to Duke.

The year before, in 1953, Mrs. Garrett asked me to give a paper at the First International Conference of Parapsychological Studies at the University of Utrecht, the first conference I had attended. I believe I was the most junior and certainly the least accomplished of the conference participants. Her confidence in me as much as the financial support was a determining factor in my staying the course.

Some time during this period, Mrs. Garrett visited the small library and ESP lab that the support of the Parapsychology Foundation had enabled me to set up at Oxford. Hers was a commanding presence. When Eileen Garrett entered a room people instinctively arranged themselves like planets circling a star. You wanted to be close but not too close; she seemed to be surrounded by something like a gravitational field that was highly attractive but also kept you at a certain distance. She was a very public person and a very private person.

Eileen Garrett was one of the most insightful and also astute writers in the field. Her *Adventures in the Supernormal: A Personal Memoir* is more than a memoir. I read it as an appeal to include the psychically gifted individual in systematic research. Her concept of the "surround," a field of information and energy that she saw around people and things deserves serious study.

Whenever I visit the Parapsychology Foundation, which is as often as possible, and see Eileen Coly and Lisette Coly, its President and Vice President, the talk invariably includes Mrs. Garrett. Daughter and granddaughter are both skeptical about the scientific evidence for life after death; nevertheless they and the visitor who knew Mrs. Garrett feel her presence. Whatever else can be said, this presence has been an inspiration for the accomplishments of the Foundation as a major center for information and research in parapsychology. Eileen Garrett would be (is?) pleased and proud.

Dr. William G. Roll

Although I met Mrs. Eileen J. Garrett only once in my life, my first impression of her was outstanding. With Mrs. Garrett and her entourage were many luminaries in an audience to witness a lecture presented by Professor Bernard Grad, and to hear my comments at a meeting of the American Society for Psychical

Research. It was totally unnecessary for her to introduce herself, for she was conspicuous: stylishly dressed in a suit and delicate fur piece, wearing a fashionable hat, and completely elegant with her British accent. She was ebullient, outgoing, and absolutely dynamic, overwhelming, uplifting, and encouraging. Her total rapport with myself seemed like we had immediately connected and genuinely known each other for years.

More peripheral than this extraordinary public contact was the clinical fact that when I was studying the renowned telepathist-paragnosts Jacques Romano and Joseph Dunninger, who had traveled the entire globe and crossed paths with the great and near-great people of the world throughout their distinguished careers, each had known about Mrs. Garrett, remembered her, and always accorded respect to her. This is psychologically contrary for these uniquely gifted people who are more frequently extremely competitive and not known to throw social bouquets to others of similar talents. She obviously had left her indelible mark of influence and personality on each of them, and others, and which also naturally and powerfully flows into her writings.

Nandor Fodor, the famous psychoanalyst-psychical researcher, once confessed to me that of all the things that we had to discuss, the most interesting were his friendly ongoing disputes with Mrs. Garrett regarding the origin of her guides, Uvani and Abdul Latif.

Although ethical restraint imposes silence in many instances, I was most deeply impressed by Mrs. Garrett's numerous completely unrecognized and seldom known acts of human kindness in extreme situations where, for example, her timely intervention once rescued a most noteworthy family from tragedy, and she obtained a home for them. As for myself and Mrs. Garrett, if it were not through the unsolicited intercession of good Martin Ebon, long-time administrative assistant to the Parapsychology Foundation, my book *Parent-Child Telepathy: A Study of the Telepathy of Everyday Life* would most likely have been tossed into the dustbin. She alone thought my research worthy of publication.

Through unselfish, exquisite examples of generosity, my hunch is that Eileen Garrett's pioneering openness — using her great talents and unique personality — will some day lead to a definitive biography and television documentary. No one could be more deserving, or more highly interesting.

Dr. Berthold E. Schwarz

Eileen J. Garrett was so unique a person that it seemed she must be immortal. When I heard of her death, my first reaction was one of disbelief — a disbelief that soon yielded to grief. A relationship composed of mutual sympathy and understanding, of common interests and tasks, a relationship that had lasted a quarter of a century — was ended, was lost.

Just a few days before, she had presided over the Nineteenth International Conference of the Parapsychology Foundation.

Other co-workers will minutely describe the historical circumstances of Mrs. Garrett's life, make a thorough listing of her writings, put accurately on record the manifold "enterprises" which were landmarks of her extraordinary existence. This will certainly be a difficult task, but perhaps a little less difficult than my own. More than once in the past, reflecting on the multifaceted aspects of her unique personality, I had been hesitant to write about her, finally turning down several requests of this or that journal or magazine. The fact is that when one evokes the image of Eileen Garrett, her diverse qualities and variegated activities appear almost inextricably connected. She was, at the same time, a medium, a researcher, an intellectual, a writer and a counselor to scores of outstanding people of our time.

However, all this had a common denominator: a boundless wish to explore unknown territories, to reach some certainties regarding the "metaphysical dimensions" of man, in other words, to understand as closely as possible some of the great questions inherent in our human destiny. This she pursued with rare intellectual power and indomitable will, as well as with almost limitless capacities of abnegation and sacrifice. Let us think, for example, of her mediumistic gifts, which attracted the attention of so many psychical researchers since she was a young girl. Many mediums are little more than passive instruments of forces which they do not scrutinize and are unable to control, and they are almost always inclined to accept the *prima facie* motivations or causes of their "phenomena." This was certainly not the case with Eileen Garrett who, from beginning to end, maintained a vigilant and inquiring attitude vis-à-vis that which for many onlookers was only a cause of wonder and uncritical belief. This desire — to deepen the study and to reach some true understanding of what happened to her as a medium — prompted her many times to put herself into the hands of physicians, psychologists, psychiatrists, neurologists. They submitted the body and the mind of their unique subject to all sorts of experiments. Some of the results have been published, and they will give considerable and important data to scientists in years to come.

To say that without Eileen Garrett parapsychology would have had quite a different face in the years subsequent to the Second World War, is really to say the least. The importance of the work done by the Parapsychology Foundation — which Eileen Garrett conceived, and to which she gave life some fifty years ago — is known to all. Very few private initiatives can be compared to this in the history of culture or science. But the very activity of the Parapsychology Foundation to the advantage of parapsychological research all over the world, has shown to what extent Eileen Garrett was far from being satisfied with her status of exceptional "subject" and to what extent, directly or indirectly, she fought in order that the phenomena about which she was intensely curious should be submitted to systematic investigation on an international scale.

The death of Eileen Garrett cannot but arouse in many a feeling of disbelief. Eileen Garrett reached the end of her path still reflecting, doubting, questioning the problems of the human spirit, its destiny, its possible survival. Many, as it is well known, think they have the definite answer to the question — be it yes, or no. Like Eileen Garrett, and after almost as many years of search, I find myself unable to reach a sure conclusion. But one thing appears certain to me: if it is given to all great humans to continue being ever present among their fellowmen because of the indelible marks they have left of their passage — in this sense, and without a shade of doubt, the soul of Eileen Garrett is still with us.

Dr. Emilio Servadio

I remember Eileen Garrett. Who, having once met her, could ever forget her? Certainly she was one of the most remarkable women I have ever met. I do not think she was particularly complex, but her several talents may have made her seem so. She was an important medium for many years, but she was also a remarkable entrepreneur in the best sense of the word. By establishing the Parapsychology Foundation 50 years ago she preserved the study of paranormal phenomena from becoming too narrowly confined to laboratories.

Of all my memories I preserve best that of my first meeting with her. It occurred soon after I came to the University of Virginia. We had dinner together in New York City. David Kahn was with us. Eileen already knew of my interest in psychical research from some book reviews I had written; we had also corresponded a little. With what I later learned was her usual straightforwardness, she asked me what research on paranormal phenomena I intended to do. I said I hoped to study the evidence for reincarnation and the aura. She said: "Those are extremely difficult topics!" She did not, however, discourage me.

About two years later, I published a summary and analysis of some 40 cases suggestive of reincarnation in the *Journal of the American Society for Psychical Research*. These cases had, for the most part, been published separately, mostly by journalists and in magazines or newspapers. No one had previously looked at them as a group and searched for common features among them. To my surprise my essay on these cases was awarded a prize and received some attention from persons interested in psychical research, including Eileen. A few months later, she telephoned me and said she had received from India a report of a case that seemed similar to the ones I had described in my article. The subject of the case was a child, a young girl, who claimed to remember details of the life of the woman who had lived in a different town from that of the child. "Would I," Eileen asked, "be interested in going to India to examine this case?" I certainly was interested. She gave me then just enough money for the expenses of six weeks in India and Sri Lanka. I went there the following summer, during my vacation. That was in 1961, and I have been studying cases in India and Sri Lanka ever since. Later I obtained much other funding; but I remain deeply indebted to Eileen for encouraging me and for making possible my first endeavors to study the children who claim to remember previous lives. Without her I could not have even started.

I have many other memories of Eileen, and they are all pleasant. I mentioned her gifts as a psychic and her acumen for business; but she had other talents. She sought to bring together people with common interests. In our earlier correspondence, which I have preserved, she counseled me to meet and become acquainted with persons who would share my interests and approach to psychical research. From her advice I met Karlis Osis and through him Gardner Murphy.

In the later years of our friendship she showed a definite coolness toward the idea of reincarnation. I had no need to guess her attitude; she did not conceal it, although it did not impair her affectionate attitude toward me. One evening we had dinner together, and she expressed her negative attitude toward the idea of reincarnation somewhat more positively than usual. Later that same evening, she went into trance and "Abdul Latif" manifested. To my surprise he began to affirm the reality of reincarnation. More than that, he rebuked me for being hesitant about it. I can still remember his saying to me "You are a thousand years behind." (I claim to remember his exact words, because their effect was painful.) What to make of that? Eileen herself was unsure of the status of her controls and so she would not mind if I am also unsure. Here this does not matter. The point is that Eileen in her commitment to psychical research showed herself hospitable to ideas that she found uncongenial. The kind of experience that I had with "Abdul Latif" encouraged some persons to call her "complex." For me, the experience only gave another indication that she was a great person.

Dr. Ian Stevenson

I want to speak of three aspects of Eileen's personality that touched my life in important ways.

The first was her generosity. Picture a scene early in 1953. I, as a young psychiatrist sitting in my office one day and going through the mail, came upon a letter I read with mounting excitement. It was from Eileen Garrett inviting me to participate in the First International Conference on Parapsychology to be held in Utrecht, Holland with all expenses paid. I suddenly became important enough to appear on the international scene! As if that weren't enough, I had the temerity to ask if Janet, my wife, who had never been to Europe, could accompany me at my own expense. Her prompt and affirmative response was to offer to defray Janet's living expenses in Utrecht. This same generous offer occurred again fourteen years later for a conference at Le Piol, St. Paul de Vence.

The second is the range of her organizational skills. If she had accomplished nothing else, the Utrecht conference would stand as a unique landmark in the history of parapsychology. It was the first time a broad interdisciplinary array of scholars and investigators (seventy-eight from thirteen different countries) met to address the challenge of parapsychological studies posed to our understanding of ourselves and the world about us. To this day the impact of so many of those who participated continues to influence my thinking.

The third is her farsightedness. 1953 was the year that marked the discovery that dreaming tended to occur during certain electroencephalographic phases of sleep and was associated with rapid movements of the eyes (REMs). At around the same time and prior to my knowing about this work, I had engaged in a number of informal dream telepathy experiments with Laura A. Dale, a research associate of the American Society for Psychical Research. Our intent was to see if our dreams of a given night would reveal any evidence of telepathic transfer between us. With each of us sleeping in our own houses, arrangements were made for arbitrary awakenings at designated intervals throughout the night in the hope that enough dreams would be captured to see if there were any correlations between our dreams. Since we did not know at the time when dreaming occurred, these awakenings did not always produce a dream. Despite this, the results were intriguing. Once the REM-dream findings came to my attention, the experiment could be refined. We now had a means of retrieving a full yield of dreams by awakening a sleeping subject at the end of a REM period and having the subject record the dream. William Dement, who had been involved in the original REM studies, agreed to come with me sometime early in 1960 to a meeting with Eileen to familiarize her with the experimental procedure that would be necessary for the dream-telepathy project I had in mind. Then and there, Eileen offered her full support. In addition to the equipment and the rooms at the Foundation needed, she made available the invaluable help of two of her research associates, Karlis Osis and Douglas Dean. The first experiment took place on June 6, 1960 with Eileen as subject. Some four months later she was again the subject. She was strikingly successful on both occasions. The rest, as they say, is history. The pilot studies we engaged in that year were intriguing and ultimately led me to leave private practice to take a full-time position at Maimonides Hospital (which later became the Maimonides Medical Center) and with the help of Gardner Murphy to set up a sleep laboratory there for the express purpose of studying dream telepathy. The work accomplished there once Stanley Krippner took over as director of the laboratory, later joined by Charles Honorton, ultimately became an important contribution to the history of parapsychological research. It was Eileen's foresight that made it all possible.

Prior to meeting Eileen Garrett, I was a psychiatrist. After meeting her, first in Utrecht and subsequently at the Parapsychology Foundation, I embarked upon a dual career of psychiatry and parapsychological researcher. For this I am forever in her debt.

Dr. Montague Ullman

❖

Although I had had some correspondence with Mrs. Garrett early in 1954 in connection with a research grant that she awarded me to carry on some psi research at Florida Southern College, I did not meet her in person until later in 1954 when she visited Durham to discuss various activities at the Duke Parapsychology Lab. She had an incredible charisma and it was impossible to be oblivious of her presence in any room. She looked quite sturdy as if she were capable of performing hard physical labor, such as that of an Irish milkmaid who toiled from dawn to dusk, but she also had a very special British accent that strongly suggested hints of royalty or someone of privileged status.

It was, perhaps, her psychic energy which was her most prominent feature. When she looked at you with those large, expressive, liquid eyes, you had the feeling that she was looking right through you, or more accurately, she was peering into your soul. My wife, at that time, reacted to her with some trepidation as she was fearful concerning what Mrs. G. might perceive in her aura. What Mrs. G. described was a rather black and muddy pale green aura, but she did not offer any comments as to its possible significance. In later years, I came to understand better what Mrs. G. had apparently perceived. The relationship with my wife eventually became a very dark and troubled one, in which my wife displayed deep animosity toward me personally and also to the field of parapsychology in general.

As I had further contact with Mrs. G., I was impressed with her ability to quickly size up a person or a situation and to get to the "bottom line" of what needed to be said or done, with a minimum amount of words or effort. Her persona, at such times, seemed to be that of an efficient CEO of an important organization, which, of course, she was. On the occasion of that first Durham visit, and in subsequent meetings, some rather artistic-looking, younger men were frequently in attendance and their behaviors suggested that their roles were that of some form of "professional escort." The images, or fantasies, that came to mind for me was that Mrs. G. could also display a sort of "Mae West" personality. Just as Mrs. G. had several distinct and enduring trance personalities when she functioned as a medium in an altered state of consciousness, she also presented a complex pattern of "multiple personalities" in her conscious waking life.

The most profound impact that Mrs. G. had upon me personally was that of being a very kind and generous benefactor. In 1954, when I was a married research assistant with three sons working at J. B. Rhine's lab, I was in a state of severe "financial challenge." Mrs. G. asked me to draw up a list of my current debtors and to send the list to her. The list totaled to $1,314.00 and she sent me a check on her personal account for this amount. My wife and I had a subsequent ceremonial bonfire, and gratefully threw into it each of the long overdue bills we had been able to pay off with her gift to us. As an indication of our gratitude, we named our fourth son in her honor, and whenever I see Craig Garrett in person or in my imagination, I am reminded of her special way of reaching out to people in need.

Mrs. Garrett continued to support me during graduate school and in some of my early academic positions. She was particularly instrumental in supporting a series of expeditions that I made to the San Blas Islands in Panama to carry out ESP field tests with the Cuna Indians who resided there. This led to the publication of several papers and my results formed the basis for my 1970 Presidential Address to the Parapsychological Association. I was hardly alone in being the recipient of her financial support. Mrs. G. served as a "fairy godmother" to many other aspiring parapsychologists, who would probably never have been able to survive their restricted financial circumstances and eventually achieve a career in parapsychology, without her help.

1970 was a landmark year for parapsychology. The Parapsychological Association was formally accepted as a member organization of the American Association for the Advancement of Science and during that same year, I, and several other colleagues, presented a symposium at the AAAS meetings in Chicago. In 1970, the PA held its annual conference in New York City and I wrote a letter to Mrs. Garrett in my capacity as president, requesting funds so that our European colleagues might be able to attend that meeting. Toward the end of that March 14 letter, I wrote: "I hope that your health has been improving recently. All of us in the Parapsychological Association look upon you as the Great Earth Mother from whom we have all sprung. I think it can be seriously questioned as to whether our association would ever have been possible if it had not been for your tireless role in encouraging and supporting the various individuals and research centers that constitute present-day parapsychology. You should feel great maternal pride in hearing that your PA family was finally graduated into the ranks of full-fledged scientific respectability just before the year began." Unfortunately, Mrs. Garrett's health declined and her transition time occurred later in 1970. We were all blessed for the time that she spent with us, and I am sure that she continues to energize us from the dimensional plane where she is currently residing.

Dr. Robert Van de Castle

Like many parapsychologists of my generation I have reason to remember Eileen Garrett with gratitude. When I first became active in the field in the 1940's, her name was legendary. Her reputed mediumistic feats, her open-minded interest in exploratory research and her access to funds for parapsychological investigations gave her a unique status. In the 1950's I had a period of hospitalization for tuberculosis and Eileen Garrett volunteered to finance a visit to Lourdes so that I could combine a pleasant convalescence with scrutiny of the medical records of miraculous cures.

My reputation for skepticism and the critical tone of the book *Eleven Lourdes Miracles* may not have been the outcome she would have liked. Some researchers complained of interference with academic independence, but I experienced no such thing, and indeed enjoyed subsequent invitations to her conferences at Le Piol. I retain a vivid memory of her appearance and dedication at the last of these when she was an old lady, clearly tired and in pain but, for me at least, cheerful, friendly and gracious to the end.

Prof. Donald J. West

❖

When I was a relative newcomer to the Parapsychology Laboratory at Duke University — I believe it was in 1955 (I had arrived in September, 1954) — Eileen Garrett with her entourage came to Durham to visit for a few days.

J. B. Rhine presided over "coffee hour" every morning, which was attended by all staff members. He told us what was new, including anything of note in recent mail or phone calls. One morning he told us "Mrs. Garrett" (his term for her) was coming, and he briefly mentioned the ESP tests he had given her years earlier and told us something about her. I had been reading her magazine, *Tomorrow,* and especially liked her editorials and other contributions. I read some of her books before she came. I was very excited not so much at meeting my first medium, but at the thought of meeting someone with psychic ability who wrote so movingly about experiences and feelings she had had. I was very impressed by her cosmopolitan lifestyle. (I was 23.)

I did not know quite what to expect, in spite of things J. B., Louisa Rhine, and Gaither Pratt had said. In any case, nothing they could have said could have prepared me for the reality. She swept in, like a duchess, flanked by her right-hand man Martin Ebon, and her friend Jean Andoire, and her presence filled the meeting room at the lab. She was a large woman, but what she projected was larger than life (and I didn't ever see her aura — in fact, I have yet to see anyone's aura).

Although she was introduced to all the new people she had not met, mostly members of my cohort, I did not get any private time with her until we all piled into cars to drive over to the dining room at the Duke Men's College Campus. (The Parapsychology Laboratory was housed on the Women's College Campus, where the buildings were more pedestrian and modern in contrast to the Gothic style of the men's campus).

Her first words to me remain enigmatic to this day! She didn't say any of the "ordinary" small chat things such as "How do you like it here?" or "How long have you been here?" or even, "Why are you interested in parapsychology?" No. Instead she patted my hand, which she took in hers (we were seated in the back seat) and she said, at least twice, maybe even more, "Poor dear, poor dear!" as if I were mortally wounded or something.

I was nonplussed! I didn't know what to say! I had been primed to ask her what Jung was like and about some of the experiences she wrote of in her books, or what did it really feel like to be psychic, but I was rendered speechless. All I could do was go through a self-inventory, wondering why on earth she kept seeing me as a "poor dear." (After all, I had been a pretty good golfer, had been praised for my writing skills, had had an NDE, and an experience of cosmic consciousness, and was very well read — had read a lot of the authors she mentioned in her writings—and I was happily engaged in learning how to be a parapsychologist. I had no major problems I was aware of. So what did she know that I didn't? I still haven't found out.)

If I had it to do again, I hope I would have the presence of mind to ask her what she meant by that. But I was young for my age, and I was very much in awe of this personage — too much so — to interact with her as if she were any other new person I'd just met. I felt on equal footing with most new people, even Aldous Huxley, whom I took out to lunch when he visited the lab. (Each staff member did something with him and in that way relieved J. B. of the duty, for he was very busy, not that he didn't spend quality time with him. But Huxley was an experiencer and J. B.'s almost single-minded interest was in experiments.)

My impression of her was that this was definitely no ordinary person. And after her first salvo, I believe I remained all but speechless until we arrived at our destination (maybe a 10-minute ride). At least, I remember nothing else. Maybe Martin mercifully switched the conversation away from me. My lasting impression of this first encounter was that when meeting most people, both parties know only what they see and think consciously, which is usually pretty superficial in the context of first acquaintance. But in meeting a Great Psychic such as Mrs. Garrett, she apparently could perceive depths of myself of which I was not then (and still am not) aware. I wonder if I ever will feel I know the answer to the koan she threw at me with the first words she spoke to me?

The dinner that evening was an enthralling experience. All of us were captivated, not only by Eileen, but also by seeing a side of J. B. with which we newcomers, at least, were not familiar. These two were both used to being in charge, both with styles that could be characterized as dictatorial, and both coming from different positions concerning psychic phenomena and their investigation. Garrett had known the inner side since childhood. J. B. was the world leader as regards investigation. He was highly rational and had good common sense (though his wife Louisa had even more), whereas Mrs. Garrett, as a psychic, sometimes came from left field. I already knew how that could throw you! Both were extremely adept at repartee and one-upmanship. Garrett was seated in the middle on one side of the long table and J. B. was opposite her. I felt we were witnessing a rare display of fireworks somewhat tempered so that no one would get hurt. Relations between Rhine and Garrett had been "on" and "off," "hot" and "cold," and we were entering a hot period following a cold one. So each one was being well disposed toward the other. Garrett was always interested in funding research; hence she formed the Parapsychology Foundation. Who better to fund than Rhine's lab? Rhine was fervently dedicated to research and the lab always needed more money to carry out all the projects he envisaged. So, on the surface, they had this very polite political conversation going back and forth. I felt like I was watching a Ping-Pong match with star players. But quite frequently, always quite subtly, a little barb would zip across the table from one to the other. Both continued to smile, but if you knew some of the background, you could feel the sting one of them must be experiencing. The exchange was definitely two-sided, and as I recall, it was a standoff. I identified with both of them! So I felt I was both punching and being punched! My adrenaline was pumping that night! I loved it. Louie Rhine, Gaither Pratt, Dorothy Pope, and Martin Ebon probably caught all of the repartee whereas the rest of us only got some of it. Anyway, it was one of the most entertaining evenings of my life. It gave all us newcomers (Win Nielsen, Gordon Mangan and his wife, Bob Van de Castle and his wife, and maybe even Karlis Osis and his wife, who had preceded us by a year or so, and myself) the feeling that we truly had been "behind the scenes" of parapsychology that night, watching the movers and shakers moving and shaking while we laughed and applauded and looked at one another, as if to say, "Did he (or she) really just say what I think he/she said?"

I was sad when it ended. I felt very privileged to have been there. I think Win had the honor of riding back with Mrs. Garrett. I probably went with Bob and Gordon, all of us jabbering all the way about what we had witnessed that night, reporting to one another some of our favorite lines that crossed the table.

At least I learned early that when Eileen Garrett was involved, you never knew what to expect. Even if you might not like it or agree with it, it was bound to be entertaining. And later, looking back, things she said would make you think a little deeper, a little broader, or sometimes, just shake your head. So, at least, it was with me.

Certainly meeting her was an exceptional experience. If I ever understand why she felt so sorry for me, maybe it will become an exceptional human experience, revealing more of my human nature than I've realized to date.

Rhea White

By the time I came upon Eileen Garrett, in the 1950's, she had made herself into a very grand figure, in a rather small world, and she reigned with true noblesse oblige. She was for me, a striking character, and a living connection to the post WWI world of Conan Doyle and British psychical research. Hers was the world of D. H. Lawrence, "a dirty little creature," as she informed me once, referring more to his hygiene than his sexual beliefs, and of Aldous Huxley, now, no longer the savage social critic but a blind, staggering giant, who tried to open the doors of perception and occasionally visited the office. It was my understanding that she had come into her own as a medium and as a woman as a result of the great interest in life after death, which followed the enormous casualties of that first great war.

Mrs. Garrett was a woman of amazing vitality, generosity, kindness and warmth, with fits of mean spiritedness, shabby pettiness and cruel rancor. She had the royal capacity to lift some lives with a smile, and cast others down into exile with a frown. Yes, she was arbitrary, but she lived by her instincts, and her wits, and who would expect she would be otherwise? Think Queen Elizabeth I, or a lustier Queen Victoria, and you have some of her spirit.

Madam was extravagant. Her office was decorated in French Provincial by Sloan's best decorators, she dressed in splendid clothes, the finest silk turbans on her well-coiffed head, the finest furs, good gold jingle jangle jewelry on her wrists, more gold flashing on her ears. When she smiled her bright hazel eyes lit up, and she showed a row of fine white teeth, as good as the expensive pearls she wore. She was overweight but pretty, and intermittently went to Switzerland for slimming down, surgically and otherwise. Stripped of her finery she could have been a handsome Irish peasant, a mother in an O'Casey play, but Eileen J. Garrett without that finery was unthinkable. She had the gift of gab, as well as her alleged gift of second sight. She loved clever talk and clever people. She was not afraid of her own doubts, or those of others. She knew that I was not a believer, but she made no effort to convert me; in fact, she often put a wink into her talk of the supernatural around me. It was not that she was a hypocrit, simply that she was not by nature dogmatic, and she liked to consider all possibilities, even the possibility that she might be a fraud. But she was no con artist. At bottom she recognized that there was something very real about her knowledge and her gifts. And her curiosity about the psychic world was driven by her curiosity about herself.

Like most people, Madam enjoyed the company of celebrities. Aldous Huxley, Gloria Swanson, and all the many notables who came to the magazine and the Foundation intrigued her, and she had strong opinions about them. Lacking a formal education, she may have given too much credence to academic credentials, but then the cause of parapsychology needed all the scientific support it might get.

When I began to grow restless at the office, she offered me a grant to study the supernatural in Shakespeare at the British Museum. That gave me a great year in London in which I wrote a study on the subject. For that year I am forever grateful. Did I like her? You don't like such people, they are so special that they are beyond liking or disliking; you dislike their arbitrary nature and their flashes of self-serving cruelty, but you do admire their zest for life, their curiosity, and their wisdom. I believe she was very wise about human nature, and that wisdom was her real second sight. I recall that her birthday was around St. Patrick's Day, and I always think of her with pleasure at that time of year. Years ago, while living in Europe, I learned of her death and I was deeply saddened, so it was clear that she had made an impact on my life. The world seemed suddenly poorer when she was gone. How I wish I did believe in ghosts. It would be fun to be haunted by Eileen J. Garrett. Come to think of it, perhaps I am.

Sherman Yellen

❖ BIBLIOGRAPHY

A SELECTED LIST OF PUBLICATIONS BY AND ABOUT EILEEN J. GARRETT

General Biographical Information about Eileen J. Garrett

Angoff, A. (1974). *Eileen Garrett and the World Beyond the Senses.* New York: William Morrow.

Borgida, L. (1948, January 17). Profile of a publisher. *Los Angeles Times*, n.p.

Eileen J. Garrett, spiritualist, dies. (1970, September 17). *New York Times.*

Hankey, M. W. (1970). Eileen J. Garrett. *Light, 90,* 177-179.

Interview. (1970). *Psychic, 1*(6), 4-6, 32-37.

Rockwell, K. (1949, October 9). Eileen Garrett lives in a world of visions. *The Daily Times Herald* (Dallas), pp. 4,7.

Dingwall, E. J., Angoff, A., & Servadio, E. (1970). Eileen J. Garrett —Recollections of three associates. *Parapsychology Review, 1* (special issue), 2-4.

McMahon, J. D. S. (1994). *Eileen J. Garrett: A woman who made a difference.* New York: Parapsychology Foundation.

Rhine, J. B. (1971). Eileen J.Garrett as I knew her. *Journal of the Society for Psychical Research, 46,* 59-61.

Servadio, E. (1971). Eileen Garrett: A personal recollection. *Journal of the Society for Psychical Research*, 46, 61-64.

Stevenson, I. (1971). Eileen J. Garrett: An appreciation. *Journal of the American Society for Psychical Research, 65,* 336-343.

Books and Articles Written by Eileen J. Garrett

Garrett, E. J. (1939). *My life as a search for the meaning of mediumship.* New York: Oquaga Press.

Garrett, E. J. (1941). *Telepathy: In search of a lost faculty.* New York: Creative Age Press.

Garrett, E. J. (1943). *Awareness.* New York: Creative Age Press.
Garrett, E. J. (1947). A medium's reflections. *Light, 67,* 339-342.
Garrett, E. J. (1949). *Adventures in the supernormal: A personal memoir.* New York: Garrett Publications.
Garrett, E. J. (1950). *The sense and nonsense of prophecy.* New York: Creative Age Press.
Garrett, E. J. (1952). The ghost of Ash Manor. *Tomorrow, 1*(1), 50-66.
Garrett, E. J. (1953). The Rockland county ghost. *Tomorrow, 1*(3), 10-23.
Garrett, E. J. (1953). What parapsychology means to me. *Tomorrow, 1*(3), inside front and back covers.
Garrett, E. J. (1953). Psychometry. *Light, 73,* 275-276.
Garrett, E. J. (1954). The aura. *Light, 74,* 303-306.
Garrett, E.J. (Ed.) (1957). *Beyond the five senses.* Philadelphia: J. B. Lippincott.
Garrett, E. J. (Ed.) (1957). *Does man survive death? A symposium.* New York: Helix Press.
Garrett, E. J. (1957). *Life is the healer.* Philadelphia: Dorrance.
Garrett, E. J. (1961). *Patterns of clairvoyance. Proceedings of two conferences on parapsychology and pharmacology* (pp. 14-16). New York: Parapsychology Foundation.
Garrett, E. J. (1963). The nature of my controls. *Tomorrow, 11,* 324-328.
Garrett, E. J. (1968). *Many voices: The autobiography of a medium.* New York: Putnam's.
Garrett, E.J., & Lamarque, A. (1946). *Man – The maker: A pictorial record of man's inventiveness.* New York: Creative Age Press.
Lyttle, J. (1942). *Today the sun rises.* New York: Creative Age Press.
Lyttle, J. (1943). *You are France, Lisette.* New York: Creative Age Press.
Lyttle, J. (1944). *Sheila Lacy.* New York: Creative Age Press.
Lyttle, J. (1961). *Threads of destiny.* New York: Dorrance.

Research with Eileen J. Garrett

Birge, W. R., & Rhine, J. B. (1942). Unusual types of persons tested for ESP. I. A professional medium. *Journal of Parapsychology, 6,* 85-94.

A book-test at a distance of 8,000 miles. (1932). *Psychic Science, 11,* 67-69.

Book tests through Mrs. Garrett. (1926). *Psychic Science, 5,* 210-213.

Carington, W. (1934). The quantitative study of trance personalities. I. Preliminary studies: Mrs. Garrett, Rudi Schneider, Mrs. Leonard. *Proceedings of the Society for Psychical Research, 42,* 173-240.

Carington, W. (1935). The quantitative study of trance personalities. II. Improvements in analysis. *Proceedings of the Society for Psychical Research, 43,* 319-361.

Carington, W. (1939). The quantitative study of trance personalities. New series, I. Revision and extension of the inter-medium experiment. *Proceedings of the Society for Psychical Research, 45,* 223-251.

Carrington, H. (ca. 1933). An instrumental test of the independence of a spirit control. *Bulletin I, American Psychical Institute,* 8-95.

Evans, G. C., & Osborn, E. (1952). An experiment in the electroencephalography of mediumistic trance. *Journal of the Society for Psychical Research, 36,* 588-596.

Goldney, K. M., & Soal, S. G. (1938). Report on a series of experiments with Mrs. Eileen Garrett. *Proceedings of the Society for Psychical Research, 45,* 43-87.

Healy, J. (1984). The happy princess: Psychological profile of a psychic. *Journal of the Society for Psychical Research, 52,* 289-296.

Herbert, C. V. C. (1937). An experiment with Mrs. Garrett. *Journal of the Society for Psychical Research, 30,* 99-101.

Hinchliffe, E. (1930). *The return of Captain W. G. R. Hinchliffe.* London: Psychic Press.

LeShan, L. (1968). A "spontaneous" psychometry experiment with Mrs. E. J. Garrett. *Journal of the Society for Psychical Research, 44,* 14-19.

LeShan, L. (1968). The vanished man: A psychometry experiment with Mrs. E.J. Garrett. *Journal of the American Society for Psychical Research, 62,* 46-62.

LeShan, L. (1995). When is Uvani? *Journal of the American Society for Psychical Research, 89,* 165-175.

McKenzie, J. H. (1929). Investigation of a psychically disturbed house. *Psychic Science, 8,* 103-108.

Pratt, J. G. (1936). Towards a method of evaluating mediumistic material. *Bulletin 23, Boston Society for Psychic Research,* 5-53.

Price, H. (1931c). The R-101 disaster (case record): Mediumship of Mrs. Garrett. *Psychic Research: Journal of the American Society for Psychical Research, 25,* 268- 279.

Progoff, I. (1964). *The image of an oracle: A report of research into the mediumship of Eileen J. Garrett.* New York: Garrett Publications.

Puharich, A. (1962). *Beyond telepathy.* Garden City, NY: Doubleday.

Puharich, H. K. (1966). Electrical field reinforcement of ESP. *International Journal of Neuropsychiatry, 2,* 474-486. (Reprinted in *International Journal of Parapsychology, 9*(4), 175-183.)

A remarkable book-test. (1931). *Psychic Science, 10,* 203-204.

Rhine, J. B. (1934). Telepathy and clairvoyance in the normal and trance states of a medium. *Character and Personality, 3,* 91-111.

Thomas, J. F. (1929). *Case studies bearing upon survival.* Boston: Boston Society for Psychic Research.

Thomas, J. F. (1937). *Beyond normal cognition: An evaluative and methodological study of the mental content of certain trance phenomena.* Boston: Boston Society for Psychic Research.

Ullman, M., & Krippner, S. (1970). Experimental sessions with Mrs. Garrett. In M. Ullman & S. Krippner, *Dream studies and telepathy: An experimental approach* (pp. 32-39). New York: Parapsychology Foundation.

Walker, N. (1929). The Tony Burman case. *Proceedings of the Society for Psychical Research, 39,* 1-46.

For further information:

Parapsychology Foundation, Inc.
Eileen J. Garrett Research Library
228 East 71st Street
New York, NY 10021 USA
TEL: 1-212-628-1550
FAX: 1-212-628-1559
www.parapsychology.org

❖ Index

❖ AN ALBUM OF PHOTOGRAPHS OF EILEEN J. GARRETT

Eileen J. Garrett,
taken circa 1931,
during a trip to New York City

Garrett lecturing
in Hollywood, California,
1933

A pensive Garrett
in 1940 in the South of France,
awaiting the outbreak of World War Two

Garrett in 1941,
upon arrival in New York,
ready to take the publishing world by storm

From the left
Eileen Garrett
in between
Creative Age Press
contributing authors
Stewart Cloete
and Mary A. Hammond,
and to the right,
war correspondent
David Cohn,
taken in 1943

Garrett
with author and associate
John La Touche,
taken in the early 1940s

Eileen J. Garrett
with her daughter, Eileen Garrett Coly,
and her granddaughter, Lisette Coly,
in 1953

Following the Parapsychology Foundation's
First International Conference on Parapsychological Studies
held in Utrecht, the Netherlands, in 1953,
Garrett greets Professor Tenhaeff of the
University of Utrecht at Le Piol.

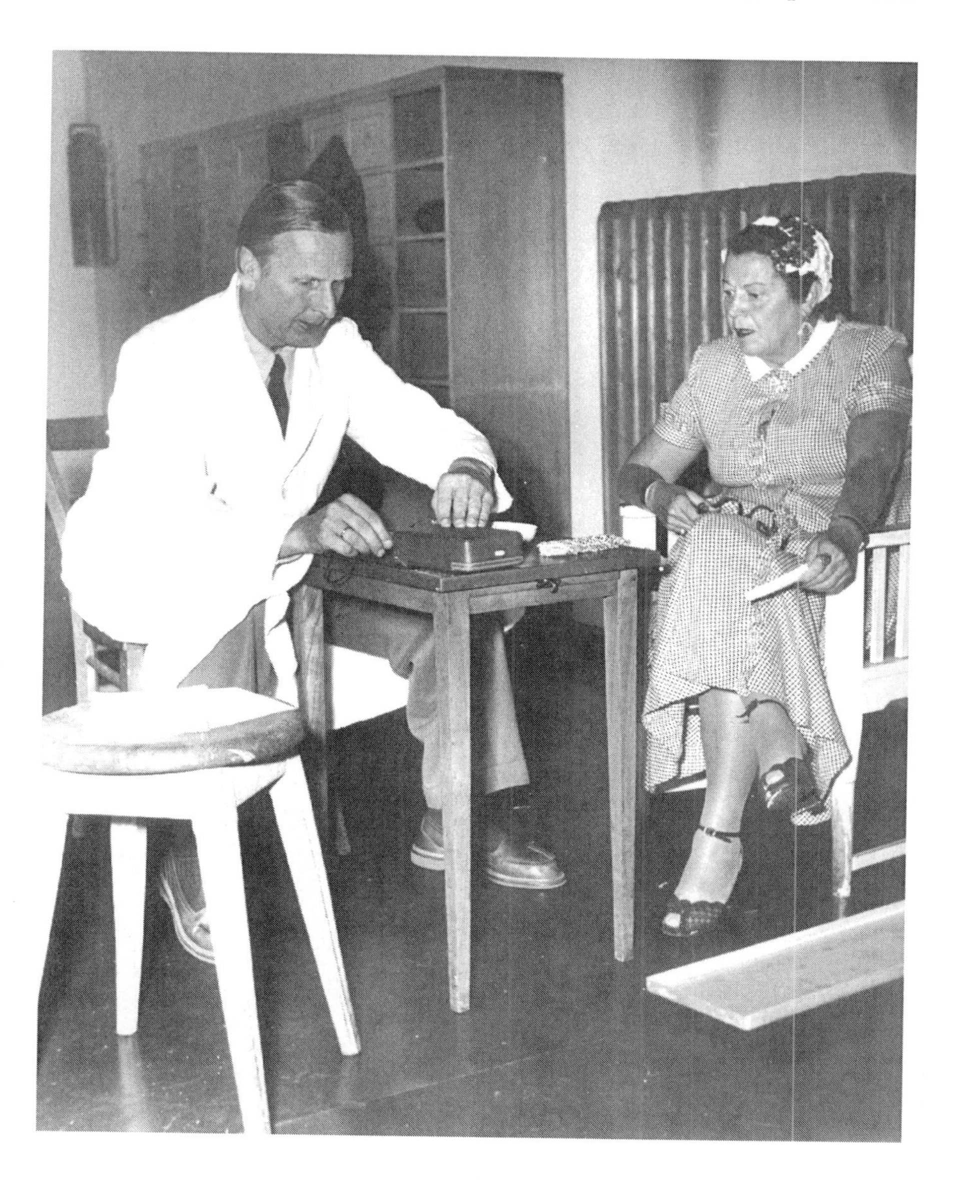

Professor Hans Bender conducting research with Garrett
at the Institut für Grenzgebiete der Psychologie
und Psychohygiene, Frieburg, Germany in the late 1950s.

Publicity photograph
taken in 1968 by Angus McBean
to accompany Garrett's last work,
Many Voices: The Autobiography of a Medium

The last known photograph of Garrett,
with Jungian analyst Dr. James Hillman,
taken in 1970 after
the Parapsychology Foundation's
Nineteenth International Conference,
held at the Lé Piol, St. Paul de Vence,
in the South of France